# The Future of Public Transportation

**By Paul Comfort**

*with contributions by over 40 public transportation leaders, associations and companies.*

Check out the book's website for updated blog posts, branded merchandise and information on future training courses:

**www.futureofpublictransportation.com**

◆◆◆

Read Paul Comfort's First Book:

***Full Throttle***
***Living Life to the Max With No Regrets***

Available on Amazon

ISBN # 9798613200986


Special thanks to Alberto Gonzales and Morgan Daniels of Pulsar Advertising for cover design and illustration and Vicky Abihsira and Blair Schlecter for editorial assistance. Also, thanks to my employer Trapeze Group for their support of this endeavor.

Thanks to the over forty public transportation leaders, associations and companies who have contributed to and sponsored this book. As a compendium book the views expressed herein reflect the opinions of the individual contributors/authors and do not necessarily reflect the views of any of the other authors, contributors or sponsors.

# Contents

# Advance Praise
**for**
**The Future of Public Transportation**

Paul Comfort is our industry's leader on what's coming next for mobility. After a thirty-year career in public transportation operations and executive leadership, he now travels the globe hearing directly from our top CEOs on what's working, what's not and what's next. If anyone can pull together a compendium on the Future of Public Transportation, it's Paul and he's done so in this book. Congrats!

> **Erinn Pinkerton**, President & Chief Executive Officer BC Transit, Victoria, British Columbia,

As a 38 year public transportation industry veteran, and former CEO and Chair of APTA, I can say that technology and mobility is adapting faster than ever to societal demands and technological abilities. Paul Comfort has his finger on the pulse of these fast changing developments and has pulled together for this book a top notch roster of executives from the public and private sector to provide their input.

> **Peter Varga**, Former Chair American Public Transportation Association (APTA) & Chief Executive Officer of The Rapid

Get on board! America's preeminent "transit evangelist" brings new optimism to a nation weary of bridges to nowhere and buses to take you there! From his extensive industry experience; global perspective; and in-depth interviews with peer CEOs on his award-winning podcast, Transit Unplugged, Paul Comfort delivers a powerful message on the path to transit's future – the construction of a mobility network that meets the needs of today and tomorrow's riders. With insights from many industry leaders, The Future of Public Transportation is a must-read for anyone who is seeking that light at the end of the transit tunnel!

**Christian T. Kent**, Principal,
Transit Management Consulting, LLC

The world's great metropolitan regions have great public transit, and over the next 10-20 years quality multi-modal mobility choices will be all the more vital to address the combined challenges of population growth, climate action and improving quality of life. "The Future of Public Transportation" is a timely addition to the global conversation about the future of mobility."

**Kevin Desmond**, Chief Executive Officer
TransLink, Vancouver, BC

It is an exciting time to be part of public transportation and transportation as a whole. Innovations in transportation are offering us opportunities to break down barriers and close gaps in our transportation networks. I see public transportation providers using apps and other technology to allow customers to seamlessly and conveniently take advantage of multiple transportation modes to expand their mobility options. Transit agencies will continue to incorporate the technology being deployed in autonomous vehicles to operate our transit fleets more safely and efficiently.

**John Sisson**, Chief Executive Officer
Delaware Transit Corporation

After reading Paul's first book "Full Throttle" and crossing paths with Paul at multiple transit industry events, I was inspired by his energy, passion, messaging and how it aligned with my beliefs as well. We instantly became friends and that friendship continues to grow. Meeting Paul, having him as an industry peer and friend, is truly one of the value adds of a career in Transit.

Paul and I spoke several times on some initiative that I was involved in, and my "Full Throttle" passion for kindness. Growing up in a home where my father (my best friend) lead by example, believing in the inherent good of people, giving second chances, and simply listening and leading with kindness, has continued to inspire me to pass that message on daily, through all facets of life.

When I am fortunate enough to be asked to speak on the topic of kindness; whether to kids, young adults, future emerging leaders/ mentors, peers or during simple daily interactions, I always try to end with the same closing remarks:

*"Every day is an opportunity to change someone's tomorrow. We are all one bad decision away from being the person in need of hope, and you don't know the impact you can have on someone's life, by a simple act of kindness. Kindness is cool, kindness is free, give it away whenever possible."*

> **Mike Bismeyer**, Regional Sales Director
> Proterra
> mbismeyer@proterra.com

With Paul's long and distinguished career in transportation as well as his current involvement in mobility through his podcast Transit Unplugged and other thought leadership, Paul is uniquely positioned to provide a clear eyed and expert view on the future of public transportation and what we as concerned stakeholders should be thinking about.

> **Blair Schlecter**, VP of Economic Development and Government Affairs, Beverly Hills Chamber of Commerce

Why I am excited to endorse Paul Comfort's new book, *The Future of Public Transportation*:

Paul Comfort has become one of the leading evangelists for the mass transit industry. From Paul's previous book Full Throttle, radio shows, and highly successful podcasts we have learned much about the current state of Public Transportation as well as the likely direction in the future. Paul's rare talent of being able to gain access to top leaders and to get them to open up and share valuable management insights are highly useful to his readers and listeners.

Paul's unique management experience, as an executive leading a major transit agency, as well as political experience having been a County Administrator, combined with his private sector experience in key business development and client relationship roles ( including in my own company Veolia Transportation North America- now Transdev ), give him an excellent vantage point to understand, synthesize ,and expertly communicate the most important trends affecting the world of mass transit.

**Mark I. Joseph**, CEO Mobitas Advisors and former CEO Transdev-North America

# Forward

By **Robbie Makinen**
Chief Executive Officer, Kansas City Area
Transportation Authority (KCATA)

When Paul asked me to write the forward for his new book, The Future of Public Transportation, my answer was immediately "yes." First of all, Paul is a good friend and I was honored to be asked. He was one of the first industry peers I met after pivoting from my role as chairman of the board of the Kansas City Area Transportation Authority (KCATA) to president and CEO of the organization.

Right away I could see that Paul Comfort was an innovator and saw things through a similar lens as me. He knows, like I do, that real change is only possible at the end of your comfort zone.

So let's get a little uncomfortable.

When I lost my vision seven years ago, it was incredibly hard for me to do business across city, county and state lines. I was thrust into a new way of life and had to learn to navigate multiple transit systems. I had to trust in the coordination of four transit agencies to help me get around the region. What I found was the system was fractured, difficult to use and broken. So at KCATA we decided to fix it. We became the regional transportation authority that we were intended to be. We fixed our paratransit system so customers with "diversabilities" (you won't find this in the dictionary!) like me could get around the region with ease and dignity.

Now, following a strategic approach to implement zero fare transit for veterans, students and lifeline customers, we are even closer to implementing zero fare transit for everyone in Kansas City, Mo.

In his book, Paul visits with industry leaders who are not afraid to step out from the pack and present their own perspectives on the future of our industry. I know in Kansas City we are charting new territory every day. As innovative approaches, like zero fare transit, loom on the horizon, we can all clearly see that the return on investment of social justice, compassion and empathy far outweigh the return on investment of concrete and asphalt.

# Preface

If I look over the horizon and see what's coming for our public transportation industry, I can get excited about all the innovation and new technology that's changing the way people get around and remain mobile. However, one fundamental has not and cannot change and that is our laser-like focus on the end user, the passenger.

That's why I got into this business over thirty years ago and what keeps me fired up today. We have the opportunity to dramatically improve the lives of tens of millions of people every day (over 50,000,000 daily public transportation passengers in North America alone) in our work. It has been said that the pace of technology improvements in transportation is faster than any other industry outside of medicine and I believe that could be correct.

Just in the past few years we have seen the introduction of game changing transportation technology such as autonomous vehicles, Mobility as a Service, the rampant expansion of e-bikes and now e-scooters, mobile ticketing options including using your cell phone, tap and go credit cards and now wearable fare payment bracelets, watches and the like. Uber and Lyft have now entered into our public mobility marketplace and are supplementing or replacing public transit services for many. Our fleets are becoming shifting to alternative fuels like electric or hydrogen, large multi-national firms are transforming how we build and operate new rail and other capital projects through Public Private Partnerships (P3), Hyperloop is looking more like science than fiction for intercity transportation, cities are becoming "smart" and eliminating traffic in the public square or charging for its usage in peak times, most transit software is moving to the cloud and privately owned electric automobiles could be the autonomous taxicabs of tomorrow.

Where will it stop and what will the Future of Public Transportation look like in just 3-5 years or beyond? Over the past couple years, I've had the opportunity to interview scores of transit executives as guests for an industry leading podcast I host, *Transit Unplugged*. In those meetings I've heard great vision and implementation plans for immediate expansion and rebooting of bus and rail networks in major cities around the world. However, I've also heard some consternation about what the role of public transportation agencies is in what's being called this "new mobility paradigm". One in which governments and traditional public transit agencies no longer have a monopoly on mobility services in their city.

As Nathaniel "Nat" Ford, CEO of Jacksonville Transportation Authority stated in his inaugural speech as the Chair of the American Public Transportation Association (APTA) a couple years ago, *"Public transportation is facing the greatest transformational 'moment' of our generation. I believe history will judge us for what we set in motion today and for the ideas we prioritize. Our industry is evolving at a pace we've never experienced. We are moving away from the traditional models and embracing new models that promote synergy between different modes of transportation, different technologies and different providers. It's time to catch up with our customers' expectations when it comes to technology and service. That is the future. "*

So, I thought I would ask some of the best and brightest to join with me in prognosticating what's around the bend for our mobility services. In some cases, they have written whole sections or chapters of this book in others they provided quotes or background information for chapters I have written. Either way, you are getting a behind the curtain look at what our industry's leaders see coming based on their vantage point. I've also included numerous industry associations as they gather intel from their members and are thought leaders on this topic. Finally, since much of this new tech is being invented and driven by the private sector vendors who supply our industry, some of them have added their voices and views to the mix.

I hope you will enjoy this overview by topic of what's happening now, where we've been and where we are going as we motor toward a bright but often uncertain tomorrow and answer the question, what is the future of public transportation.

*Paul Comfort, Esq.*
*On Maryland's Eastern Shore*
*December 2019*

# Part I –
# Practical Improvements

## Make it Work Better

### By Paul Comfort

### VP Trapeze, Host Transit Unplugged

When I first arrived at the Maryland Transit Administration (MTA) as Administrator and CEO, I went to a meeting of business leaders in Baltimore City and the theme of the meeting for me was that many of these employers had instructed their employees not to take MTA bus service to work because if they rode they most likely would be late to work and that could cost them their job.

Ugh…that hit me hard. Of all six public transportation modes MTA operated (bus, commuter train, metro subway, light rail, commuter bus and paratransit) our bus system with 250,000 daily riders had the most passengers by far and yet had the worst overall performance. Additionally, ridership for the bus, metro subway and light rail had been on a multi-year decline. We decided to take the highest ridership bus routes to higher frequency (between 10-15 minute headways), change them to color coded names instead of numbers and consolidate bus stops by using ridership, passenger productivity and proximity to other stops to guide our decisions instead of requests from politicians and interest groups.

The bus routes themselves were laid out over 50 years ago when most of the jobs and activity in the region was in the downtown Central Business District (CBD) and many buses still followed the old streetcar/trolley routes. Now however while there were still 145,000 jobs in the CBD, many more had located around the 495 Beltway and into the suburbs yet they were underserved by our bus routes because 2/3 of our 65 routes, using about 560 peak buses, all went to the downtown CBD. This had to change if we were going to better serve our ridership and use the transit system more as an economic development engine to get employees to job centers.

So, we proposed a new bus route network that would create about a dozen high frequency, color coded routes and be branded City Link. These would pulse into and out of the downtown area on 10-15 minute headways so that riders would not even need a paper schedule. They could ride these City Link buses just like the Light Rail or Metro Subway, waiting on shorter frequencies. Then we would develop about 50 routes (Baltimore Link) serving the neighborhoods of Baltimore that would connect in with the City Link, Light Rail and Metro Subway routes to get them into and out of downtown. This would also reduce the "bus bunching" that occurred on heavily traveled routes on the four main downtown West-East streets.

While the bus network was largely developed fifty years ago, the Metro subway system (with ~45,000 daily passengers) was only 30 years old and the Light Rail system (with ~25,000 daily riders) was just about to turn 25 years old. So these rail networks were laid out after the bus network was yet no administration had ever comprehensively tried to connect up the bus routes to the rail stations/stops, nor had they done so for our MARC commuter train service (with ~35,000 daily passengers) that went through Baltimore on its way to Washington DC.

We wanted to comprehensively re-route the entire bus network to create better connections to these three rail modes as well as create inter-connections between them using bus. I also rode the service a lot in those days and spoke to passengers who told me their number one complaint was that the bus service was unreliable. They often would wait for a bus that would be very late picking them up or actually never arrive. They also told me that the buses were dirty inside and out and that drivers were often rude.

These were themes I heard over and over again not only from passengers on the bus but at community meetings I attended. We had to address bus cleanliness and provide world-class customer service to our passengers. I also knew that any system redesign had to be coupled with a focus on not only improving the reliability/on-time performance but also the efficiency of the routes – which meant reducing the friction that slowed our buses down.

We had a very low miles per hour (Mph) system average in city limits that made it quicker in some instances to walk than ride our bus. So, as part of planning the implementation of this proposed bus route network redesign, we worked closely with City Government on how to reduce the friction our buses experienced in the CBD by identifying over 30 intersections throughout the region for installation of Transit Signal Priority (TSP). We proposed to fund/acquire the new equipment necessary for their light poles and traffic light systems to allow our buses to get through these intersections quicker by green lights longer and making red lights turn green faster.

As part of this process we also made detailed plans to move many bus stops to the far side of intersections so the bus could use the TSP to get through the light quicker and then stop for passengers. We also proposed miles of bus only lanes on the main downtown east-west and north-south corridors. This would mean eliminating on street parking for some main thorofares one which many businesses were located (who would not take kindly to this proposal). We would provide the funding for Baltimore City to paint these streets red and put up other markers/identifiers for these roads, thus eliminating any further impediments to this important but controversial part of the plan.

We added a bus cleanliness component to our program. We found that while buses were being cleaned at night, if they stayed on a route all day, often trash would accumulate inside the bus by the afternoon rush hour. So, we added roving vans with cleaners on board who would meet buses at the end of their line and sweep and clean the inside of the bus during their short layover.

We identified that major improvements could be made to our faring system. At the time, our day passes were often purchased by passengers on board the bus at the farebox. This process took about 30 seconds for the bus driver to punch in the info and print out a day pass. We calculated that this process wasted over 53,000 hours of productivity (buses moving) and slowed the whole system down significantly. To reduce this, we put in place a plan to improve the usage of our quicker, multi-use pass called the "Charm Card" (so named because of Baltimore's unofficial moniker as "Charm City"). Market penetration for the Charm Card was under 5% of our passengers. Part of the reason was that they were only sold at five locations in the city. We added dozens of new locations for our Point of Sale (POS) system where passengers could purchase the Charm Card and we started advertising the benefits of using the card. We moved the 26,000 school children who utilized the transit system daily from day passes to our Charm Card system which allowed for quicker boarding.

We also began the process of moving toward implementing fare payment from passenger smart phones. For our high-frequency routes we focused on getting better headway management through technology. This would help reduce bus bunching and buses leaving stops too soon. We added in dozens of new bus shelters at high use bus stops and created new amenities for them including bus driver bathrooms, better informational and wayfinding signs for bus stops.

This was the plan with the why and how. We had proposed comprehensively remaking not only our bus routes but our whole agency. To make it purpose driven and give all 5,000+ plus employees and contractors a north star to sail by and guide their daily actions. That was the beginning of a long, eighteen-month process implementing these dramatic changes to a legacy bus and transit agency that would affect the over 111,000,000 passengers per year on our statewide transit system.

This process included gaining approval from the Maryland State Legislature for our proposed budget and programs, holding over 200 meetings and briefings with the public, elected officials and community groups, the hard work of an engaged staff of dozens of employees, contractors, consultants and volunteers developing, adjusting and implementing our new plans along with support from a department-wide group of leaders across the Maryland Department of Transportation that assisted in shaping and supporting the plan.

**From There**

From there I started with our people and directed the creation of a "Five Star" Customer Service Training Program with five levels of competency. We required this training for all our receptionists, administrative assistants and others who interacted with the public, including bus operators. We also revamped new employee training to include a day where all new staff (i.e. IT, Finance, Media Relations, Human Resources, Procurement, Engineering, Legal etc.) visited the operations facilities and met with employees there, to ensure they had at least a basic understanding of what business they were in now.

I had found that many employees in the administrative functions never visited operations or rode a bus, so I felt they did not have an appreciation for our core business. This one day bus tour to several garages and the Operations Control Center at the end of their week long orientation (shortened down from the two weeks it had been and many classes moved to self-paced online videos to be completed within the first 90 days of employment) became a favorite for most new employees and took the adage to heart – a picture is worth a thousand words.

I did regular television, radio, newspaper interviews preparing the public for our upcoming changes. We had developed our own MTA radio station, WTTZ FM 93.5 to help spread the news and explain the details that regular media might not cover. We also had our own home- town football star, Baltimore Ravens Quarterback Joe Flacco hold a press conference, do interviews and have his likeness on the side of five of our buses (his jersey number was 5). We figured this was a way we could get the news about how the service changes would improve trips to our football and baseball stadiums on game days to even the guys who only read the sports page of the newspaper. The Baltimore Symphony Orchestra held mini concerts on our routes to draw attention to how route changes would help patrons get to the arts throughout the city.

We even had a fare-free Information Bus travel each and every route of the system on which our Service Ambassadors (employees and contractors trained on the new system features) would explain the proposed routes changes to individual passengers one-on-one and hand out info.

For City Council and State Legislators from the region, our team met with them individually and gave them one-page route comparisons that showed the existing bus routes in their district and the proposed new ones. We took their feedback on routes and made some adjustments. We invited these elected representatives to welcome the public and speak at our community meetings. We also gave them enough copies of the route comparisons that they could provide these to their constituents and have them in their district offices. This enabled the local legislators to be part of the process and have ownership of the new routes and the overall Baltimore Link system.

Then in June 2017 the MTA ripped the band-aid off the old system and overnight there was a new bus route network with a new name, logo and design, new bus stop signs, schedules, shelters, web site, buses and employees - shining. We had followed our guiding principles but made smart compromises with community groups and other's feedback by not adjusting some routes where there was significant community push back. This was our plan edited by our passengers and key stakeholders and open to future adjustments as necessary.

## The Takeaway

Many transit agencies are looking to reshape their agencies to make them more relevant to today's riders. Passengers today demand that their system is safe, efficient, reliable and provides world-class customer service. Many transit agencies believe that if they build those factors into their system....they (the passengers) will come. In order to do that, they often are looking for guidance on what has worked and what didn't from other systems.

Our team actually spent a day in Houston with Houston Metro's CEO Tom Lambert and his whole leadership team, who provided us a symposium on how they had performed their system reboot. It proved highly beneficial as we laid out how we were going to implement our lofty plans. We wanted help from someone who had already done a route network reconfiguration to learn from them. And were looking to the future for help in shaping how our agency could become more cutting edge.

That's what many transit agencies are also looking for today. That's what this book aims to provide. Some historical context for how we've gotten where we are as an industry and a look over the horizon by some of our best thought leaders. In this these next chapters of our first section we will hear from leaders of various disciplines of our public transportation industry on topics that you have to deal with every day – contracted transportation solutions, paratransit, safety, rail, bus maintenance, operations, data reporting and more. What will the next two to five years bring in these areas? Here are the experts to tell you.

# Chapter 1

# The Contractor's Role in the Future of Public Transportation

## By Justin Pate
## First Transit, Senior Vice President –
## Global Business Development & Marketing

*I've known **Justin Pate** for many years. We both worked together at the same company while I served as Director of Operations for the WMATA Paratransit contract in DC and he was VP of Business Development. I have always found him very insightful about our business.*

*Because so much of our industry's work is contracted out to private companies (most often paratransit but also fixed route, campus/corporate/airport shuttles and more), I asked him to share what the future of this part of the industry looks like. What he gave me is a great overview of the entire topic, so I decided to use his chapter first. Enjoy.*

**Getting Here**

L ike many others whose stories I've heard over the years - when growing up in Dallas and imagining my future career path, I never envisioned myself in the bus business. I initially went to college to study business and then went on to study hospitality. When I graduated and left NY, I went to work for Four Seasons Hotels & Resorts, where I had the opportunity to work in amazing places like Palm Beach, FL; Kona, Hawaii; Scottsdale, AZ and Nevis in the West Indies. The Manager in Training (MIT) Program through Four Seasons instilled in me a dedication to thinking outside the box, developing a culture of excellence and focusing on the needs of the customer, which have been keys to success throughout my career.

After working for Four Seasons for six years, I was recruited in 2011 by a transportation contractor on the sales and strategy side. Armed with my passion for innovation, quality and customer service, I dove into the transportation industry, learning everything I could from everyone I could. I was fortunate enough to have wonderful mentors who took the time to teach me everything they knew. My skills and strengths translated well to our industry and brought a unique perspective to the business. After six years of progressively building my transportation career, I was recruited by First Transit President Brad Thomas. It was a time when I had been considering a change and weighing options, and for me, First Transit was the best overall fit. I liked the focus on innovation and keeping pace with the changing landscape of transportation, the global footprint of the company and the stability of the Executive Team. As Senior Vice President – Global Sales and Marketing, it has been a great opportunity to lead growth, strategy and development efforts for an industry-leading, global transportation provider.

Although transportation wasn't my original plan, it's an industry I've come to love. Every day we get to solve another challenge and the work we all do has a lasting impact on millions of peoples' lives. It's a vital and evolving industry that is gaining tremendous momentum. I'm excited to be part of the renaissance of transportation, as the industry is attracting many innovative and visionary leaders with various backgrounds and experiences. Transportation has become sexy again and is the darling of investment firms and innovative startups alike as more and more municipalities, communities and companies rethink the way to best meet consumer expectations.

## Our Responsibility as Contractors

As global transportation contractors, we are uniquely positioned to leverage our scale, resources and experience to the benefit of our clients. We can and do identify solutions for our partners that would be nearly impossible otherwise. I see the contractor's role as the think tank, aggregator and incubator for ideas and innovation. We have the ability to pilot and test many new ideas and unproven concepts that further the forward mobility of the industry as a whole.

Often the best ideas come from a simple need to overcome challenges – as contractors, we have the resources and expertise to develop sustainable solutions, such as our "Techs Helping Techs" program. With a few key strokes, a technician in Columbus, Ohio can diagnose a reoccurring maintenance issue with the assistance of an iPad and a counterpart in Portland, Oregon who has solved the problem on the same bus at his or her operation.

We have the corporate resources to place individuals in roles such as Regional Driver Recruiter and Employee Retention Engagement Specialist to devote their careers to overcoming the driver shortage challenge currently plaguing transportation agencies across the globe. We share knowledge gained through training, conferences and involvement in groups such as the American Public Transit Association (APTA), Mobility on Demand (MOD) Alliance and the Conference of Minority Transportation Officials (COMTO) throughout our workforce. We have the capability to invest in the future of transportation, with resources dedicated to exploring new modes of mobility, prospective strategic partnerships and new technology tools, evaluating them and introducing to our clients only those we know will have real benefits for their specific operation.

This level of expertise has fueled our ability to innovate not just for the sake of introducing the next big thing, but to provide real solutions to overcome challenges and improve mobility in the communities we serve. This ability has become even more important, as our clients' expectations of their contractors has also evolved. While a contractor's role was formerly focused primarily on best practices, sharing proven expertise and handling day-to-day operations, these responsibilities have expanded to include innovation, integrated mobility solutions, service design and system planning. We now work with our clients to see that their transportation systems are meeting the evolving needs of passengers we serve, anticipating future challenges and overcoming them. The contractor's role in the future of transportation is forward-facing, keeping our clients at the forefront of the rapidly changing industry, bringing them not only the expertise, tools and solutions needed, but also the confidence to change the way it's always been and to move the transportation landscape in their communities forward. It's humbling to think about how much influence our industry has, and will continue to have, on the daily lives of billions of people across the globe.

I see the contractor's role in the future as not just as an operator of services, but also as an aggregator supporting the client (public or private) in incorporating many different services into one platform while ensuring system efficiency. This isn't just confined to vehicles on the road transporting passengers but also incorporates vital tools such as software services, maintenance services, logistics and package delivery. A successful transportation system will no longer be comprised of separate transit services operating completely independently in silos. True mobility means integrating multiple modes of travel – from traditional fixed route and paratransit services, to autonomous vehicles, microtransit, on-demand and micro-modes such as bike sharing and scooters. It also means collaboration between multiple agencies and jurisdictions – public transit, school transportation, airports and private industries.

In the Houston, Texas area, my firm has aligned with community stakeholders including municipalities, transit agencies, universities, private industry partners and regulatory agencies, to further regional mobility goals. Like most large cities, congestion is a real challenge in Houston – with each individual commuter in Houston spending an average of 75 hours a year sitting in traffic, a statistic that's expected to get worse in the future. In addition to the personal, business and economic impacts of this wasted time is the gallons of extra fuel consumed each year. An integrated, well-designed and forward-focused transit system is at the heart of efforts to combat the negative impact of traffic congestion.

First Transit provides fixed route and paratransit services in the City of Houston and several surrounding agencies, as well as transportation services at George Bush Intercontinental Airport, and school bus transportation for several districts in the Houston area. Additionally, in partnership with Houston METRO, in 2019, we began operating autonomous vehicles on the campus of Texas Southern University. This slow-speed shuttle service operates on campus pedestrian pathways, connecting students and faculty to key points on the campus on a pre-programmed route.

This varied experience in multiple modes of transit services in Houston gives us a keen understanding of regional transit challenges and the obstacles to keeping the community moving, as well as the City's goals to improve mobility and alleviate congestion. As a true partner in the overall transportation landscape in Houston, we are able to have a greater impact on mobility issues and provide insight that goes over and above daily operations.

# The Future Transportation Landscape

### Mobility as a Service

The concept of Mobility as a Service (MaaS) has forever revolutionized the transportation industry. It is also changing the role of the Contractor in the mobility space – our responsibility has expanded to incorporate new and innovative approaches, integrating multiple modes of transportation and introducing new technology tools to keep communities moving.

Additionally, MaaS changes the way riders and agencies interact, allowing for passengers to select among ride-sharing, bike-sharing, public transit services, and private transit services to fully customize their travel preferences and choose the solution that fits their needs through an integrated network. As a partner to our clients, we share in the responsibility to facilitate that evolution.

APTA recently undertook a study mission looking into MaaS systems in Europe to gather data and evaluate the readiness of American transit systems to fully embrace MaaS. The study, released in June 2019, emphasized the importance of a solid, sustainable public transit system as the backbone of the MaaS concept. According to the study, a clear vision for enhancing mobility, a high quality, well-integrated public transportation system and mobility partners/contractors who share the agency's mission, are all vital components of effective MaaS initiatives.

The study also identified that regulatory policy and lack of governmental support, not technology, is the key challenge when it comes to MaaS. It is clear that technology is outpacing policy developments with many options currently available for real-time mobility apps that integrate a community's transportation options. It's important that contractors like First Transit stand with our clients to support policy changes that facilitates the Mobility as a Service movement. I believe we are just beginning to scratch the service of what will come to fruition over the next 3-to-5 years.

One of the changes I expect in the near future includes the regionality of mobility. As cities grow and begin to overlap, the traditional boundaries of public transportation are blurred. I envision a future where a city or metroplex releases a Request for Proposal for turnkey mobility solutions for all modes, looking for a partner to handle all aspects of mobility. Clients will look for the best overall solution for their community's complete transportation needs - covering fixed route, paratransit, university and private shuttle, on-demand, school bus, contact center, rail, fare payment, maintenance services and more. Additionally, clients will look for a contractor who can aggregate all services together on one platform, through one payment channel, to create seamless journeys powered by artificial intelligence and data, while also providing additional revenue streams.

## On Demand Transit

On-demand transportation is one of the more popular solutions to increase mobility, improving system flexibility, efficiency and convenience. On-demand options, which take many forms, are successfully incorporated into both fixed route and paratransit services, sometimes including the services of Transportation Network Companies (TNCs) and other third-party providers. Some of our first on-demand transit operations included late night services at colleges and universities, designed to ensure students have a safe ride home after traditional transportation services end for the evening. On-demand services have also been successful as a first-mile last-mile solution to increase ridership in fixed route operations and have also shown to improve passenger satisfaction and efficiency at paratransit operations, facilitating the ability to take same-day trip requests. More recently, on-demand services have expanded again with service for passengers needing wheelchairs or other mobility devices. The additional capability of on-demand services in wheelchair-accessible vehicles (WAVs) not only increases mobility options for individuals with disabilities, it also allows for better overall service delivery by freeing up resources and increasing productivity.

One specific type of on-demand transportation – microtransit – has proven to better connect various communities and/or zones to increase the use of public transit. In many of our microtransit operations, our company partners with our clients in evaluation, planning, service design, and implementation to achieve the desired results.

Technology is a vital component of microtransit operations, and there is no shortage of passenger apps available for this purpose. Through these apps, or via a designated phone number, passengers can request trips. Passengers and dispatchers can see the real-time location of their vehicle, making commutes and trip planning much easier and convenient on the part of the passenger.

The expertise of transportation contractors assists clients in identifying areas that can benefit from microtransit services, design parameters of service delivery, choose appropriate technology tools, and develop successful marketing of new initiatives to increase public awareness.

In one successful example in Redding California, First Transit and long-time partner, Far Northern Regional Center (FNRC), a nonprofit organization, worked together to improve access to jobs for individuals with disabilities. In 2017, First Transit began providing an on-demand program, Redi-Ride, for FNRC clients needing transportation to and from work or employment-related functions. As job opportunities increased for the community, the need for safe and reliable on-demand transportation quickly arose. The program now provides 600 rides per month, opening up opportunities for FNRC clients that did not previously exist.

**Shared Autonomous Vehicles**

As perhaps the most publicly-recognized sign of the evolution of the transportation industry, autonomous vehicle technology has grown expeditiously over the past few years and will continue to expand in future years. As regulatory policy continues to evolve, the public perception improves and technology continues to develop vehicles that are more reliable, safer and less expensive, autonomous transportation options will continue to increase.

Shared Autonomous Vehicles (SAVs) are a viable alternative to traditional buses and can currently be used in a number of applications and operating environments, including:

- Integration with public transportation system as a circulator
- University or corporate campus shuttle
- Airport shuttles, baggage, or cargo movers
- Residential and commercial developments
- Retirement homes
- Hospitals
- Theme parks or other event centers
- First mile/last mile solutions for rail and fixed route bus service

To me, one of the most exciting aspects of AV technology is that the advancements in safety necessary for driver-less technology can also be applied to the industry as a whole in the future. Instances of drivers turning into the sun and not seeing a car because of low light, or unfamiliarity of a certain section of the road, could be reduced with the help of technology being developed for autonomous vehicles.

Autonomous vehicle technology is a new and emerging market for everyone, with both regulations governing their use and technology options available constantly evolving. In this environment, most clients feel more comfortable entering the AV world with a partner they trust – enter transportation contractors like First Transit.

**Artificial Intelligence**

I believe the future will also bring automation of other aspects of transportation service delivery – to include smart reservations and scheduling in contact centers. Incorporating automated call taking, smart applications and scheduling technology will likely become more and more common in on-demand operations and transportation call centers of all types, to reduce overall call center costs and improve passenger satisfaction.

Through contact center automation, or artificial intelligence, customers can be given the option to have their calls taken and trips scheduled automatically. Technology tools take trip requests from callers, schedule trips automatically, and confirms trip time with the passengers, tying in directly with paratransit scheduling software to identify the most efficient option for trip scheduling. Understanding our clients' desire to identify efficiencies that will not negatively impact the customer experience, automated call taking and scheduling can achieve this goal. I've had direct experience with new call automation technology that has become so advanced, I thought I was talking to a live agent, when in fact it was a computer sitting in the cloud.

Call automation is gaining popularity amongst many types of contact centers, not just in the transportation industry. According to the International Customer Management Institute, a leading B2B information group with more than 500,000 members, automated call centers are a growing way to keep pace with evolving customer needs. They estimate that 25% of customer service and support operations will integrate some degree of automated or AI technology across their engagement channels by 2020. As contractors, it's our responsibility to look into technology partners to facilitate this automation and provide our clients with options to consider as they look into automating call center functions.

## Micro-Mobility

Another component of Maas that contractors must embrace moving forward are micro-mobility solutions, including non-traditional technology modes such as scooters and bike sharing. These micro-mobility services can operate as first-mile, last-mile solutions for public transit systems and, to be successful, must reflect the mobility preferences of the community. For example, successful micro-mobility services could include bike sharing in a downtown environment where biking is popular, or incorporation of transportation in open-air golf carts to fixed route pick up points in a beach community.

According to the Mobility as a Service Alliance, a public-private partnership dedicated to creating the foundation for a common approach to MaaS, micro-mobility solutions can help fill in the gaps in public transportation for commuters, making public transit a more attractive option for many. These solutions can also have tangible benefits for transit agencies, including reducing parking congestion and improving ridership on fixed route systems.

In many larger cities, commuters are able to rent bikes, scooters and other micro-mobility vehicles on a convenient app. In some cases, including scooter service in Cincinnati, Ohio where First Transit is headquartered, customers can use their mobile phones to locate a vehicle, unlock it, and pay their fee. This level of convenience is designed to appeal to today's commuter and offers services available on-demand, at any time the passenger is ready.

As contractors look to provide more complete mobility management services to our clients, the future will likely mean more subcontracts with micro-mobility providers like scooter and bike sharing companies, providing our clients with management of these partners and taking accountability for their performance and adherence with applicable regulations.

**Sustainability and Corporate Responsibility Initiatives**

With the influx of new transportation initiatives and options comes the responsibility to ensure that we are conscious of how those changes are impacting our cities and environment. It is our corporate responsibility to consistently look for ways to increase sustainability with conscientious service.

Contractors can serve as the expert on alternatively-fueled vehicles for our clients, leveraging partnerships with vehicle manufacturers, understanding all fleet options available and the costs associated with each. This includes maintenance considerations, such as vehicle life and costs of preventive maintenance. Additionally, we can facilitate the implementation of technology tools that support environmental stability, including systems to monitor fuel usage, and paperless technology for record keeping and storage.

We can also bring in financing partners to assist with a conversion to electric vehicles, where a city or agency may not have the right funding sources to accomplish their goals. In 2020, we will begin talking to current and future clients about how innovative strategies around capital constraints can help them achieve their sustainability and green initiatives much sooner than we all thought would be possible even a year or two ago. The move to electric is underway and in full swing, we are excited to bring our expertise in electric vehicle maintenance to our clients.

## Moving Forward

There has never been a more exciting time to be in the transportation industry. Many of the transportation options available today did not even exist a few years ago. Most transit agencies realize that the status quo will not continue to meet passenger expectations in the future. Progressive, sustainable transportation systems will embrace new modes, approaches and technologies to provide mobility as a continually evolving service to its customers.

At the forefront of this shift are the global transportation contractors – companies like mine who impact regulatory policy, set industry trends and continue to provide an invaluable resource for the clients we serve. The expectations of both the transit agencies who contract with us and our shared passengers are changing and evolving – with the desire for more convenience, innovative technology and flexibility in service delivery. The time to provide mobility as a service is here – and we must be proactive and forward-thinking to meet this demand. For those of us driven by the need to do things better, faster, safer and more efficiently, not relying on the status quo, we're committed to meeting this challenge head on.

*You can reach Justin through his company website*
*www.firsttransit.com*

# Chapter 2
# The Future of Paratransit

**Christian T. Kent**
Principal
Transit Management Consulting, LLC

*I've known Christian Kent for 25 years. While he was working for DAVE Transportation I was working for Mayflower and both our companies were acquired by Laidlaw. We were both young guys in our twenties working our hardest to make a difference in this business. He went on to manage numerous operations and ended up in Washington DC as AGM of WMATA leading the paratransit service while I worked for their contractor MV Transportation. He was always thoughtful and brilliant, and I am so happy to continue our friendship in our new career phases.*

*He is now Chair of APTA's Access Committee and one of the nation's leading minds of the paratransit industry. Hear him speak on its future:*

# The Future of Paratransit

For nearly 30 years, we have been providing ADA complementary paratransit service to ensure equal access to public transit for our customers with disabilities. Many of the parameters of this federally mandated service are reflective of the technology and operating methods that were available at the time the ADA was enacted. Thirty years later, we are still attempting to schedule service the day before travel even though we know that our productivity will evaporate overnight. And as more systems adhere to the required minimum service area of a ¾ mile "corridor" around the fixed-route system, what happens to people who live in communities with limited or no fixed-route service? And about fixed-route service – will we be expanding these systems to correspond to urban sprawl, even if the distribution of ridership is not conducive for doing so? Who had the vision in 1990 that thirty years later, the industry as a whole would be fighting to retain fixed-route ridership, or that the gains in paratransit ridership would be unsustainable?

Much has been said recently about public transit agencies "reimagining" their roles in the industry and transitioning from service providers to *mobility integrators*. What exactly does this mean? Simply put, the transit agency must recognize that it will no longer be the principal provider of transit services in a region, but it can still be the central coordinating arm of a larger ecosystem of providers. This concept makes some people uneasy because they believe it portends an end to public transit as we know it. I do not subscribe to this point of view, and I was pleased to hear a fellow transit luminary emphasize this point at an industry conference. Chicago Transit Authority's CEO, Dorval Carter, was asked to address the trajectory of transit in the face of ridership and funding challenges.

Carter responded that our industry has been and will continue to be the best provider of *mass transit*, and the growth of our nation's cities will have an ongoing need for us. The decision before us is what role we will play for smaller, more individualized trips that do not require the capacity provided by traditional public transit. In those areas, there will be more players, and we would do well to integrate those services into a larger set of options for the riding public. I couldn't agree more.

> **The truth is that the models for both fixed-route and paratransit are no longer viable, and their futures are inextricably woven together in a single vision – fortification of accessible fixed-route service for the masses; and the development of on-demand services everywhere else. Operating in tandem, this is a new transportation ecosystem called,** ***Integrated Mobility.***

We have seen the deterioration of our transportation infrastructure in recent years, and perennial political battles that take place over funding it. If maintaining our current infrastructure is already challenging, we must think very carefully about how much more we build if we hope to sustain it. The main component of paratransit infrastructure is the wheelchair accessible vehicles (WAVs), and the more ubiquitous these vehicles become throughout society, the less ADA paratransit will have to shoulder the burden in providing them. This includes fixed-route transit vehicles and most recently, *autonomous vehicles*. Making these systems accessible from the start eliminates the need for supplemental services to be created to accommodate accessibility, and ultimately, this should contribute the increasing availability of capital dollars for larger infrastructure projects that serve more people. Meanwhile, the supply of individual WAVs must be leveraged from their respective demand-responsive services, but this can only happen when their use is properly *coordinated*.

### Failed "Coordination" and the Rise of On-Demand Services

"Coordination" in the paratransit genre is an old and unpopular term because it is an idea that never seems to get off the ground. But the excuses for not achieving coordination have become as dated as the concept of coordination itself. Why? Because new technologies, developed in the last few years, let alone what has evolved in the last 30, enable shared resources and much more efficient and dynamic scheduling of WAVs that are owned and operated by separate entities within a common or overlapping service area. This is especially advantageous since the provision of accessible services to the public is a shared responsibility. So what is stopping us from accomplishing this?

45

The agencies responsible for ADA paratransit and non-emergency medical transportation (NEMT) are separate departments in the federal government's executive branch, and for this reason alone, they are funded separately and barely interact with one another. The Coordinating Council on Access and Mobility (CCAM), established during the Bush Administration in 2004, was intended to make recommendations and implement activities that would improve access to transportation for people with disabilities, older adults, and those with limited income. In the 15 years since its inception, it has made recommendations, but there has been little to no implementation of new activities as a result of this group's efforts.

> *A legislative and regulatory innovation is needed to incentivize coordination of paratransit and NEMT resources, and it should be politically palatable because it is not a request for new money. Two examples: Allowing funds from HHS and DOT to be reciprocally available as the "match" for grant funds; and adjusting Medicaid transportation criteria so that the regional ADA paratransit fare is not characterized as a "lowest cost" trip option for Medicaid brokers.*

Fortunately, the private sector is motivated to enter the picture and effect change. Public transit agencies looking to manage the rising costs of ADA paratransit service have initiated numerous pilot programs across the country in partnership with taxi operators and transportation network companies (TNCs) to create on-demand services that run parallel to their ADA paratransit service, but at a substantially lower cost. Powered by on-demand software that schedules and dispatches trips in real time to nearby vehicles is infinitely more efficient than the traditional paratransit schedule approach, but the pilot programs quickly fill to capacity because the demand still outpaces the supply of vehicles and drivers that public transit agencies can offer. They are still attempting to shoulder the cost of all the paratransit demand in their region without *decentralizing* their control and sharing the responsibility with the broad array of small operators that are available and equipped with WAVs with other funding streams for which these same customers are eligible, and this approach remains unsustainable.

### *Progressive Solutions for Funding and New Operating Methodologies*

Meanwhile, the private companies that are managing health care are finding that the lack of access to transportation is costing them big money; therefore, they are looking for ways to improve this situation. Some are even investing substantial funding into coordinated transportation partnerships because the cost of fulfilling an evening trip to take a patient home from the hospital is a fraction of the cost of an additional night's stay. Additionally, the cost of missed appointments alone is in the billions of dollars, again prompting health care organizations to take more than a passing interest in how medically related transportation services are provided. They are beginning to seek out public transit as a partner to remedy this situation, and slowly but surely, we are beginning to see integration of paratransit with NEMT resources.

In Richmond, Virginia, the Greater Richmond Transit Company (GRTC) has established one such arrangement in which a private-sector broker, RoundTrip, was hired to integrate health care related transportation with ADA paratransit. RoundTrip enables transportation for medical appointments to be arranged through third parties, which include health care organizations. RoundTrip in turn distributes the ensuing trips to various fleets which are inclusive of vehicles owned by the transit agency and others that are not. These are the seeds of coordination being planted, and the future of paratransit beckons us to continue in this direction to include referrals to services that are operated separately from the transit agency altogether. Meanwhile, GRTC built a highly successful bus rapid transit service, "The Pulse," which has achieved national recognition for generating ridership increases as other agencies struggle to retain ridership.

## The Long View

Some transit agencies are missing the point of this evolution of our industry. They see the rise of on-demand services and think they should attempt to replicate the on-demand model in their own services. Recall Carter's comment about our core competency – we are the providers of mass transit, not the individualized trips that are served by on-demand systems. Transit agencies do not need to invest their capital dollars in a fleet of sedans for paratransit service when those vehicles are available from taxi and TNC providers, and even they are slowly partnering with NEMT providers to increase the accessibility of their fleets.

> *The future of ADA paratransit service provided by transit agencies should be one in which public dollars are invested to procure fully accessible fleets that represent more of a last-resort option for customers who are unable or unwilling to use the significantly increased number of alternatives that will be available to them.*

Over time, the growth of paratransit service will slow, and if managed properly, could even decline as customers select more convenient options. There is little doubt that the transit agencies will find other infrastructure needs to make up for the reduced spending on paratransit fleets, and those vehicles that are purchased through this mechanism can find their way into the NEMT and private sector markets after they have completed their useful public sector life cycle, thereby increasing the number of WAVs that are generally available for all kinds of public transportation services.

Becoming a mobility integrator will be easier for some transit agencies than others due to a number of factors. Technology is an essential ingredient, and the rapid evolution of mobile apps and on-demand software, with their self-service transactions for trip reservation, payment, and tracking; and dynamic scheduling will afford agencies many more choices if they are willing and able to invest and commit. Some agencies have a better environment for coordinated services. Indeed, rural communities have had the best track record in this area because they have had little choice but to connect all of the resources and funding streams available to them.

Transit agencies in larger, urban environments have had the luxury of operating separately from other transportation providers for some time, and many regional transit authorities are plagued with unending differences over jurisdictional preference, resource allocation, and even culture. But the traditional model of centralized paratransit service is increasingly proven to be unsustainable, and the stark reality of scarce resources will force agencies to reconsider their long-standing methodologies. Furthermore, as decreases in fixed-route ridership threaten the ongoing relevance of public transit, it will take visionary leadership (transit CEOs) to guide the agencies toward more progressive thinking.

Transit leaders must have a much better understanding of their constituency – it is not a baseline of indigent, transit dependent riders supplemented by whatever "discretionary" riders one can find. The new reality is that ALL of our customers are discretionary, and agencies must offer a value proposition to every kind of customer that makes more sense than traveling in a single-occupancy vehicle. Empower the customer with better choices, and you empower your agency to produce better outcomes.

> *The future of ADA paratransit as we know it is its own death and reincarnation back into the complementary, supplementary service that it was always intended to be. It will become an unremarkable option against the backdrop of a system of accessible services that allow people with disabilities to travel with their able-bodied brethren without delay; without nearly as many "accommodations" because the system will not need them.*

*You can contact Christian Kent at his website www.christiankentconsulting.com*

# Chapter 3

## The Future of Passenger Rail in North America

### By **Paola Realpozo**
Product Director, Rail Solutions
Trapeze Group

*I used to listen to Paola Realpozo speak at transit conferences and always enjoyed her presentations and found her insights valuable. Then one time we were both speakers on the same dais at a Conference in New Jersey. We struck up a friendship that continues to this day. So happy we both work for the same company and often collaborate on projects.*

*She has a great background in rail and managed the implementation of the first automated train control system for a major train company in Mexico over a decade ago. Hear her thoughts on the future of Rail:*

## Part I: Introduction

Passenger rail services promote mobility and accessibility, allowing millions of people in North America to travel to work, school and other places for tourism, recreation and commerce in areas where no other mode of transportation is always available, convenient or affordable for some people.

Close to one hundred rail systems operate in North America today. Streetcar, light rail, heavy rail or subway, and commuter rail form an important part of the regional transportation system to support daily commutes. These modes join the more conventional intercity railroads in their effort to develop the rail market and relief other means of transportation.

When I think of the future of passenger rail in North America, I see a highly integrated mode that is critical to seamless passenger mobility. Rail continues to promote economic growth, sustainability and green initiatives of cities, and supports the vision of a truly reliable, convenient and frictionless experience, commonly known as mobility-as-a-service.

Due to its inherent benefits and the positive impact that rail has on communities, it is paramount that the role of rail is promoted and not neglected, especially with a growing population, changing demographics and an increased pressure to reduce carbon footprint.

The more commuter-oriented rail modes will have the highest impact on people's daily life with the delivery of improved services and customer experience. A shift in city planning and environmental goals will drive commuting behaviors that will relieve congestion in urban areas, mainly through these rail modes.

The intercity rail network will see the creation of new corridors that deliver true high-speed transportation between regions with high population density. Long-distance travel will become more convenient and competitive offering comparable alternatives to cars and airplanes.

However, rail faces a reality that is different from other modes of transportation. The aging infrastructure, the considerable capital investment required to build fast and efficient rail systems, and the difficulty in increasing service with limited track capacity, present more significant challenges to the future of rail.

For a real transformation in the long term, the industry must embrace innovation in all aspects of the business. This way, the challenges that rail faces today can become the driving forces that will shift the future of passenger rail at last.

**Part II: Benefits**

Given the benefits that rail systems provide to the cities and communities that they serve today, many more systems area already under construction and planning phases. Three primary benefits of rail are mass transportation, energy efficiency and economic growth:

**Mass transportation** – Rail is the only transportation mode capable of moving a massive number of people reliably at high speed. This unique capability, which is essential to alleviating a big surge in demand over a short period, makes rail a critical component of mobility-as-a-service.

**Energy efficiency** – Rail is three times more efficient compared to cars when it comes to per-capita resource consumption. It helps reduce road congestion and greenhouse emissions by taking vehicles off the road. The industry has made strides to adopt more efficient engines, cleaner fuels and electrification to further reduce the carbon footprint. By choosing cutting edge technologies such as regenerative braking, which helps to capture power from braking, the industry continues to drive higher efficiencies.

**Economic growth** – Studies show that rail systems generate two to four dollars equivalent economic growth per every dollar invested. The construction and extension of rail systems stimulate the local economy and provide a source of working-class jobs. People can work, study, and seek entertainment in large urban areas while living in more affordable houses outside the city, knowing that they can rely on rail transportation day in and day out.

Many cities are quantifying the positive impact of rail systems in the community. It is not surprising to see a better collaboration among city planners, local, state and federal government, and the private sector to explore the future development and economic growth of regions through the introduction of new passenger rail lines.

## Part III: Challenges as Driving Forces

Even with a growing number of passenger rail systems to be built in the next five to ten years, North America falls behind on rail passenger-miles compared to Asia and Europe, for example. This prompts a common question of whether rail in the United States will ever compare to the service in those regions.

Economic and cultural factors drive the development of rail networks in each region. For instance, population density determines the type of service and the scale required, and policy often influences the direction and pace of innovation. By studying the characteristics of a country one can understand why rail systems between countries may not be comparable in volume, modes or passenger experience.

Aging infrastructure and a capital-intensive operation are top challenges in the rail industry, but particularly in North America a significant car culture, traditional funding practices and a lack of customer focus have been critical reasons why our passenger rail system lags compared to other systems worldwide. The industry now is transforming though innovation, and rail is part of this transformation.

**Safety and infrastructure** – Infrastructure to provide rail services is expensive to procure, maintain and upgrade. It requires significant capital to run safely. At first instance, to replace rail assets that are currently in poor condition the industry requires tens of billions of dollars. On top of this, commuter and intercity railroads have gone through a labor intensive and expensive implementation of Positive Train Control, a Federal Railroad Administration mandated train protection system by the end of 2020.

Even when funding is available, agencies cannot solely focus on expanding the system or improving the customer experience. They also need to allocate the right amount of capital towards keeping existing infrastructure in a good, safe condition and comply with rail safety regulations.

**Funding** – To run a safe operation railroads need funding that is mostly supported by the government. Funding is also required to modernize the system and fulfill new customer demands. Thus, the industry continues to seek more participation from the private sector and to develop innovative funding strategies to support their current operation and modernization plans, for example:

- Funding new technology through digital advertising at stations and onboard trains
- Creating new revenue sources by adding new delivery services and stores at station to increase passenger value and convenience

- Making creative deals with real-estate developers for the construction of new rail stations in exchange for new commercial or residential space above it
- Attracting private investment and partnering with local corporations that require transportation alternatives to attract talent

**Adoption** – Though many people in North American ride public transportation and, more specifically the train, in general people prefer to use their vehicles. New mobility services are causing a shift in car ownership. People will continue to buy cars, but their reliance on alternative transportation modes will increase as they face increasing congestion on roads, mainly as more cities introduce dedicated bus lanes and congestion pricing for personal vehicles.

The shift from mostly using vehicles to also taking the train, starts with service availability, communication and excellent customer experience.

When rail services become available, ridership follows. In addition to increasing service, public transportation agencies can design communications targeting all segments of the population to educate them and guide them on their adoption journey. They must inform the community about how riding public transportation supports the city's environmental goals.

The changing demographics are resulting in new customer demands and service expectations. Rail agencies must innovate and put customer experience at the forefront. This is the essential driver to adoption and advocacy for rail.

**Customer experience** – The mobility industry is innovating to deliver better services and excellent customer experience, all driven by a demographic, cultural and technology shift. Rail is no exception. Industry leaders are working towards improving overall service and experience. Information and convenience will become the key drivers in the effort to making trains an integral part of people mobility.

Accurate, real-time information is essential for commuters. Riding the train will become part of their journey as the service becomes more intuitive and integrated with other modes. Rail passengers will experience a smooth transfer to other connecting services with on board and at station information systems and through mobile apps. Public transportation agencies are implementing modern ticketing systems that work across multiple modes and enable users to use their smartphones. The convenience for the rail user will further increase with the introduction of new services at rail stations, from parking and multi-modal services to grocery delivery and fine dining eateries.

Long-distance travelers will also enjoy a better rail experience with an increase in non-stop trips, better onboard services and new partnerships with airlines and local transportation providers. The introduction of innovative services such as high-speed railroads and the Auto Train* will make passenger rail for business and leisure more attractive and convenient than ever before.

Rail operators continue to gradually introduce ways to connect with their passengers and provide a more personalized user experience.


**Part IV: Conclusion**

The future of rail is bright. There are plenty of opportunities for rail agencies and operators to improve the service for the millions of riders in North America. Innovation in all aspects of the business will be key to a meaningful transformation of the rail industry. Technology, marketing, and data are some of the tools that the industry will leverage to transform the way business is conducted and communicated.

The challenges that are unique to rail will not go away and the industry is already working towards new ways to fund their operation and capital investments. Providing a safe, reliable, informed and convenient service to riders is and will continue to be the industry's number one priority.

Rail in all its modes can and will become the most appealing means of transportation in North America.

# Chapter 4

# The Future of Safety

## By Timothy Tyran
### Chief Safety Officer (CSO)
### MDOT Maryland Transit Administration

*Timothy Tyran is fast becoming an industry safety expert in public transportation. He spent his first career in aviation with American Airlines becoming their Manager of Safety Management System (SMS) in Technical Operations, then was at WMATA shortly as Manager of their Rail and Facilities Safety and now heads up safety for the 11th largest transit system in America, the MDOT MTA in Baltimore, Maryland.*

"What is safety?" asked an anonymous voice on the conference line. That's a good question to ask in transit because there are so many different opinions on what the definition of safety should be. Now there is no question on who is responsible for safety, right? If you answered, "The Safety Department!" then we have a lot of work to do together to change that view in 2020. Safety is everyone's responsibility and is always the top priority, the first thought in any decision-making process. There's no question about that, is there? Safety should be more than that, though. It should be a core value you hold in your heart and at the very heart of your organization, from the top to the bottom. Now several seconds of awkward silenced passed after the question was asked. I then confidently answered the question on the call with an answer that probably sounded long-winded. I proclaimed, "Safety is the proactive identification of hazards and risks with mitigations implemented to either eliminate or reduce those risks to as low as possible in the operation to keep our people and our customers free from harm." I think I heard ten more seconds of silence after I spoke up. Eventually I heard a, "Sounds good to me.", by a timid, unfamiliar voice. I immediately thought I needed to rephrase my definition. I went against my rule of keeping all-things simple. I went on to say that safety is all about "risk management". We can't run a transportation operation without zero risks, so let's do everything we can do to identify hazards and risks before they become something unsafe and unacceptable. Let's do everything we can to truly run a safe operation where everyone in the organization knows their role in safety and feels supported to speak up when something doesn't look quite right to stop bad things from happening. You see, safety really is about so many different things. Simply put, in my humble opinion, safety is about managing risk. One thing is certain though. Safety in mass transit is evolving at a rapid pace.

I come to the wonderful world of mass transit from the ultra-safe world of commercial aviation. I spent almost thirty years with a major airline. The last position I held in aviation was that of Safety Management System (SMS) Manager in Technical Operations. My job was partly focused on change management processes and completing Safety Risk Assessments (SRAs) to ensure any unforeseen, unintended consequences with proposed changes were identified and mitigated before they had a chance to become reality. This ensured the success of many projects. But I must tell you, when a project wasn't implemented because the Safety Risk Assessment showed levels of unacceptable risk that could not be mitigated to an acceptable level, I celebrated those no-go project decisions even more. I became a true believer in SMS when I saw how it, the system and its processes, prevented bad things from happening repeatedly. SMS also knocked down departmental silos, improved cross-departmental communications and empowered all employees to report hazards with ever-increasing numbers over time without the fear of management retaliation. SMS in aviation is maturing. It is making an already extremely safe way to travel even safer. The great news is that SMS is coming to transit with the Federal requirement of the new Public Transportation Agency Safety Plan (PTASP), 49 CFR Part 673. The many benefits that aviation has enjoyed for over a decade with their Safety Management Systems in place will also benefit mass transportation. It's where we are going now with mass transit safety. It's why I am here as a Chief Safety Officer (CSO).

As the deadline approaches for mass transit agencies to implement the new PTASP and SMS requirements, I see great cooperation and sharing of ideas between the Federal Transit Administration (FTA), American Public Transportation Association (APTA) and the many mass transit agencies throughout the country. There should never be competition in safety, only the sharing of lessons learned and ways to do things better. Mass transit is benefitting from its close-knit, helpful community of committed people who want to become safer and are willing to share their ideas. One of the ideas we are sharing at my agency is the implementation of a Safety Management System (SMS) Ambassador program. As is true with many Safety departments, the current staffing levels may not be enough to effectively run an SMS focused on proactive safety risk management. Safety Officers can't always be everywhere at once. We have established our SMS Ambassador program by deputizing a member of each organizational department to help be our direct connection and to represent Safety in their respective work areas. They educate their fellow employees on how to report hazards and risks. They may even bring hazard reports to the monthly SMS Ambassador Meetings run by our SMS Manager. They are educated in SMS to the same level as our Safety Officers and can perform hazard analysis processes. We have over thirty SMS Ambassadors. Those are, in effect, thirty more members of the Safety department. That's a benefit of SMS worth celebrating. In addition, SMS requires an Employee Safety Reporting Program (ESRP). This program helps change your safety culture for the positive. We are also sharing the many ways we encourage and empower our employees, vendors and contractors to report hazards and concerns into our SMS. In keeping with our "keep it simple" theme, we have four easy ways to report. We have an easy to remember toll-free phone number to call, a simple email address to send a report to, a QR code to scan with your Smart Phone, and we have placed boxes throughout the facilities where paper reports can be dropped in anonymously. All reports and hazards are assessed and tracked to completion with a big emphasis on submitter follow-up. We even recognize our submitters when they report a hazard that could have been disastrous in potential outcome. This encourages more reports and, in turn, makes the operation safer. This may be the biggest benefit of SMS coming to transit. If we can get more hazard and risk reports into the SMS and addressed in a timely manner, all numbers in safety, quality and on-time performance should trend positively. I believe this is the future for transit along with a huge new focus on data collection and analysis. Data, data, data. That's where we're headed to make us even safer.

I talk a lot about hazard reports from employees and the need to increase those, but half of the true transit safety equation when it comes to proactive safety risk management efforts is obtaining hazard reports for riders. Riders can report system abnormalities in real time, not just security threats, by using technology such as apps on their smartphone. They can report a rough ride on the rail that may actually be a broken rail. They can report that a Bus Operator is operating in a reckless manner or who is on the phone. They can even report simple facilities issues such as icy platforms or parking lot lighting issues. These are all risks that need to be investigated and possibly mitigated. Those rider hazard reports in turn can be trended and analyzed. As organizations, we must look at rider safety and security feedback as much as we look at customer service feedback with the same amount of vigor. Not all possible system hazards will be seen or found by our employees. I see an increase in rider hazard reporting systems that are simple and user friendly making transit systems safer for all.

Let's now talk about data and innovation in safety.

It may be the most challenging task in implementing a Safety Management System. Finding all the current (and future sources) of information the organization has and bringing them together with the purpose of proactively identifying trends that show risk and safety performance. That's what I need to know every day as the CSO. Where is the risk in our organization? What is its level and if it's unacceptable, what is our plan to mitigate or eliminate it? If we mitigate it, are there any new, unintended risks introduced? Who and what over time is going to ensure our risk mitigations have been successful? Risk is in places you don't know about yet because maybe you haven't seen the data that proves it's there. Has risk been there for a while just simmering quietly, undetected? Let's not let it simmer any more. Take the cover off and expose it. Maybe there needs to be new sources of data brought in and analyzed to find those highly desired leading indicators every safety professional wants to review to prevent the next accident or incident. In our agency alone we have identified over three dozen sources of data that can help us proactively identify risk. That process of locating them and their respective owners took over six months. Now that we have the data sources identified, the future focus is in getting it all analyzed in a way that provides us with those valuable leading indicators. Getting those data sources to talk to one another is another challenge we must overcome. As we look to hire new people into the Safety department, solid data analytical skills are going to be a must have. Once we get a truer picture of operational risk based on data, we then will selectively assign our Safety Officers and Field Supervisors to focus their efforts on the areas of highest risk. Soon, risk-based inspections should play a vital role in ensuring the safety of transit assets and facilities. This is the natural tie-in between the FTA's required Asset Management program and Safety Management System (SMS). Both have risk thresholds that, if crossed or ignored, could lead to an accident, incident or tragic outcome. It is imperative to look at these two systems closely in terms of hazard analysis and risk management efforts.

The most exciting part of transit is the pace of innovation. From my position as the Chief Safety Officer (CSO), I see new products and services being introduced with the goal of improving the safety of all people, employees and the general public. In Safety, we do everything we can do to keep risk as low as possible by working with our internal and external customers. We also want to work to bring new engineering solutions to reality. Is there new technology that could detect patrons that have fallen into the track area and immediately alert the oncoming train operator in real time to stop the train preventing a strike? Is there new technology that could identify trespassers along long stretches of commuter rail tracks that would also alert train operators especially at night? We must keep asking the question, have we done all that we can do to lower risk or are there possible solutions out there that have yet to be designed and engineered? Positive Train Control (PTC) implementation has taken years to become a reality. I believe safety technologies in mass transit will be embraced at a quicker pace in the future as the requirement of having an SMS will require high levels of risk to be mitigated in a timely manner.

I can predict that with the implementation of SMS and the advancements in safety technologies, accident and incident rates will decline across the board. It will take time, but with a new laser focus on unacceptable risks, a commitment to safety and support of safety from the very top of every organization, and personal safety accountabilities held like never before, improvements will be evident and will be celebrated! Change management will also be a normal part of doing business with Safety involved at the beginning of all proposed projects and/or asset purchases. Automation of SMS systems will be widely in use making it simple. Additionally, the SMS Manager will be the most wanted person in the industry. You will also see Safety departments grow and expand to keep up with all the demands of an effective Safety Management System (SMS). Safety Data Analysts are going to be in great demand. I can also see a shift in track inspection methods. Instead of entire track systems being inspected by time schedules, they will be inspected on risk. Risk based inspections will become more acceptable in the industry for tracks and other assets. I am hoping to see new buses designed and delivered to fully protect the Operator behind a shield to eliminate the troubling operator assault issues. The future is bright for safety in transit, especially for those who question the way things have always been done.

To summarize my thoughts on mass transit safety, it's about managing risk in our risky environments. Let's all focus on being more proactive in our organizations by digging deep into the data. Let's never stop promoting the importance of the Employee Safety Reporting Program (ESRP). It's time to really engage our employees. They need to be heard and their reports valued. I will keep shouting from the mountaintop to the subway tunnels that safety is everyone's responsibility. Everyone needs to think and act like a risk manager. If the job is done the right way, in compliance to rules and regulations, we all will benefit from it. Let's keep working together by sharing our ideas on how to increase transit safety. Finally, let's commit to living safe every day, at home and at work. It's exciting times in transit. It's going to get safer by the passion of the transit professionals who value safety above all else. There is another definition of safety that I like. It is similar to the definition of integrity. It's doing the right thing, the safe thing, when no one is watching. What is more valuable than safety integrity? The answer is simple, nothing.

# Chapter 5

# The Future of Data Reporting

### By **Dave Jackson**
President
TransTrak

*Reporting our data has always been an important part of public transportation. I remember on my first job as Transportation Coordinator for Queen Anne's County I learned all the reporting procedures for NTD, UMTA and MTA grants, for Medical Assistance funding and for local requirements. I did them all by hand in rudimentary spreadsheets and hand typed the forms. Wow have times changed.*

*Dave Jackson has become a good buddy over the past couple years and is a leader in the industry as Chair of the IT Committee for APTA and head of a company focused on this key part of our business. Listen to his take on where this is going:*

The task of gathering, managing and analyzing transit operational data is one of the largest challenges facing transit agencies. Our industry has always had an interest in reporting tools, whether it is:

- Basic operations reporting e.g. incidents, on time performance, miles and hours of operations, ridership on a daily, monthly or annual basis;
- Monthly reporting for board reporting and for funding agencies or;
- Reporting for the National Transit Database (NTD), which was formed in 1974 for transit agencies receiving Federal Transit Administration (FTA) funding to report on performance to the FTA, congress and researchers.

Data is meticulously collected for NTD and Board Operating Reports, but precious little time is spent in analyzing the data because it is collected from multiple systems in a labor intensive process that leaves staff little time to actually step back and analyze the data in order to make important management decisions on service design and delivery policy.

Often transit agencies have looked upon all their data collection and analysis needs as a formidable task that is executed only when required. Many of these tasks take weeks or must be manually performed to meet the needs of the agency. The challenges of balancing supply and demand, that is, matching service levels to the financial resources allocated to a transit agency requires full time attention.

In the 70's and early 80's much of this data was gathered manually starting with the basic timetable information to calculate hours and miles, and exception reporting to add or deduct service as appropriate based on actual operations. While some of this data made its way to mainframe computers, Vax workstations, etc., most of the data gathering, summarization and reporting was largely manual.

With the advent of the personal computer in the mid 80's the mighty spreadsheet began to take life as the tool of choice for many reporting functions. While specialty programs started to be developed that covered the basic parts of the industry such as rail, fixed route and paratransit scheduling, some of the basic reporting became automated through these applications, but most fell short of the basic reporting needs of the agency, let alone the regulatory NTD reporting required by the FTA. The spreadsheet is the predominant reporting tool at many agencies today.

Collecting and maintaining data is expensive and time-consuming. Each department typically maintains a separate data system and these systems may not be integrated. Basic data, such as number of passengers, may have three separate and disparate numbers – one passenger number from the automated fare system (AFS), another number from automated passenger counters (APC), and a third number based on manual counts used to validate APC data. Data may reside in separate systems and no two numbers ever agree. In this case, the basis for performance data is inaccessible or fragmented and thus credibility and reliability are often impacted by data inconsistencies.

Consolidating data in an easy-to-use reporting system is a starting point for addressing data overload and fragmentation. In discussions about the numbers, there should never be any confusion about the accuracy of the data. The goal is to have data immediately available for tactical decision-making.

Wikipedia defines business intelligence as the "transformation of raw data into meaningful and useful information for business analysis purposes." Business intelligence (BI) is characterized by:

- A set of clear performance indicators that concisely convey the financial, service and safety performance of the agency
- The tools, processes and personnel to continually evaluate and improve agency performance
- The capability to identify challenges and opportunities, as well as the knowledge to take appropriate action

What this means in practical terms is that management wants a system of Key Performance Indicators (KPI's) and dashboards that provide accurate and timely information for strategic decision making. Supervisors and mid-level management want information for tactical decision-making to improve performance. Managers require information in enough detail to make daily decisions with confidence and assurance that the data is correct and accurate. This implies more detailed reporting and dashboard drilldowns. Data managers require an effective process to collect and report information that does not involve re-keying data from multiple databases and sources. IT Managers require systems, tools and services to support the BI program.

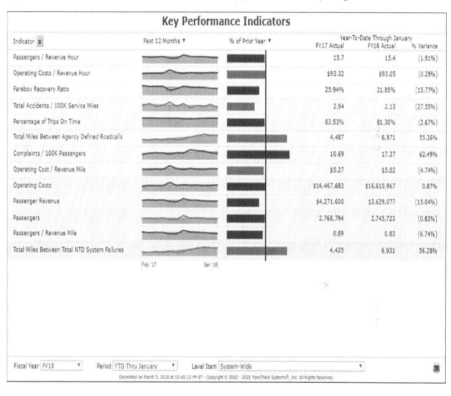

Numeric and trend graphs appear to be the predominant symbol for executive level dashboards designed to focus attention on a performance issue or issues. These are the pointers and trend identifiers; not the answer or reason for performance results. New BI tools focus on conveying the maximum information at a single glance.

BI applied to the transit industry can help reduce costs, increase passenger revenue, streamline operations and improve safety and service quality. Implementation of a successful BI program requires:

- Involvement by top management and full participation by data managers and process owners throughout the life of the BI program
- Identification of key indicators for measuring performance and agreement on data definitions and sources
- Elimination of time-consuming data reconciliations by obtaining data at the source and centralization of data storage and reporting
- Involving the entire team in a collaborative effort to establish targets, analyze performance results and develop of improvement strategies

The successful implementation is a mixture of people, process and technology. Technology is often the easiest part of the equation. The proper processes must be put in place to ensure that the data is properly collected and managed such that the results are consistent for each time period that the data is measured. People must be properly engaged and motivated to ensure that the data is correct each day, week and month to support the BI tools. If each level of the management team regularly reviews the dashboards and associated data, and identifies to staff when there are anomalies, and focuses on making sure the data is accurate, accountability is the direct result as staff will know the importance of the data and will prioritize making sure it is correct as part of their normal routine.

A successful BI implementation empowers employees at every level of the organization to make better decisions. Critical transit data needs to be accessible to all employees so they can perform their own analyses and collaborate with team members on fact-based improvement strategies. With access to relevant data, displayed as useful information, employees can find opportunities to operate more effectively.

Successful BI implementations are setup to handle agency data from a variety of sources and can manage data from legacy systems as well as the new systems as the older systems are replaced. Trying to build these tools in house is not cost effective to build or maintain as technical staff need to fully understand not only the technology but the business processes and needs as well. Additionally, many of the manual processes and spreadsheets that are prevalent in the business need to be accommodated within the BI tools themselves to provide an effective way to manage these aspects of the business and include them within the reporting tools provided with the BI implementation.

Successful BI implementations are also supported by staff that understand not only the technology and the business, but also the industry best practices of all facets of the BI tool deployed.

*You can contact Dave at www.transtracksystems.net*

# Chapter 6

# The Future of Labor Relations

### By David Vinson

### Labor Negotiation Specialist

*I first met Dave Vinson about a decade ago while we both worked for MV Transportation. He was National Director then Vice President for Labor Relations and helped me renegotiate the collective bargaining agreement (CBA) with our union in DC. Then when I became CEO of MTA in Baltimore, I recruited him to assist us there in the role of a consultant for the same function. We received over 70% yes votes of the union members for ratification of the proposed CBA, while the previous three negotiations had all ended up in Interest Arbitration.*

*I have found him to be one of the most literate, engaged and caring labor relations experts in the nation. It probably helps that he started his career as a Teamsters Local President so he truly understands and relates with union members and their leadership and can communicate with them from a position of credibility and respect. His contribution here rings true for me and I think it will help position our industry to better anticipate some of the coming changes in this important field of work for the public transportation industry.*

## The Past, into the 2020s - and Beyond

The changes happening within the Transit Industry are not and will not occur in a vacuum. As a career Labor Relations executive, I may be a bit biased, but virtually every area of change this upcoming decade will in fact be affected by the relationships and negotiations outcomes with Organized Labor. Data from the Bureau of Labor Statistics reveals the general union membership rate for 2018 was 10.5%, which is about even with the numbers from 2017. However, that percentage represents a precipitous overall decline in union membership since comparable data was first released in 1983. That year, more than 20% of workers belongs to a union. Over time, that number has dropped steadily by almost half.

Historically, the Transit industry has had a considerably higher percentage of bargained employees than the overall private sector – a fact that will probably result in a rather exaggerated influence by Labor in relation to the changes occurring throughout the industry. Change will come, but many areas of transition will necessitate negotiation with Union partners – thus, the speed and efficacy of the changes will be affected by the skill, strategy and planning of those Labor Relations practitioners that are tasked with negotiating the Labor Agreements of the 2020s and beyond.

To further drive this point regarding Labor's influence, let's take a quick look at how a Collective Bargaining Agreement (CBA) affects Transit operations and those whose management and oversight ensure the routes are on time, safe and efficient. The Agreement directly determines employee assignments (bidding), time off, PTO, the ability to sever ties with bad or unsafe employees – and a majority of economic levers that affect the cost of running a Transit entity: wages, PTO, benefits, pension, etc. I've had to state and reinforce these facts a number of times through the years when some operations leaders don't understand the absolute necessity of smart, strategic, well planned, data-driven Union negotiations.

In this chapter I will present my perspective regarding how overall Labor Relations has – and will further change within the Transit industry between the 2010s and 2020s. My first experience in the Transit world of Labor was in late 2005. I had just made a career change from the Union side of the table and had many years of bargaining and overall experience in every aspect of LR, and in many industries. However, I quickly found out that Transit LR was indeed a "different animal." In the early 2000s I was confronted (mostly in California and the Northwest) by rather aggressive Transit local unions that seemed hungry for membership and whose bargaining priorities were to protect their members from the onslaught of new drug/alcohol testing regulations, heightened Agency concerns regarding overall driver safety and trying to achieve compensation and benefit breakthroughs that would help keep up with inflation and other bargained industry standards. Confronted with these realities, it quickly became apparent that in order to be successful in the Labor Relations arena, the Transit sector required considerably more effort than most regarding establishing and growing good working relationships with Union representatives. It was not my experience or opinion that this had been a priority in my region for quite some time. Thus, I set about meeting and trying to establish good, positive working relationships with every Union leader – at every level, that my business was tasked to deal and negotiate with on a regular basis. Yes, this takes a relatively steep investment in time, travel and emotional energy, but the returns were substantial. I experienced and witnessed a fairly high increase in cooperation between Transit Unions and the management I supported during this period. It seemed many of the more militant and aggressive Labor Relations practitioners and Union officials were either coming around to a more cooperative mindset or retiring. Then came the Great Recession.

The Great Recession of 2007-2009 affected Transit Labor Relations like most other areas of the economy – drastically. Direct federal funding for Transit Agencies was frozen or cut, property tax revenue that frequently went to local Transit fell, and with the spike in unemployment ridership also dropped almost universally. Transit Labor negotiations during this period were interesting to say the least, and I recall very few economic issues coming to a head. The Unions realized the financial situation the Agencies were facing, as well as a reduction in ridership, thus wage and benefit increases were minimal, at best at this time. (1% or annual wage freezes were common.) The negotiation landscape had changed and just like

81

the rest of the nation (and a good part of the Western world), sacrifice and getting by with gains from better times would have to suffice for a while. There actually seemed to be a "comradery" between the parties during this time because of the catastrophic economic events that most had never seen before, nor since. We sensed that we actually were "all in this together" and must partner in order to get though those tough times.

When the 2010s came along there was a new issue arising within Transit Labor Relations. An issue that started small, has gotten bigger and now is front and center – Technology. As the dual focus of safety and cost became larger and larger – negotiation and day-to day Labor strategies had to be reimagined. The Transit units I supported, initially across the Western USA, were fixed, paratransit and employee shuttles. Very different types of operations, but the focus on safety from a Labor Relations perspective was rather universal. Around 2008, as safety related technology was becoming more and more the norm, new and re-negotiated CBAs had to reflect this reality. One of the first major tools to be implemented in this direction were the on-board camera systems. These early systems were initially G-force or driver activated and became the subject of my initial foray into negotiating the necessary Technology language with the Unions. The fact that these on-board recording systems could and would be used as evidence in employee disciplinary actions necessitated a skilled negotiation approach. These early systems would "activate" an onboard camera system if there was a certain amount of G-force exercised on the vehicle – such as hitting another vehicle or fixed object, or a hard break. Today many people have Ring Doorbells and other camera technology around their homes and personal cars – but in the 2008-2010s period, this was pretty high-tech and game changing stuff. My approach was to carefully craft then bargain "Technology" language into every CBA that I or my team negotiated - regardless of the technology level that an Agency or company's vehicles possessed. It was clear that this tide was going to rise…and I preferred it to not be a Tsunami, rather a wave I could ride in more of a controlling manner.

Thus, Transit Labor negotiators in this period who saw what was coming and acted at the table at every negotiation had a relatively smooth ride. I had very little pushback from my Union partners, as they also knew that this would need to be dealt with sooner or later. As many employed strategies regarding Technology language in the 2010s, newer and more sophisticated systems were coming online. GPS based systems that could track vehicle location, speed, traffic law compliance, on-time route performance and other areas were hitting the market rapidly. For those Transit Labor practitioners who had the foresight to see what the new norm could be, things have gone well. The basic Technology language that I crafted in 2007 for relatively simple camera systems has morphed through re-negotiation to change with the technologies. The key here with technology, and in other mission-critical areas is to get ahead of the curve by being intuitive and understanding the landscape as it exists – and how it might change.

Tomorrow's Transit industry Labor Relations landscape will be a very different place then the one I entered in 2005. Many of the same issues – technology, safety, employee attendance and conduct, funding restraints, etc. will still be on the negotiating table baked into proposals from both parties. I believe in the Transit Labor world the "what" and the "how" will be transformed in a number of ways. Let me explain a bit.

There have always been drivers or "operators," but what will their job description be in 2030? AI's influence is exploding in our economy, and Transit is one of the industries that could be affected the most and the soonest. Autonomous transit vehicles have already been launched and / or are being expedited for use in Public Transit at a breathtaking pace. (https://www.apta.com/research-technical-resources/mobility-innovation-hub/autonomous-vehicles/) This will ultimately require a huge investment in strategy and effort at the bargaining table with all Transit Union partners. The "operator" of the next decade may in fact be an onboard "software operator" that assists or backs up a vehicle's AI driven system. They may simply act as a backup driver in case of system failure, or even customer service representatives – or some combination. Thus, these affected job classifications must be completely re-written and the affects on existing operators negotiated. My 2000's Technology language is starting to look rather quaint. Not only will existing job classifications have to be re-written rather drastically, there will be entirely new tech-driven classifications across the board. Unionized Transit maintenance employees will not only do bus repairs and vehicle maintenance. There will be a need for computer and software techs that "fix" and maintain this new AI driven (literally) hardware. Updates will need to be installed, Agency apps maintained, system data downloads...well you get the idea.

The potential for the number of (dues paying) operators to dwindle in the coming decade(s) is real, therefore, Union organizers can be counted on to set their sights on these new tech-heavy classifications. Remember, any reduction in bargaining unit members also means a reduction in contributions to affected Health & Welfare and Pension Funds – many of which are already underfunded. The time to begin preparing for strategic bargaining in the area of changing classifications is upon us, both in re-defining existing classifications and in inoculating new ones against potential organizing. Looking ahead, as CBAs expire in 2020, these issues, even if in the embryonic stages, must be addressed with extreme foresight and intuition.

Technology will also change collective bargaining in the Transit industry as more options become available to riders. App based transportation, increasingly productive dispatching software, changes in city traffic policy, Transit dedicated lanes and an increase in overall competition in the industry will all have effects on bargaining in the next decade. In 2010 who could have imagined app-based companies like Uber and Lyft would transport millions of riders door to door on demand with a few taps on a smartphone? Unions that represent Transit workers would be wise to see the competition handwriting on the wall. The large Transit corporate players and agencies should do the same. In the USA we have entire industries that have been devastated by poor responses to increased competition as a result of new technology - and poor collective bargaining strategies that hastened a number of these demises. No one wins long term when this occurs. People will always need to move from one place to another in our society and economy, and if the Labor Relations practices, especially CBA negotiations within the Transit industry are not updated to be more proactive, intuitive and strategic, there may well be some rather difficult challenges ahead.

*You can contact David Vinson via LinkedIn: https://www.linkedin.com/in/david-vinsonba4115/*

# Chapter 7

# The Future of Smart Infrastructure Asset Management

## By Brett Koenig

Industry Solutions Manager, Enterprise Asset
Management, Trapeze Group

*Brett Koenig has nearly 20 years of experience
implementing public transit and rail asset management
systems. He and I both work for the same company
and often collaborate on projects together that deal
with asset management and state of good repair. He
helped me prepare for my speech this year to most of
Australia's top transit asset managers.*

*Below he gives some insight into what you can do
practically to improve in this important part of effective
transit management over the next few years.*

## The smart infrastructure revolution

The business of transit is incredibly infrastructure intensive. Look down the street in any major city and you see buses and trains, stations and stops, all operating along a vast network of streets and rail corridors. For a transit system to be running on-time, countless mechanical systems need to all be functioning smoothly together. With so many interrelated pieces of equipment, the margin for error is very small: All it takes is one major component failure on a commuter train to trigger a cascading series of events from which it's difficult to recover: rider delays, leading ultimately to lower satisfaction and potentially lower ridership. So, as we look to the future, one industry challenge is: can agencies deliver more consistently-reliable service, by significantly reducing (even eliminating) service delays due to mechanical failure?

In what is being called the latest Industrial Revolution, the (Industrial) Internet of Things (IIoT) offers the promise of dramatic increases in transit service reliability. So exactly what is IIoT? What started out years ago as simply "telematics" (sensors communicating data/faults to another system), is becoming a massive network of asset health monitoring devices embedded throughout your bus/rail network. As more and more of this "smart" infrastructure comes online, it is providing real-time actionable intelligence so that agencies know which

88

assets are healthy and which may be on the verge of failing. In short, IIoT is the equivalent of today's smartwatches: it puts the agency's finger directly on the pulse of its transit infrastructure's health. Among the benefits of IIoT are improved asset reliability, prolonged asset life, decreased costs from fewer component failures, and ultimately higher customer satisfaction.


Rolling Super-Computers and State of Good Repair
Today, a convergence of political and technological trends are driving the IIoT revolution in transit. The conditions are ripe for change due to the international ISO 55000 standards and the timeline imposed by MAP-21/FAST Act, which mandated that agencies comply with State of Good Repair requirements by 2018. The most significant trend, however, is technological. We are in the midst of a "smart infrastructure" revolution, with more and more sensors embedded into new transit infrastructure coming online. New fleets of vehicles (railcars, buses) have become rolling supercomputers, capable of monitoring their own health in real-time. Installed on those vehicles are a multitude of telematic sensors embedded in electrical and mechanical systems. Common bus components capable of self-monitoring include: engine, transmission, brakes, retarder, and body controllers, to name a few. For railcars, a multitude of systems include propulsion, HVAC, door, and braking systems. But it's not just rolling stock. For rail wayside, SCADA alerts are commonly generated by power substations, interlockings, and elevators.
 Major Systems Alerts A key benefit of tracking fault data in real-time is the ability to detect an equipment failure and alert maintenance before it occurs (e.g. conditions have reached a user-defined min/max

threshold). This notification gives operations staff time to proactively swap-out the component before failure, thereby avoiding the disruption to service. In addition to fault monitoring, IIoT also tracks operational characteristic data to better understand the expected useful life of a system under your local operating conditions. For example, switches/motors, can be can be counted for how long they operate before failure. Leading agencies are embracing this trend to the point of creating the role of Data Scientist (in function, if not in name) to turn the growing mountains of IIoT data into "actionable intelligence". This information can then be used to optimize your maintenance intervals which are often based upon very conservative manufacturer-recommended intervals.

So, how can you fully benefit from these advancements?

## Four Step Approach to Transit IoT

1.    Your equipment is talking, are you listening? Include telematic requirements in your new equipment specifications, so that any new, safety-critical infrastructure (vehicles, facilities, wayside) that you bring online has these capabilities from day 1. For legacy equipment, engage with your equipment vendors to tap-into the telematic condition monitoring data that may already exist. If none exist, investigate the many third party telematic options available in the marketplace.

2.    Get integrated. Explore building interfaces to send fault codes from high priority systems (propulsion, brakes, elevators, SCADA, etc.), to your enterprise asset management system to alert maintenance and

generate work orders.

3.      Don't be afraid of the data.  Over time the largest gains are realized through a comprehensive IIoT approach involving analyzing patterns in the data.  This is typically achieved by integrating your critical streams of health monitoring data into a single system such as commercially available Business Intelligence, or Predictive Analytics tool.

4.      Evolve your maintenance regime.  For transit Maintenance divisions, IIoT is seen as a catalyst to evolve the industry from standard fixed (time/mileage) maintenance to the newer condition-based and predictive paradigms.  With a deeper understanding of your infrastructure's health patterns, ask yourself "Are there ways we can optimize our maintenance program?" Real-world examples include:  switching certain inspections from fixed-interval to condition-based, and refining the frequency of selected services (increase interval for component rebuilds, etc.).

A significant reduction in service delays due to equipment failure is within reach if you listen more closely to what your infrastructure is telling you.  Asset health monitoring technologies are something your maintenance division should be investigating now.  For many agencies a fully-integrated IIoT system may feel like a lofty goal, so start by focusing first on your most safety critical systems.

*You can contact Brett through his company website:*
*www.trapezegroup.com*

# Chapter 8

# The Future of Public Transportation .... Talent!

## By **Daphne Le Blanc**

Principal / CEO
TALENT SEARCH CONSULTANTS, LLC

*"To prepare for a new mobility paradigm, we need the best and the brightest skilled workforce. We must professionalize many of our front-line jobs by linking them to skills-based certifications and measurable competencies at every level of our agencies. It's simple - industries that use transformational times to their advantage are usually the ones investing in their employees." - Nathaniel P. Ford, APTA Chair (2017-18) and CEO, Jacksonville Transportation Authority. October 9, 2017 – APTA Annual Meeting & EXPO (Atlanta, GA)*

*We all know there is a real shortage of drivers and mechanics in transit agencies across our industry as many of the baby boomers and Gen Xers (my generation) in these jobs have begun to retire. But there also is a general issue of keeping our staff and executive positions filled with competent, qualified employees with the "fire in the belly" to relentlessly pursue excellence. Daphne Le Blanc has dedicated her career to helping agencies find just these kinds of applicants. I'm excited to have her share a little of her*

*approach and how we need it more than ever to staff*
*the transit systems of tomorrow.*

H ow and where do we find future leaders of the
transit industry?
You'd be surprised at the talent that has been
languishing just below the surface. That perhaps with
coaching, could be a future leader. And when your
institutional knowledge needs to be replaced, perhaps
we should look to other industries where mass
transportation has something in common...High Risk &
Highly Regulated. Aviation, Health Care, Oil & Gas,
Nuclear, Aerospace and Utilities, to name a few.
(Safety, procurement, risk, operations, etc.)

How we do what we do, and who we do it with...Two
words: Process & Talent

I am presented with this reality on an ongoing basis as
I conduct the next search and matching talent
accordingly. The transit industry is moving slowly but
surely toward a more proactive approach to mobility,
anticipating what our service delivery must be in order
to improve the customer experience and maintain
ridership. But as we change external needs we must
also change or enhance our internal needs. Our talent.
Leadership with a working understanding of continuous
improvement or performance management, workforce
planning are in great demand in general. We must go
where the talent is. Functions such as safety,
procurement, planning; risk management, human
capital, financial, etc. In fact more and more leadership

positions with in surface transportation are being filled by professionals within air transportation (aviation).

### Retain Talent (Bread & Butter)

Look first in your own backyard; don't let good talent get away in the first place. Assess your talent, find your stars and set up a meeting!

Employer: Investing time in your team and actually asking them what they would be interested in doing within the organization as a next step, be it a promotion or lateral move gathering knowledge across departments… it shows your interest in their future.  The 30 year employee may be a thing of the past, but we can do more to retain the good talent that we have. Establish a development plan complete with career aspirations and ask your star talent a key question… Put these three things in the order of importance: Position, Location & Money (if they say Position, drill down and ask them how much money they would leave on the table to get it or ask…so you would go anywhere for the right opportunity?) It might start out a bit shaky but through the conversation you will get a better idea of what's important to them.

Employee: I have said many times to candidates as they complain that their employer doesn't care about them. I say…your family and your God care about you… your employer pays you for a job well done. It's your responsibility to make sure to get everything from of this employer that you can.  When you see things changing like legacy talent retiring and transitioning, find out how you might transition into a better opportunity, as well. And...always attend the APTA Annual Conference, even if you have to pay for it yourself.

## Attract (Future)

When the market place knows that your organization cares about the career development of its employees enough to create a development & retention plan in addition to a great benefits package, it adds to what makes you an employer of choice.

And, as we encounter an even more multigenerational workforce (baby boomers, millennials, Xgens) we must learn to get the most out of working more collaboratively together, making necessary adjustments. Ex. An employer said to me that millennials are not interested in working in one place for more than a couple of years. I said to that employer, fine than let's make sure you get the most out of that couple of years in talent, ideas and energy... and move on.

I'm a sports enthusiast and have always noticed that **most teams work best with veterans and rookies!**

## Reclaiming My Time (Legacy /Transitioning Personnel)

Employers could schedule meetings with potential retirees (3 to 5 years) and find out about their plans moving forward; if they would find an interest in a planned gradual "tapering off" schedule complete with identifying select team members to shadow specific function(s) of that potential retiree… "Legacy Shadowing". Taking back your time.

## Make Use of the Full Range of Talent

Much like a transit system takes advantage of multiple modes (bus, van, light rail, scooter), we much intentionally utilize a full range of talent including: full time, part time, interns, consultants, and previously retired "active seniors". And finally have each department head cultivate a solid #2 and hold them accountable for doing so as part of the structured job description.

## Bridging the Gap

It has become a national challenge and we must now work nationally to bridge the growing gap, at a time when transit is at its most dynamic, increasing infrastructure; mobility and connectivity. The problem … not enough operators, mechanics, trainers, etc. Generally, we are not attracting sufficient talent to maintain and continue our increase in service. It is creating choices that include possible reductions in service. Everybody has an opinion and here is my two cents: Intentionally create a plan to:

- Create more cluster collaborations and/or regional style clearing houses to funnel applicants into a system that screens, tests and shares within the cluster/region applicants that make it through the process.

- Join with a collection of technical schools and junior colleges to create the curriculum with them and develop a certification course and thus a pipeline.

- Establish a sustainable full range systematic and <u>ongoing approach</u> to recruitment for similar positions.

- Use a team that includes an active senior recently retired from the transit industry and an emerging transit talented professional to engage with high schools; junior collages, and trade schools. <u>Ongoing Effort</u>.

*You can contact Daphne by email at transearch@aol.com*

# Chapter 9

# The Future of Transit Fleet Maintenance

## By **Richard Haukka**
### Director of Maintenance
### Pacific Western Transportation Ltd

*I met Richard through LinkedIn and then in person this year at the CUTA Conference in Calgary. He is Director of Maintenance for the largest privately held people transportation company in Canada.*

*When we talked, I thought he had many interesting insights into where bus maintenance was headed in the next few years and I asked him to share some of them with us here.*

The majority of specialty skillsets that employers hired for in the 1990's and 2000's are tailored for engine and fuel technologies (like diesel engines) are at the end of their development. The future of bus maintenance, especially in Transit will change drastically as new technologies are implemented into service.

Implementation of AVL, cameras, driver telematics, onboard diagnostics, contactless pay systems and onboard wifi have challenged the maintenance divisions to diversify their skillsets and adapt to new technology at a steady rate. Some transit companies have divided labor between mechanical and electrical technicians to solve a short-term problem. However, this has created a new dynamic which has divided an organizations ability to adapt to future changes in technology.

In recent years, transit agencies have begun piloting new types of propulsion systems such as battery electric, hydrogen fuel cell, compressed natural gas, and gasoline powered units. Small scale switching over to alternate fuels, battery and fuel cell electric go largely unnoticed from a maintenance standpoint because the manufacturers can support these initiatives. When a new, dominant propulsion technology emerges and displaces the bulk of a major fleet (500-2500 buses), it will change the type of infrastructure and workforce required to support it.

The problems that a transit agency may not think about when changing to a new fuel/propulsion type are around the lifecycle and sustainability of the technology as it was intended. Often large transit agencies have substantial maintenance operations with unionized shops where technicians that have defined scopes of work. The clean boundaries of these jobs are being blurred. Electric drive systems don't nicely line up with these old definitions and threaten the stability and suitability of an established transit workshop because the areas of expertise completely change. The reluctance to revamp exiting maintenance operations are magnified by the difficulty to hire and train new people into the Transit specific environment.

Long term success (and realized savings) of transitioning to an electric or alternate fuel like CNG hinges on successful transition of the maintenance operations and the people within it.

In the last 15 years, I've seen normally agreed upon business metrics like repair times, bus to mechanic ratios and fleet spare ratios become political hot potatoes within the management/union relationship when non-conventional vehicle types are injected. Often the lack of industry knowledge becomes the greatest enemy to adapting an alternate power source and knowing how to budget for and maintain it.

The electric bus is the best example of this. Many of the options for propulsion in North American electric buses are sourced from European sources, mostly German. The manufactures of these systems insist that the hood should only be opened by an engineer. In North America, this is not practical as these types of technicians are not common and cannot be hired at sufficient quantities. Specialized training to support these drive systems in North America must be performed locally to bring technicians accustomed to working on diesel bus and truck systems up to speed. In this model, quality of work on new technology, qualifications for safety and warranty compliance become additional factors that the transit agency need to consider.

*You can contact Richard through his company website www.pwtransit.ca*

# Part II

# CEO's Speak

*Now let's hear from some of the Public Transit CEOs who have to put it all together and make sure that bus/rail service gets on the streets every day. As a former CEO of America's 11th largest transit system, (the MTA in Baltimore) I know the burden these CEOs have to bear every day to keep the public, their boards and key stakeholders happy (or at least only mildly to moderately dissatisfied - thanks Leland).*

*So, it takes a bold leader to adopt new approaches but here are some of the best in the business - I know each of them and have visited their operations - giving us their approach to these new transit trends and how they are going to create the Future of Public Transportation in their own cities:*

# Chapter 10
# MJ Maynard

Chief Executive Officer
Regional Transportation Commission of Southern
Nevada (RTC) in Las Vegas, Nevada

*If there ever was a woman made to lead transit in Las Vegas/Southern Nevada, it's MJ Maynard. She cut her teeth in the city as VP of the Hard Rock Hotel and Casino then spent over a decade as Deputy CEO of the RTC with the great Tina Quigley. Now given the reigns she is galloping forward at fast clip ready to assume the mantle of leadership in our industry into the new Roaring 20s!*

*To recount all their innovations at RTC would take multiple pages – here are a few: RTC, in concert with the City of Las Vegas and Keolis North America, led the country in the implementation of shared autonomous vehicles (AV), running an AV on a route to Fremont Street (which I got to try) and are now ready for their US DOT-funded autonomous circulator between downtown Las Vegas and the Las Vegas Medical District. The RTC partnered with ride-sharing company Lyft on a first-mile/last-mile program to help employees of a local business located in an area not served by transit.*

*The RTC launched a new, affordable, on-demand, shared-ride service called Trip to Strip. The RTC has a partnership with Lyft that has provided hundreds of paratransit customers with a same-day flexible service option that is also saving the RTC hundreds of thousands of dollars. The RTC's mobile ticketing and trip planning app, rideRTC, already integrates multiple transportation options to help people plan their trip, including public transit, bike share, and Uber and Lyft rideshare services. The RTC also oversees the local Traffic Management Center, the nation's first truly integrated Intelligent Transportation System (ITS) operating across all jurisdictions in the region. It's an amazing facility (that MJ gave me a tour of last year) that combines law enforcement, road and traffic management and public transportation.*

*This chapter is her take on how to really transform transit in this next decade. Read it and be inspired.*

## Transforming Transportation

Transportation as an industry is evolving faster than ever before. Today, new and emerging transportation options like autonomous vehicles, electric scooters and private rideshare services are transforming how people get from one place to another. As we look to the future, we know that no one mode is going to solve all our transportation issues. We need to leverage a broad mix of advanced technologies and multimodal options to build a synergistic ecosystem of mobility services that are flexible and can work together to address the needs of our residents and visitors.

As a result, public transit agencies and municipalities are working overtime to test advanced mobility solutions to help meet the transportation challenges currently facing their communities, while also planning for the future to ensure investments complement or are compatible with new technologies. With these goals in mind, the Regional Transportation Commission of Southern Nevada (RTC) launched On Board, a comprehensive community transportation planning initiative to help address our region's transportation needs and priorities for the next 20 years.

With substantial community engagement, data analysis, and expertise from local and national mobility leaders, On Board outlines eight bold mobility moves to improve the quality of life in Southern Nevada and prepare our transportation system for the expected growth over the next two decades. These include building high-capacity transit; expanding transit service to maximize access to jobs and homes; enhancing the safety and security of all travel options; making short trips easier and safer; expanding dedicated services for seniors, veterans and people with disabilities; improving resident connections to major destinations; providing reliable transit for the city's hospitality employees; and leveraging new technology to improve mobility and sustainability.

These mobility priorities will help provide more sustainable transportation options for Southern Nevada, which is seeing sprawling economic diversification and population growth. Like other innovative transit agencies, we are already testing technologies to meet the mobility needs of a diverse and expansive region.

For example, we have forged public/private partnerships to offer more point-to-point, on-demand transportation services. Through a partnership with Lyft and a local employer, we are bridging the first- and last-mile transit connectivity gap in a user-friendly and highly cost-efficient manner. With costs shared among the partners, employees can take subsidized Lyft rides from transit to work, equating to thousands of miles that employees would have walked to and from bus stops. These rides often include more than one employee, reducing the number of single occupant cars on the road. Another partnership with Lyft has provided hundreds of our paratransit customers with a same-day flexible service option that is also saving the RTC hundreds of thousands of dollars. It is clear from these programs that transit and rideshare can co-exist and even complement each other to enhance mobility.

In the future, the continued development of such partnerships, as well as the addition of neighborhood and mobility hubs that marry multiple forms of transportation, including microtransit, to meet the individual needs of a commuter will likely become more commonplace. Yet, to support a higher level of multimodal connectivity, single-platform ticketing, mobility on-demand solutions and real-time travel information at high-volume transit stops will need to be developed.

The RTC's mobile ticketing and trip planning app, rideRTC, already integrates multiple transportation options to help people plan their trip, including public transit, bike share, and Uber and Lyft rideshare services. As we move forward, we are looking to add other transportation operators to create an integrated payment system across multiple transportation services. Then, with just one app and a few clicks, a rider can find out how to get from point A to point B in the most efficient way possible and pay for their trip, too.

One mobility option that will likely dominate the future of transportation and transform transit is the autonomous vehicle. The successful pilot of the nation's first autonomous shuttle in mixed traffic in downtown Las Vegas led to federal funding for GoMed, a groundbreaking advanced mobility project in the Las Vegas Medical District. Set to launch within the next few years, the program will use three self-driving shuttles to connect patients, employees, students and some of our most vulnerable populations, such as the elderly and persons with disabilities, to essential health care services, employment, and education opportunities in this fast-growing area. Paired with state-of-the-art pedestrian safety technologies and nearly two dozen smart transit shelters, GoMed epitomizes the future of transit by leveraging emergent and automated technologies in a complex urban setting.

GoMed's success, like that of its predecessor pilot, requires significant coordination and cooperation among numerous agencies, jurisdictions and private partners. To achieve sustainable multimodal mobility in the future, we will all need to work together and beyond our individual silos to implement flexible, integrated solutions to connect people to opportunities and services, reduce traffic congestion and increase safety.

While On Board charts Southern Nevada's mobility course for the next 20 years, a lot can change between now and 2040. The development of a flexible and interconnected mobility system will require continued monitoring of emerging technologies and transportation disruptions as well as the identification of trigger points for course corrections to keep the plan "future proof" long-term.

No one has a crystal ball to see what the future holds. But it is certain that technology will continue to revolutionize transportation and that consumer preferences will continue to change. We only have to look at the last ten years of urban mobility to know the future will look dramatically different from the past. Emerging next-generation mobility solutions are evolving rapidly and call into question the appropriateness of solutions the transportation industry has relied on for decades. As an industry facing a transformative future, we need to listen to our customers, evolve with the changes, and work together to create a safer and more connected transportation system for all.

# Chapter 11
# Phil Verster

### President and Chief Executive Officer
### Metrolinx in Toronto, Canada

*Phil Verster is a rock star in our industry. Coming from South Africa with a long, rich history of leading rail in the UK, he now heads Metrolinx in Toronto and is the operator of GO Transit: GO bus, GO commuter train, and UP Express (airport). Metrolinx is the Toronto's regional transit planner and is responsible for two massive capital investment projects: GO expansion with 4 consortiums for $30B and the Toronto subway expansion. An interesting tidbit is that Metrolinx is the largest free parking provider in North America with a total of 70,000 free parking spots across all their facilities.*

*He also has a unique customer service concept for GO Commuter Train passengers that I got to see first-hand. This service allows passengers to order their groceries online and have them delivered to their local GO Train Station for pick up from a refrigerated locker on site when they get back to the station after work. Metrolinx developed this unique partnership with Canadian grocery store giant, Loblaws, to make GO Stations the first outpost for Loblaws' "Click and Collect program". This creates a strong value proposition for transit amongst commuters who are seeking to save time in their day.*

*Phil Verster is a very progressive, business-like CEO that has a clear plan to achieve his service goals. The priority for Metrolinx is to expand and Phil wants to shift the agency to operate more like a business, so it requires less and less public subsidy. When I visited him in his offices at the Toronto Union Station, I had just finished a day-long tour of his operations and found his massive team responsive, engaged and focused on safety and operational excellence. Phil has a definitive operational philosophy that guides him and his agency. He calls it the Four Musts and it can help any agency or transit system improve and grow.*

## The Four Musts

Hereby my thoughts on the "Four Must's" transit organizations must espouse of Safety, Business culture, Customer and Innovation:

- Every transit organization MUST have an intense, passionate and systematic core business philosophy of "Safety First"

- Transit organizations MUST operate as and adopt the behaviours of commercial businesses, in everything they do and must not become "departments" or "agencies" or bureaucracies.

- Transit teams MUST focus on customer benefits and must innovate in order to excel at satisfying customers

- A positive focus on responsibly and effectively adopting innovation MUST be used to reinvent operations, increase customer satisfaction and revenue while reducing costs.

110

Taking these in turn:

## 1. A core transit philosophy of "Safety First"

Transit organizations that develop deep, authentic and tangible safety behaviours are most likely to serve their customers best, have better community relations, have better supply chains and be better at managing their own operations, revenues and costs.

There are very practical reasons why this core philosophy, when adopted, fundamentally changes the fabric transit organization - safety is a "high agreement" core value, as leader you can build continuous improvement capabilities around improving safety which can be redeployed to benefit other parts of your operational performance. You can link your organization's focus on safety to your focus on customers.

In Metrolinx we adopted a an integrated "Customer and Safety Charter" (attached) while driving significant change programmes to develop and refocus our teams to make safety a real, daily commitment - and to focus those same behaviours to excel at satisfying customers. We do a "Safety Moment" at the start of every meeting where individuals talk to their peers about their home, work and personal safety experiences, we have invested huge efforts into safety performance indicators and we systematically review and act on these from the frontline right up to the CEO and senior team, and we have established an industry wide CEO-level "Safety, health and Environment Leadership Team" to drive safety innovations such as

RFID motion sensors for worker safety and locally operated warning systems for railway operations safety.

## 2. Transit organizations must operate as and adopt the behaviours of commercial businesses

While it may sound too obvious to say "operate as a business", it is remarkable how many transit agencies operate as "departments" or "divisions" with a policy/bureaucracy culture rather than with a strong business culture. There are four important "operate as a business" features, in my view, that transit agencies must invest in to have a strong business culture:

- Develop the marketing capability to deliver revenue plans that are based on a deep understanding of customer behaviours, customer requirements, market segmentation, marketing channels and price/adoption sensitivities. The GO train and bus revenues are growing at 6.2% per year and ridership by 5.5% because of a systematic market segmentation into 7 "Journey Purposes" and separate marketing campaigns for each of those segments that entice new riders to adopt transit.

- Create a confident commercial capability that can extract the appropriate balance of benefits from the complex supplier and stakeholder agreements in place, including defending against complex construction claims. Metrolinx recover around 2.5% of its operational cost base, per year, from commercial management. But most of all, the construction of a new line (the "Freight Bypass") at a cost of $4.5 billion has been avoided through a commercial solution reached with an infrastructure owner in the same geography.

- CEOs must manage their transit businesses to a "bottom line" that is not all about costs. Metrolinx implemented and manage, every month, the whole enterprise using 85 "Key Performance Indicators" and a Risk Management framework which supports reviews and action planning of everything from returns from revenue campaigns through to time to recruitment new employees, customer satisfaction and employee engagement. Most importantly, the "bottom line" is about the level of subsidy or level of profit and literally everything the organization decides crystallize into that bottom line - and it is a mistake to focus on costs only if you want to build a sustainable, long-term, transit business that is both robust and profitable.

- Lastly, and most importantly, have clear and workable sustainability strategies that makes your organization robust through gender balance and inclusion, development of high potential leaders, creating a sense of internal community and cultivating a very strong focus on external communities. Metrolinx increased its women in senior management positions (top 200 positions) from 24% in 2017 to 38% in 2019 simply by focusing on gender neutral job descriptions, balanced interview panels and an unconscious bias campaign. A multi-year campaign to support a local charity created both an internal community of colleagues collaborating to collect donations and a strong sense of supporting the less fortunate in the external communities we operate in.

## 3. Excel at satisfying your customer

By focusing on "value differentiators" in our offer to our customers, we have pushed our level of customer satisfaction for our UP Express to Pearson airport to 89% and for GO to 83%. Value differentiators are anything that enriches the customer's transit experience: we introduced "quiet zones" on the top of our bilevels for nap time, we launched "same day delivery" lockers at selected stations for on-line grocery orders, we implemented free WiFi, we are systematically expanding self-serve through fare card terminals and freeing up frontline staff to engage with customers better, we are improving way-finding at our stations, but, most of all, we have created an "Operations Centre of Excellence" where we teach our people "Voice of The Customer" and LEAN management techniques to reduce waste in how we operate and to increase value by increasing revenue and selectively reducing non-value adding costs.

## 4. Innovate!

Sometimes innovation is seen as how quickly organizations are adopting new technologies. This is part of transit innovation, but the more important part is to innovate in those areas of your transit business where performance targets are not being met. It is innovative to reduce your time to close-out call centre responses by 12 seconds through better routing of calls, to improve punctuality of train performance by 1% through standardized operating plans to disruptive events, to do two large scale emergency exercises every year so as to improve your teams command-and-control and business continuity planning.

But it is also very much about new technologies. We are implementing a number plate recognition system to improve our management of reserved parking at our stations, our use of memes and gifs to market our new train services to Gen Z customers are growing this market segment by 9% per year, we are experimenting with an electronic system to detect oncoming trains and to evacuate rail workers safely, our e-ticket solution is growing fare revenue by at least 0.5% per year, our fare management card on mobile devices rather than plastic will increase customer satisfaction and fare revenue by an estimated 1% each.

# Chapter 12
# Jeffrey Arndt

President and Chief Executive Officer
VIA Transit in San Antonio, Texas

*Jeffrey Arndt is a good pal and leader of our industry. He has been in the transportation profession for over 40 years (he must have started when he was about 10) and still views every day as an opportunity to learn and improve their system. I visited with him in late 2018 in San Antonio and toured his operations and phenomenal transit center.*

*VIA Metropolitan Transit's ongoing commitment to invest in innovation for smart transit solutions has earned a national Innovation Award from the American Public Transportation Association (APTA). The award honored VIA's GoCodeSA Codeathon, a regional coding competition for transit solutions. Some of VIA's other recent smart transit initiatives include implementation of free, systemwide, high-speed Wi-Fi, introducing its VIA goMobile app, and development of the VIA goCard, a reloadable smart card.*

*Jeff is the current Chair of Southwest Transit Association and Visit San Antonio (The convention and visitors bureau for the region).*

## Transit Stands at an Exciting Crossroads

I n 1789, Benjamin Franklin wrote "…nothing can be said to be certain, except death and taxes". I believe "change" should be added to that list. Change is a constant thread throughout our lives – we learn to crawl then learn to walk. We learn to talk then learn to talk back. So simply, to change, we must learn.

And these times, we must learn more quickly with every passing day. Technology is enabling broad change across multiple sectors. In the span of the Baby Boomers, we have gone from three TV networks and antennae, through satellite TV, Betamax, VHS, DVD, Blu-ray, cable TV and streaming content. My granddaughters cannot fathom having a land line, let alone a party line. And in the realm of mobility, we have gone from a for-profit mobility transit services through development of the interstate highway network with the attendant suburbanization of American cities, introduction of TNCs and the emerging world of micromobility. And automated vehicles are beckoning from the future.

History is full of examples where change was ignored to the detriment of the blissfully ignorant. Ask Blockbuster (if they still were around to be asked), or visit your local mall. We were not all that good at predicting those changes either. Five years ago, electric scooters were not on our radar. On the other hand, the 1990s prediction that transit would be on fuel cells by 2020 has not really panned out.

Transit has not always adapted quickly or well. The "law of the hammer" states that when the only tool you have is a hammer, everything starts to look like a nail. Transit's hammer was the basic model of fixed-route/schedule service and we pushed that model outside of the urban core for which it was created into suburban communities whose very design and form made that model unworkable.

But the good news is that the transit industry is fast realizing that what worked in the past environment does not work universally in the current. Technology improvements and disruptive competition have played a part in that wake-up call. The important thing is that we are now awake, alert and responding.

One San Antonio example is the introduction of VIA Link services in May 2019. VIA Link is a recognition and response to the fact that suburban communities are not a "nail" to our "hammer.". Instead, we identified an area where our hammer was not working and developed a different mobility tool.

In a 17-square mile suburban area in northeast San Antonio, VIA ran three fixed route services. All ran with 40-foot buses, all ran once an hour, and all terminated at a transfer location in an area called Naco Pass. At Naco Pass, customers essentially tied into the remainder of the VIA network. Unfortunately, the three routes served few riders and therefore incurred a disproportionately high cost per boarding compared to the system average.

The new tool we are piloting is our version of on-demand mobility. The dollars required to deliver those three hourly services were used to instead deliver "Lyber"-like demand response service ("Lyber" is my

118

name for a TNC). Using the VIA Link app, customers request a trip from their origin to destination (those who do not have app-friendly phones can instead call into the system).

The app will return the name of the VIA Link driver; the model and license plate number of the vehicle; the estimated time of pick-up and the estimate time of arrival at the destination. The customer will be directed to a virtual stop. The customer can track the progress of the vehicle as is approaches.

The customer can also pay their fare on the app, using passes or pay cash. The fare is the base bus fare, with all discounts also honored and customers have free transfers to the fixed-route bus system. VIA dropped a transfer charge in early November 2019.

All vehicles have bicycle racks and most are wheelchair accessible. About 66% to 75% of the time, the driver will stop to pick up another passenger along the way. Upon arrival, the customer will be prompted to rate their driver, much like Lyber does.

The three bus routes ran concurrently with VIA Link for a couple months. VIA staff rode every trip on every vehicle on those routes, informing those riders about how to navigate the new system. Those who do not have app-friendly phones can instead call into the system. Interestingly, many of those who continued to ride the bus said they were used to the bus but realized that they would be moving to VIA Link shortly.

The results of this pilot service have been remarkable. While the fixed route services ran hourly and did not all have weekend service, VIA Link operates seven days a week. The average wait time between requesting/accepting a trip and the vehicle arriving to pick up the customer is only about eight minutes.

The customer reviews are very favorable. The average scoring of all trips is 4.6 to 4.7 out of 5.0. It is very easy to spot drivers who are not providing the expected quality of service and respond to any improvement opportunities.

Economically, the cost per passenger is between 20% and 40% lower than the cost associated with the fixed-route service. VIA Link carries up to 700 daily passenger trips which reflects an increase of roughly 20%, with a larger increase on weekends.

We plan to introduce this model in other outlying areas, essentially using it as a first/last mile solution. At the same time, VIA Link may serve as a local circulator route – about half the trips in our pilot area remain inside the area in fact.

So, you see, transit is not just buses or bus and rail. Transit is mobility and the we have more than buses in our VIA toolbox. In many ways, the technology and models introduced by rideshare trends laid out a pathway for transit to provide a broader array of services. Much of what we are doing, both locally and an industry, on apps, fare payment and trip planning has been driven by the things that these models introduced. So, within the list of things disrupted by Lyber, is the complacency of transit.

Transit stands at an exciting crossroads today. We are/can be both a mobility provider and a mobility facilitator. We can combine high quality transit and rapid transit corridors with scooters, e-bikes, rideshare, autonomous shuttles to extend the reach of those services we provide. Building partnerships for shared payment systems, fares and trip planning between our systems and other providers is the next level. Using the partners to coordinate with our provided service allows resources to be deployed to enhance those services rather than to spread them out.

Our VIA Reimagined Plan is not just a re-branded Comprehensive Operations Analysis, but a vision for such an integrated system. The Plan has three key components – Better Bus. Advanced Rapid Transit and Smart Transit. Smart transit leverages what each mobility partner can do best to create more comprehensive mobility solutions than we each can provide individually. Synergy (I knew I could use that word someday) is real.

And Smart Transit is not an end, it is a commitment. Few of us anticipated the scooter craze of the last few years; how likely can we foresee what lies five, 10 and 20 years ahead of us. But I am confident that we can develop a framework that can incorporate whatever we cannot see. We future-proof our systems as long as we are never content or rigid in doing it "our way" but instead are constantly learning and experimenting. Our customer and our communities deserve nothing less.

# Chapter 13
# Lauren Skiver

Chief Executive Officer & General Manager
SunLine Transit Agency in Thousand Palms, California

*Lauren Skiver heads SunLine Transit Agency which leads American transit in hydrogen based, zero emission fuels for buses. She and her team have built the largest hydrogen production plant in transportation in the United States (that I recently got to tour) and not only uses it for her fleet but is working on selling it on the open market for other fleets and vehicles. She developed and built the West Coast Center of Excellence in Zero Emission Technology (CoEZET).*

*Lauren and I also share a transit heritage having both served as executives of the Maryland Transit Administration (MTA) in Baltimore after which she became the CEO of the Delaware Transit Corporation before heading to sunny southern California. Lauren not only is a great industry leader she also has created an employee-centric culture at her agency that allows everyone to participate in key decision making.*

*I admire her vision and ability to implement it.*

# Zero Emission Fuels

When we think about alternative fuels as an industry, we sometimes get worried when there's a big change especially if it's a mandated change. But we need to start being better risktakers - doesn't mean crazy work Risk Takers but it means at least looking at opportunities and figuring out what's best for your organization. The future of zero emissions is not going away. In fact, we only believe more sectors are going to have to move this direction. For us it's about more than just zero emission fuel it is about bringing to the street what customers want that is environmentally sound and in a thoughtful application.

So why not be like Sun Tran we're already looking at how we're going to capture the trucking market by selling them hydrogen and then taking that profit from those revenues and putting it into more service for our customers. Fuel cell cars and rideshare is in our future too because we're going to be producing this hydrogen fuel so why not use those fuel types to get zero emission vehicles into neighborhoods. Especially those that have bad air quality or economic challenges in which they deserve a ride and a zero emission car.

We don't need to put the oldest thing on the road. To give them a ride in hydrogen is definitely going to be part of the conversation. Not only is Transit going to hear more about it but big energy companies from around the world are looking at the US for wind, for solar and to be a part of the where they generate large amounts of hydrogen. We are already being

124

approached by them you know we live right next to the oldest windfarm in the country.

I did a paper on it that's how I know and there are many companies very interested in taking that stranded land under that wind farm and creating hydrogen with it and then using that as electric. To feed to customers you can transport it so if it's liquid you can transport if it's gas you can transport easy to transport if it's liquid. So they're seeing the benefit of taking what's not happening right now with wind energy and create a revenue source with it that actually provides clean energy to users. I think the other thing that's important when we talk about zero emission is that most people don't realize that you could have an electric bus that's zero emission but it's not completely clean if you purchase your electricity from coal fired plant. Yes, you're still getting a benefit to air quality by not continuing to pollute the air with emissions from the tail pipe but you haven't bought a renewable source and so transit agencies we've got to learn about energy.

We know about fuel but we haven't started to realize that energy is our new fuel and so learning about energy Power is now what we've got to transcend into as professionals and incentivize our employees to learn more about it and become energy managers. You know when we are going to power something the first thing we look at his what's the feedstock, what's the source. Because we can't say zero if it was from a polluted source when we put it into the bus and we want more transit agencies to learn from us and from others in the field and space of zero emission vehicles.

I hope for the rest of the country that doesn't have the California mandate what we see happening in the next 2 to 5 years for America is an increase in the usage of alternate Fuels in public transit. We are seeing more and more states adopt a zero emission protocols and it may not be to the degree that California is but it's a fun subject to learn about so instead of saying we will never do that, it's not happening, I'll retire before it happens, it's actually exciting to see or understand a new way we can operate. Even if it doesn't happen for your agency there's nothing wrong with understanding how an electric bus works.

Learning about electricity is really important thing even for your home. Like most of us before I came to here I didn't know about how much how much I was paying per kilowatt and how much it was costing me to have a light on. My dad used to say "turn off the lights!" Now I know exactly how much does it cost right I think those kind of things are important for us to delve into and to be curious about. Being curious is just understanding that you want to know more and have your agency know more about how our energy is generated and powers our fleets and facilities.

I think sometimes in transit we think if we're curious it means we agree and I think we need to separate that curious means you are you are getting your agency ready for something should it happen. Then you are ready for decisions. You are ready for money should it become available and we always need to be doing that even if we don't think it's the right thing for our agency right now. I see a lot of agencies having to scramble to put together a plan now because they really never thought this state mandate would happen. Now in California you have to have a plan filed in the next year and so instead of proving the concept wrong now you're having to describe how you're going to conform.

I just say start doing it now. It just makes it that much easier. You translate these needs to say in the next few years I need to start bringing onboard staff that can help us think differently so there's a lot of disciplines involved in this. Your human resources and risk management teams need to start learning about energy management and start staffing up in these areas. I think that you need internal champions that you just need to inspire is that's one way to go. I think setting up an innovation office is another.

It's exciting for the agency people get excited when as the director your going to set up an innovation office like we said we kind of lean on the folks in our organization to do a great job every day for what we're doing but if you were to give them the opportunity to do something different and dream about something different, actually bring something different to the organization they would just rock it with that that opportunity. Yes and I think that if we pay more attention to sort of a sleeper cells that are just waiting to be incentivized – you many not have to hire outside help. You may have one or 10 people on your staff that would die for a chance to work in the innovation office.

I know I would if someone came to me years ago in my career and said I've got a job for you in the innovation office I would've taken it in a heartbeat. And I think sometimes it's all in how we put together opportunity and talk about it and then give our people a chance to dream and inspire them to explore that we're not always good at of this in this industry. I think we're getting much better at it though every day.

So many thought leaders in this industry so many CEOs are starting to open up to the notion of risk-taking and allowing their people to dream and create more than my first 20 years in this industry. So I'm hopeful. I don't think you have to necessarily staff or look for new staff I think you need to start by starting an office and it could be an office of no one in the one people see an innovation office on the org chart they start to get interested and they start to get curious about where you're going with that. I always found that's the best way to start getting interest in something to show it on the org chart if you don't have the money to staff it you still are starting to get a signal to the organization on where you're going as a CEO that you're going in an area to inspire people and allow them to help create the direction you're going. We have a lot of young people that are passionate about the environment and if they had a chance to kind of do that as a sideline with what they're doing they would do the regular job you have that exact label here they do a job in finance but are on project action teams on the hydrogen program because someday they want to do that and someday they want to work maybe in the environmental field. And they know that Sunline is doing that and so were able to to give them opportunity even though they're doing a job as accounts payable they still feel like they are involved in the decision making of the agency.

I think those are small things we can do that incentivize people to create a career in transit which we had a struggle to do. We've got to tap into those things that people are looking for an environmental on creativeness and being environmentally friendly and sound is one thing that we know millennial's are integration so we should talk and have conferences about what are we going to do this in the workforce. I say unleash them on the things that they're interested in and maybe incentivize them for a lifelong career in an industry they might not otherwise stay in that's great.

# Chapter 14
# Stephen Bland

Chief Executive Officer
Nashville MTA/WeGo in Nashville, Tennessee

*Steve Bland is leading public transit in America's Music City of Nashville, TN. It's a fun, upbeat and fast-growing region that includes such cultural iconic locations as The Grand Ole Opry and Music Row.*

*However, his city's voters turned down a referendum a couple years ago to invest billions in expanded transit infrastructure. What lessons did the city's transit advocates learn that can translate to our entire industry? They turned to their transit leader Steve Bland, a veteran CEO of multiple transit operations including at Pittsburgh and Albany, NY.*

*Steve has helped the city's new Mayors and political factions come together in new partnerships to rebrand and improve their service headed into this new decade. I recently had the opportunity to tour WeGo Transit's operations and meet with their senior leadership staff and found their motivation and commitment to excellence higher than ever. With new innovations in areas like gamification in transit, improved technology and TNC provided first and last mile solutions, Steve is leading the charge to reposition the agency and its multiple county transit services for new successes into the near future.*

## Partnerships Form Nashville's Transit Future

I think a lot of folks are focused on the technology for the future of mobility. I'm kind of focused on and excited about some of the new partnerships that will emerge among local transit agencies and complementary development partners. Those development partners can be in education, law enforcement, with social service agencies or even developing around our stations by getting complementary real estate uses.

We are particularly proud of an ongoing and emerging relationship with the homeless agencies in our community where we reciprocate with bus passes to get people into programs to help get them out of chronic homelessness. That's actually showing about a 75% success rate for the first six months and in return we're also getting terrific support from the homeless agencies on interventions, where we have homeless folks who are for all intents and purposes using our facilities as places to live, which doesn't work out too well for anyone.

Another partnership we have emerging is with our Metro Nashville Police Department. We don't have our own transit police force so we trying to get them a better understanding of how our system works and how transit security works. Another area we are seeing great results in is with educational partnerships. With some of the pending new technology we're finding great partnerships with our community colleges and tech institutes. Again, it's not always a partnership where each of us pays for services from each other.

131

Very often its sort of a barter relationship where we exchange things like transit passes for students and get in return seats in classes for our technical or IT staff, where our team can improve their skill sets.

While we are working on improved technology, improving service models, mobility on demand and Mobility as a Service, like I'm sure many other agencies are doing, our focus is going to be about partnership and making friends. As we need to build support for funding measures the more friends we have out there, the better.

With the rate of growth Nashville has had, while it's still a much more affordable city to live in than the coastal cities, the cost of housing has gone up astronomically. So lower income folks are kind of getting pushed to the fringe. We have seen a lot of developers pop up with a specific niche in the affordable housing market and working in partnership with us.

One of our current strategic plan initiatives is to develop a network of transit center around our service areas so we've actually gotten a couple terrific partnerships with developers who are donating land toward those centers. We also have received support from our metro city council, mayor and other funding agencies to develop the centers with close adjacency to their subsidized and affordable workforce housing. We are finding it even increasingly difficult for bus drivers to find places to live. So partnerships with those types of groups who put low income and workforce housing in close proximity to transit stations with dense transit lines helps our own employees. It also kind of gives it a double whammy and makes a little bit easier for people who are paying a higher percentage of their income on housing if they can lower the percentage of their income they spend on transportation by being able to go to a one car household.

We also are partnering early and upfront with our school district and working on partnerships that will essentially help place youth on a path to working in public transit. We have youth action teams formed in almost all of our high schools to educate kids about transit and transit etiquette. With about 5,000 individual public school students who use our system on a daily basis it's important they learn about how to ride the system and also about potential employment with us. We give them an orientation to careers in transit and its various occupations. We highlight summer appointment with us doing things like cleaning shelters and emptying trash at bus stops to get them acclimated to the organization and to showing up to work each day. This is with the hope that as they get old enough to pursue commercial drivers' licenses and technical education that they consider us as an employer of choice.

**Partnerships form the future for the Nashville WeGo Transit Services.**

# Chapter 15
# J. Roger Morton

## General Manager
## Oahu Transit Services, Inc. in Honolulu, Hawaii

*J. Roger Morton has led public transportation on Hawaii's most populated Island of Oahu (where Honolulu, Waikiki and Pearl Harbor are) for many years. He has served under many different Mayors and legislatures and remains respected and effective. His transit system called Oahu Transit Services (OTS) has routes and paratransit service that run shore to shore, covering the entire Island and it's million inhabitants and many visitors.*

*Now there is a renaissance of more public transportation coming to the Island including raised guided rail and a revamped public bus system. I recently got a chance to see all of it in person. Ever the innovator, Roger is taking his agency into the future with bold approaches to serving the public. Read them here:*

## What the Future Holds for Honolulu and Oahu Public Transportation

I n Honolulu and more broadly on the entire Island of Oahu we have a rich transit history. That history goes back over 150 years when the first passenger railway connected the rural communities of Ewa, Waianae and the North Shore to Downtown Honolulu. An electric streetcar system opened in 1901 and became the historical antecedent to Oahu Transit Services. Since then, Honolulu has always had a reputation as an innovator in good public transit and I believe we will continue to innovate in the future.

Oahu is really the perfect laboratory for doing a lot of good transit stuff. We are a 600 square mile island in the tropics and our primary urban corridor is among the densest in the United States. Our urban population is about 1,000,000 residents and more than 100,000 tourists at any one time. We have fantastic weather. We don't have snow. We have a consolidated City and County government without separate municipalities or counties. Our region is very well defined. It is the entire Island of Oahu and our region ends when it meets the Pacific Ocean. We don't have all the other impediments that frustrate transit in some places. Our civic leaders have always supported transit. We also have a riding population that has never lost the habit of riding public transportation. We operate an intensive bus and paratransit system and our per-capita ridership is the fifth highest in the country for major metropolitan areas. Honolulu has one of the lowest costs for an unlinked transit trip. This is all the more remarkable since Honolulu is a high-cost region.

**New fixed Guideway Rail Transit System**

We are less than one year away from opening the first segment of our 20-mile-long, grade separated, driverless, rapid transit rail system and that's going to be a huge shot in the arm for public transit on Oahu. The rail system traverses our dense urban corridor from the Ewa plains to Waipahu, Pearl City, Aiea, Pearl Harbor, Honolulu International Airport, and Kalihi connecting these communities with Downtown Honolulu and the Ala Moana Shopping Center – the largest open-air mall in the country and the gateway to Waikiki.

The first segment of the rail system to open will be about 10 miles long running through several neighborhoods and college campuses and ending at Aloha Stadium in Honolulu. We'll offer high-quality bus service to connect the interim terminal with Downtown, Waikiki and the University of Hawaii. Then probably two years later. A second segment will add another 5 miles to the system and will terminate at our Kalihi Transit Center at Middle Street. Currently, the rail contractor is constructing part of the station interface to our transit terminal which will be connected to the rail station by a pedestrian bridge over a major street. Then about two or three years later we should get all the way to Ala Moana Center. That's a 20-mile-long system.

## Rethinking the Bus System

In preparation for rail we are doing a lot of exciting things. Our bus system will undergo a massive restructuring to transform a largely trunk-based system to a feeder bus network with extensive improvements in the neighborhoods adjacent to the rail system. This will be the largest bus network change in our history and is designed to get our residents to the places they need to be faster, safer more secure and on clean transit vehicles. We are in the midst now of a large-scale test of our HOLO card (our tap and go account-based fare system) with thousands of active users trying it out. Full scale launch of the new fare system is programed for 2020 so that the system will be up and ready for rail when it opens.

We are also testing electric buses now and will soon begin introducing battery-electric buses to our fleet. Honolulu's Mayor Caldwell and the Honolulu City Council have made commitments to have 100% renewable energy public vehicle fleets, including transit vehicles, by 2035. Our infrastructure plans for charging stations are well underway. We have one charger currently installed, and we have a plan for 26 more going in during 2020. Additional charging facilities will be implemented incrementally over the next ten years as we roll out battery-electric buses to replace diesel buses. We're trying to make sure our infrastructure is there as we purchase the electric buses.

We've been collaborating with our local electric utility for the past few years and they have just published a pilot E-Bus tariff that incentivizes us to recharge our buses at times when there is abundant renewable energy available on the grid. That's during the day between 8:00am and 5:00pm when solar energy is produced at scale and after 10:00pm when consumer demand declines and where wind energy will play a large role. The State of Hawaii has made a commitment to utilize 100% renewable energy to produce electricity by 2045. For transit, it will be a challenge to devise bus schedules and operational procedures to ensure that the electricity we consume is not simply generated by fossil fuels. We need a generator to the wheel mentality to accomplish this, but we are committed to reducing the carbon footprint of our system.

**Technology**

We are putting a lot of effort into improving our technology including our data infrastructure. We were an early adapter of GOOGLE transit and worked with GOOGLE, along with a couple of other West Coast systems to develop the GTFS standard that has now gone global. We are constantly working on our back office to make our public feeds more accurate for our riders. Recently, we installed routers into all of our buses and have converted about half of our GPS data to a cellular system replacing a slower data radio system.

On the operations front, we are trying some new approaches for street operations. In partnership with our AVL supplier, Trapeze, we have developed a dynamic operating system run out of our Central Control Center and directly integrated into our CAD system. For frequent service routes, we've thrown away the public timetable and instead operate frequent bus service on a dynamic schedule where we attempt to keep all the buses on these routes evenly spaced and not bunched. Currently, we operate two busy routes dynamically. With this approach, we can do a lot of neat things like if we have particularly high ridership on a day, we can inject more buses into the route and automatically space them out. If we have a breakdown and a bus goes out of service, we can adjust the route so there isn't a huge gap in service. We are very excited about that. We think that maybe 30-40% of our service could be moved to this dynamic operating approach in the next few years. We are also planning to be able to devise emergency schedules on the fly for such things as major detours, emergency bus bridges between rail stations, rockslides cutting off parts of the coastal highway system, etc.

## Recruiting the Best People

One of our challenges is recruiting and retaining good talent to become our future transit leaders. We are attempting to improve our image in the community and get the word out that transit is a multi-billion-dollar industry and that we do exciting things in transit. The folks that we hire are often surprised at the technology we use in IT, Planning, Scheduling, Maintenance, and Human Resources. We recently had a lot of retirements of senior managers on our staff. While we lost a lot of experience, we were able to hire a lot of younger, talented leaders for our system. For our front-line folks, we are partnering with local high schools and community colleges to make sure the public education system exposes our students to the exciting world of public transportation. That is my legacy to the system – that the people that come behind me will continue to provide the best possible service to the people of Honolulu.

# Chapter 16
# John Lewis

## Chief Executive Officer
## Charlotte Area Transit System (CATS)

*John Lewis has been a CEO at three major US transit systems starting with GRTC in Richmond, VA, then Lynx in Orlando and now CATS in Charlotte, NC. Previously he also served as a senior executive at my alma-mater, the Maryland Transit Administration (MTA).*

*He is a sought-after conference speaker and real community leader. John was named Charlottean of the Year in 2018 by Charlotte Magazine and received the 2019 Most Admired CEO Award from the Charlotte Business Journal.*

*His success in expanding the light rail in the city and now improving its bus service is making Charlotte a real mobility haven and example for growing cities across the nation.*

## A Paradoxical City

To understand the transit landscape in Charlotte, you first must step back and understand the paradox of the city.

Charlotte, North Carolina is a primarily "blue" city in a largely "red" state.

The region is experiencing an unprecedented rate of growth and private development with 60 people moving to the city a day, while concurrently experiencing an affordable housing crisis.

While it is ranked a top destination for millennials and tech talent, it's simultaneously ranked 50th out of the 50 largest metro areas when it comes to upward mobility.*

It is both a wealthy banking town and one of the most difficult in which to climb out of poverty.

When I became Chief Executive Officer of the Charlotte Area Transit System in 2015, I took on a perplexing set of challenges. Over the past few years, we have seen much success in beginning to solve these challenges while seizing future rapid transit opportunities.


## Charlotte's Transit Landscape

What many don't realize, is that this southeast city has had some form of transit since the early 1800s. Streetcars first traversed the downtown area, followed by public bus service in the 1930s. But, the current transit landscape as we know it was born when CATS was established 20 years ago.

Over the past two decades, CATS has altered the transit landscape by leaps and bounds. We've completely restructured our bus system through an initiative called "Envision My Ride," and have reintroduced rail service with the LYNX Blue Line light rail and CityLYNX Gold Line streetcar.

While bus service continues to be the backbone of our transit system, it is the power of rail that has really changed the infrastructure and identity of this former textile industry town.

The LYNX Blue Line became North Carolina's first light rail alignment when it opened in 2007 with just under 10 miles of service. Since then, a 9-mile extension of that line has opened, along with transit oriented development, and has been a catalyst for economic development.

## How'd We Get Here?

Prior to the establishment of CATS, Mecklenburg County citizens voted to approve a referendum in 1998 to dedicate a half-cent sales tax to expand transit. This dedicated-funding source, in conjunction with the newly drafted 2025 Integrated Transit/Land-Use Plan primed CATS and the City to begin implementing rapid transit technologies, including light rail.

Over the past two decades, there have been various iterations of long-range rapid transit plans leading to the current 2030 Transit Corridor System Plan. Today, the plan calls for two light rail alignments, one streetcar line and one heavy commuter rail line.

One of the biggest things the City of Charlotte got "right" was projecting and planning for the region's future growth.

## The Power of Light Rail

When the southern portion of the LYNX Blue Line opened, few people understood how great the magnitude of the city's investment would be. The line was built through an industrial area south of Charlotte. Warehouses and old mills were scattered across brownfields with little economic growth activity.

In the years since, and with the opening of the Blue Line's northern extension, Charlotte has seen well over $2 billion in transit oriented development surrounding the 19-mile alignment. The South Corridor has become a vibrant center of activity and sought-after destination for retail, residential and trendy corporate offices.

We've not only constructed a successful light rail line, but have revived a city corridor into a place where people want to eat, work and play. Charlotteans have seen the development and placemaking opportunities that come with light rail. Residents have observed first-hand the transformative power of light rail infrastructure. And they want more. We heard the message and aim to do that through the 2030 Transit Corridor System Plan-- CATS' long-range rapid transit plan.

The 2030 plan calls for several transformative projects including the LYNX Silver Line. The 26-mile light rail service will connect two counties while making critical stops in Center City Charlotte and Charlotte Douglas International Airport which is ranked among the top 10 busiest airports in the world.

Compared to legacy transit systems like New York, Boston and even Atlanta, it might appear that Charlotte is coming in late to the rapid transit game. But for this city, we're right on track. We have the opportunity to implement lessons learned from legacy systems, explore new technologies, and build up our public infrastructure hand-in-hand with private development.

**Bus: The Backbone of the Transit System**

Yes, light rail is a major economic catalyst. Yes, light rail provides reliable travel times. And yes, light rail is a more "green" or sustainable travel mode. But, what about bus? Bus has the freedom to travel on any road and can be rerouted when service needs change. For CATS, it's how we transport the majority of our riders.

That doesn't mean bus transportation is perfect. When I arrived at CATS, our bus system was still operating on a classic hub-and-spoke system. Our riders were having to make two-to-three transfers just to get to their destination. Some, spending hours on the bus every day. I knew that CATS was capable of providing better service than that.

In 2016, we launched a complete bus system redesign called Envision My Ride. Our goals through Envision

146

were to increase route frequency, provide more cross-town connections and provide more direct service. And, we're doing just that. Since the launch, we've restructured over 46 bus routes and now provide greater access for more than 22% of our community. We no longer see bus ridership falling in the double digits and making the turn to increasing ridership on some of our routes.

But, we've still got a long way to go to achieve all our goals. To best serve the Charlotte community, CATS has committed to make bus just as reliable as light rail. That's our next step. We're currently piloting a bus-only lane while continuing to increase frequency on routes across our bus network and studying the latest technologies.

## Challenges and Opportunities

Cranes fill our skyline as major developments continue to grow across the city, yet there is a critical segment of our population that remains underserved. Charlotte is in the midst of an affordable housing crisis. As of September 2019, it was estimated that the City needed over 34,000 affordable housing units to meet the current demand. Not only that, but former center-city residents are being pushed to the outskirts of our city as they become priced out of their homes.

While this is a major challenge for the City, I believe that our public transit system has a hand in creating affordable housing solutions that so many U.S. cities are struggling to find. CATS sees each challenge as an opportunity. As we begin early design of the LYNX

Silver Line, we will also be looking at how to preserve land to accommodate mixed-income and affordable housing close to the station areas.

In looking at populations that are underserved, our agency will use the Silver Line to help connect some of those areas to better opportunities by linking to the Charlotte Gateway Station. The Charlotte Gateway District will be home to a multi-modal station including connections to the LYNX Silver Line, CityLYNX Gold Line, bus service and Amtrak. With regional, statewide and local transportation connections and networks, the district will be a vibrant employment center for the city as well as a welcoming place for people from around the world.

**What's Next?**

CATS has made a promise to the community to deliver the 2030 Transit Corridor System Plan and we are primed to deliver on this promise while continuing to provide safe and reliable service to our customers daily.

CATS is entering into a new phase and must prepare to serve new generations of Charlotteans. In preparing for this phase, the City and its stakeholders must prioritize collaboration and innovation. And, if we do it right? Charlotte will continue to grow, thrive and evolve into a city dedicated to providing equitable opportunities for everyone.

# Chapter 17

# Gordon Maclennan

Chief Executive,
Strathclyde Partnership for Transport (SPT) in
Glasgow, Scotland, UK

*This past year I got the chance to tour the United Kingdom and meet with some of their greatest public transport leaders for my podcast, Transit Unplugged. While on this trip I rode most of their transport modes including an overnight sleeper train to Glasgow, Scotland, where I got to know one of the most entrepreneurial public transit managers I've ever met, Gordon Maclennan.*

*He has turned his amazing operation into a revenue making machine, charging private bus companies for the right to use his bus terminals. He also runs the third oldest subway in the world and has been able to raise hundreds of millions of dollars to renovate it.*

*I became enamored with his city and his leadership style as he walked me to their beautiful City Hall, through old city squares and major rail station improvements. We even visited their downtown Central Train Station, where I got the chance to play piano there for the crowds of passersby. I still consider my time with Gordon one of the most memorable visits I've ever had with a CEO. I think you'll see why when you read his vision of transit tomorrow for Scotland.*

Glasgow and the west of Scotland have been blessed with a transport system that would be the envy of many similar sized cities and regions across the world.

An extensive motorway network going right through the heart of our urban core, the largest suburban rail network in the UK outside London, a significant bus network, an underground railway – the Subway, more of which later - connecting the city centre to western and southern suburbs, a well developed walking and cycling network, ferries, two international airports, freight terminals, and much, much more.

So with that kind of system you may be justified in thinking we should sit back, relax, put our feet up. Job done!

But nothing could be further from the truth.

While we do count ourselves lucky in being the fortunate inheritors of a transport network that reflects Glasgow's historical status as a progressive, modern city, we are by no means resting on our laurels. Our region's survival and growth over the last few hundred years has been based on its ability to adapt and change, to be flexible, to respond to the needs of a changing society, and that approach continues today.

But the challenges facing our city and region now are some of the biggest we've ever taken on. The urgent need to respond to the climate emergency. Some of the poorest areas not just in Scotland, but the whole of the UK. A health record that has led to us being known as the 'sick man of Europe', with some of the lowest life expectancies across the continent.

So no, no resting on laurels, no feet up, no relaxing.

I firmly believe that transport is at the heart of addressing these issues and in helping Glasgow and the west of Scotland fulfil its potential as a modern, ambitious, dynamic world city and region, where all its citizens and visitors feel part of its success story, and where businesses grow and thrive.

These beliefs have been the driving force behind our approach in SPT over recent years. Keeping a razor-sharp focus on meeting the needs of our customers, maximising our efficiency – delivering "more for less" - and innovation in all its forms have been at the core of our work.

Modernisation of the Subway system in Glasgow has been a good example of how we have applied that approach in practice. The 15 station underground railway network, the 3rd oldest in the world after London and Budapest, had last been modernised back in the 1970's and was beginning to show its age. Our proposal for modernisation, endorsed and co-funded by the Scottish Government with a total cost of £288million, took a holistic, transformative approach in seeking to ensure future generations could reap the benefits of this amazing asset.

The first multi-modal commercial smartcard in Scotland, new driverless trains, state of the art refurbished stations (some integrating with other modes), platform screen doors, and new control and signalling systems, are just some of the changes we are bringing to the Subway. Crucially though, we have also adopted a position of 'modernisation' with our workforce. The Subway is nothing without our fantastic staff, and so we have taken the opportunity of the modernisation project to work with them to ensure they feel part of the new, modern 21st century version of the Subway, through better training and improved working arrangements. A timely reminder that yes, technology will play a huge part in the future of transportation but people, be they staff or customers, will always be at its heart.

**So where are we going next?**

Well, in these unquestionably exciting times for the future of transportation, it is important to keep cool, calm, and level-headed. It is too easy to get carried away with and seduced by new tech.

From a policy perspective, addressing the climate emergency will undoubtedly be the dominant force in all we do in future. It will inevitably mean tough choices and hard decisions for all in changing how, when and where we travel and, indeed, how we live our lives. The key challenge for transport planners will be in making that transition as smooth as possible, and in exploiting the wider economic and social opportunities which we know will arise from a 'net-zero' future.

From an infrastructure point of view, I firmly believe we need to make the most of what we've already got. How can we better use the capacity of our existing transport networks? Is there a better way of delivering a service? Are we using roadspace in the most effective way possible? Are we being truly cost effective? Are customers getting the best value we can give them? Is there another way to pay for transport? Is there a digital solution to a problem?

That last question leads me to my final point about where we are going next. Digital technology is by no means the be all and end all for the future of transportation, but it will play a massive role. As an industry, are we "skilled up" to make the most of it? For me, not yet. We still take too traditional an approach in solving transport problems. We must exploit all the opportunities digital tech affords but remember to keep our feet on the ground. Rhetoric, as experience unfortunately tells us, all too often does not match reality.

At SPT we are in the process of writing a new Regional Transport Strategy for the west of Scotland, so many of the issues I have written about are currently at the forefront of our minds. I remain positive about the future, ambitious for transportation, and ever more determined to ensure the people and communities of Glasgow and the west of Scotland get the transport system they need and deserve, enabling them to thrive for many generations to come.

# Chapter 18
# Bill Carpenter

Chief Executive Officer
Rochester Genesee Regional Transportation
Authority, NY

*Bill Carpenter was my first guest on the podcast Transit Unplugged so I thought I would give him the last word in my book from the CEO's perspective. He has been at RGRTA in Rochester, New York as CEO for nearly a decade now, having been brought in as COO. He knows how to lead through change and has a bent for service and innovation.*

*Their agency provides transportation services in the eight-county area in and around Rochester, New York and oversees the daily operation of eleven subsidiaries. They serve over 10 million customers annually in their phenomenal $50 million, 87,000 square feet transit center in downtown Rochester that I got to see firsthand a couple years ago. Bill has a knack for pulling it all together nicely and shows how his agency is responding to the disruption, innovation and paradigm shifts that new mobility has brought us.*

**Disruption. Innovation. Paradigm shifts.**

About a century ago my family delivered milk because many homes did not have an ice box (today known as refrigerators). Early in my career, I sold Yellow Pages advertising in something called a "phone book." Today, the public transit industry is involved in a similar period of dramatic change.

What caused the milk delivery business to end was not the method of transportation changing--from horse and buggy to delivery vans-- but rather the ubiquity of refrigerators (Disruption). The phone book was an invaluable partner to the stationary phone, but cell phones and the internet required--and enabled-- resources to be available on demand, wherever you are (Innovation).

Public Transit is being impacted by both Disruption and Innovation. Transportation Network Companies (TNCs) compete with transit for a variety of trip purposes. While bikes and scooters have been mobility options for decades, the integration with smartphone apps created a business model that makes these options convenient and affordable. At the same time, trip purposes are being cannibalized by Disruption and Innovation. Look no further than Amazon, Uber Eats, On-line Learning, MD Live, and many more for examples.

In the Rochester, NY area, we are reimaging our public transit system to better meet the needs of our customers. Over the past few years we have surveyed thousands of area residents, businesses, car-driving and bus riding travelers. We spoke with and visited transit agencies in communities across the country that are implementing new mobility solutions.

What we learned we are implementing as Reimagine RTS. Our new system is based on five guiding principles:

| | |
|---|---|
| a. | Maximize Ridership |
| b. | Enhance the Customer Experience |
| c. | Coordinate with Community Initiatives |
| d. | Ensure System Sustainability |
| e. | Expand Public Transit to Include More Mobility Options |

Our fixed route system, RTS Connect, will have fast, direct routes running frequently seven days a week. Our innovative On Demand mobility option is ready when you are to take you to your destination or to RTS Connect. The new system will include state of the art transit app, software and mobile ticketing capabilities. All our vehicles will be accessible, all of our systems will be inclusive, and all eligible Military Veterans will ride free! It is a transformative time at RTS.

This transformation is really about preparing for the future of mobility. I am not the first executive to state that to be the mobility leader in our community will require transit agencies to think "outside the bus." TNCs are a reality. Autonomous Vehicles are close to being integrated into the mobility landscape. Bikes and E-bikes, scooters and car rental by the hour, all provide the opportunity for customized mobility without the excessive cost of owning and operating a personal vehicle.

For our service area, RTS will build on the success of a robust fixed route network. When many people want to travel in the same corridor, public transit is the right solution! Increasing the frequency means customers are able to travel on public transit without a schedule, as if they were in their own car. As the demand decreases, our mobility options need to scale to serve customer requests. On Demand solutions offer real time mobility in a more limited geographic area when there are a handful of customers making their journey.

Public transit agencies have a higher responsibility to ensure our mobility options can serve all abilities of the population. In our society, mobility enables personal and community success or it constrains favorable outcomes. Transit agencies must concern ourselves with the overall mobility of the communities we serve, not just segments of the population.

Looking further into the future, population centers will increase in density, making public transit even more appropriate for mobility. This will not be your parents' bus system! The new generations of buses running in fixed route corridors will offer more and more technology: Paperless ticketing; Wi-Fi to surf the internet while riding the bus, real time information for when the bus will pick you up AND when the bus will reach your destination. Fuel systems will evolve to offer greater favorable impact on our environment. It will be cool to ride the bus, light rail or subway.

This year our transit agency added "agility and innovation" as a core value. Private sector solutions for personal mobility will become even more customized, offering features specific to each individual. The ride might just as easily be to a movie theatre, concert hall, internet café or meditation room, with the difference being that you will arrive directly at your destination! Public transit agencies will maintain prominence in shared ride solutions. Our ability to attract customers to a shared mobility solution will require increasing innovation. Implementing the solutions quickly requires the agility that is all too often missing in bureaucratic institutions. A key part of that agility involves our ability to recruit and retain the workforce of the future. As we look out five to ten years, we need an innovative culture and the kind of work that draws more people to the industry.

Public transit is fortunate that industry leaders share their best practices with their peers. While innovation in the private sector is a competitive advantage to be maintained with secrecy, our industry has regularly reinvented itself, shared learnings from both successes and failures, and has never had a brighter future than we have today!

The team at RTS is excited for that future because we have reimagined our system to meet current customer needs and we are positioned to be able to exceed their increasing expectations. Fast, frequent, direct fixed route service complemented with On Demand service will provide a robust transit system.

Innovative, accessible technology and fully accessible vehicles will serve our entire community. While we are working urgently to implement our new system, we are creating the culture to be agile and innovative to drive our success into a transformative future.

# Part III

# Industry Associations Views

*I remember my first transportation conference in the late 1980s. I had begun working as my county transportation coordinator for the Department of Aging and started our county public bus system. I felt like I had been looking through a keyhole into a large room called public transportation and when I attended my first conference it was as if the door had been opened and I could come in and participate in all that this industry had for me and my system.*

*That was then and this is now. Our industry associations provide more than just training and camaraderie, they now are literally our voice in Washington DC (or Ottawa) and state/provincial capitals, they are public spokesmen for our industry and are helping to lead the charge into our era of new mobility.*

*Hear from them on what they feel the future of public transportation looks like next:*

# Chapter 19


# Paul P. Skoutelas

**President and CEO**
**American Public Transportation Association**
**(APTA)**


*Paul Skoutelas has done it all – from serving as the CEO of two major US transit systems to being the National Director of Transit and Rail for WSP USA to leading the American Public Transportation Association (APTA), the largest industry group in North America representing all modes of public transportation. He truly is a "man for all seasons" and a passionate champion for transit.*

*I'm delighted to count him as a friend and so happy to have his and APTA's support for this book. Paul's chapter is a comprehensive look at the public transit industry and its top trends. It's a better overview and look forward than almost anything I've seen on the topic ... and it's a pleasure to read.*

*Enjoy the dive into this deep well of knowledge and information about public transportation and mobility by our industry's top leader.*

# The Renaissance of Public Transportation in the New Mobility Era

There is nothing more fundamental to the human spirit than the need to be mobile.

It is the intuitive force that sparks our imaginations and opens pathways to life-changing opportunities. Our nation was born and built on the movement of people and goods; mobility propels the promise of prosperity. It is the catalyst for progress and personal freedom.

Public transportation has been a vital mainstay of that progress and freedom for more than two centuries. Our industry, even in its infancy, has always done more than carry travelers from one destination to another. We connect people, places, and possibilities. We provide access to what people need, what they love, and what they aspire to become.

In so doing, we grow communities, create jobs, strengthen the economy, expand social and commercial networks, improve the environment, reduce congestion, save time and energy, make travel safer, and help millions of people achieve a better life. How many industries can make similar claims?

At a time of unprecedented social, economic, and technological change in almost every sector, the question for public transportation is: What must we become to continue to serve the public, to improve the quality of life for users and non-users, and to fulfill an expanded, vibrant, and valued mission in society?

**The State of Public Transportation:**

The state of public transportation in America today is strong and growing stronger.

For much of our history, public transit's evolution and growth mirrored the changes in America. Horse-drawn carriages gave way to vehicles propelled by steam, electricity, and fossil- and alternative fuels. Service swelled within and beyond urban centers as more of the population moved to newly developed suburbs – and then back to revitalized downtowns – and as smaller towns sought to be connected to jobs and commerce.

When the Highway Revenue Act of 1982 secured a permanent federal role in funding urban mass transit, public transportation's future changed. For the first time in our nation's history, public transit was acknowledged to be a vital and integral element in America's growing mobility infrastructure.

The unofficial codification of a federal, state, and local funding partnership offered great promise —for better long-term planning, smarter spending, and new priorities to meet changing public needs and preferences. Over the past nearly 40 years, public transit seized the potential of that promise in myriad ways. As funding increased at all levels, public transportation expanded to other communities and delivered more services, thereby leading to more jobs and more social, economic, and environmental benefits.

**U.S. Public Transportation Industry At A Glance**

➢ A more than $72 billion a year sector that generates $4 in economic returns for every $1 invested.

➢ Over 430,000 direct public transportation employees and millions of transit-related private sector jobs across all 50 states.

➢ 21 percent increase in the number of people who used public transportation since 1997, exceeding the growth rate of the U.S. population during that same period.

➢ Nearly 150,000 railcars, buses and vans in service daily, with more than 9 of 10 accessible to persons with disabilities.

➢ 10 billion trips delivered annually in large and small communities by more than 1,300 rural transit systems and 925 urban transit systems.

➢ 9 in 10 trips on public transit trips impact a local economy – by taking people to a job or an activity that generates commerce and taxes.

➢ Public transportation is lowering carbon emissions by 73 percent, and reducing fossil fuel consumption by over 4 billion gallons a year.

➢ Our industry is a leader in the use of clean technologies. Nearly 55 percent of the transit bus fleet are powered by alternative power systems, including hybrid technology and alternative fuels like natural gas, biodiesel, and electric battery, compared to about 3 percent of private vehicles. Five public transportation systems run trolleys and electric buses powered by overhead wires. And while battery electric bus technology is in the early stages of deployment, there are 300 of these buses in service.

> Communities with robust public transit – defined as more than 40 trips per resident annually – are twice as safe from traffic fatalities as those with little or no transit (fewer than 20 trips per person).

Since the varied benefits of public transportation are more widely understood and valued today than they were 40 years ago – both by people who ride transit regularly and by those who do not – support for the industry is expanding in old and new communities. More than 74 percent of Americans – nearly 3 in 4 – want Congress to increase federal investment in public transportation. At a time when there is little consensus on most public policy issues, this sentiment shows the broad, growing demand for transit.

The public's view is also evident in local funding measures. Since 2000, voters in large and small communities have approved more than 70 percent of local funding measures – in 2019, the success rate reached 80 percent.

Many cities, towns and suburbs are expanding their transit offerings to meet growing customer demand, thereby increasing public transportation's relevance, responsiveness, and reliability. In 2018, there were seven new BRT openings or extensions totaling 86 miles, and eight new passenger rail openings or extensions totaling 115 miles.

And while new private ridesharing services have been multiplying, it's telling that 77 percent of Americans view public transportation as "the backbone of a multi-transit lifestyle."

What does that public transit "backbone" mean to big cities and small towns? Take a stroll through Dallas, Texas, Portland, Oregon, Lawrenceville, Georgia or St. Cloud, Minnesota, and you'll experience a uniquely American desire to rethink and reinvent mobility from the perspective of the customer, with modern buses, new rail lines, and paratransit services playing a central role today – and for tomorrow.

There is an abundance of creativity and inventive experimentation underway in public transportation in the U.S. and around the world. The focus is on today's customer: from subscription travel services and the bundling of public and private modes to passenger amenities and apps that cover the entire passenger experience from planning to payment.

Across the country, innovative thinking and experimentation is making the future of public transportation a reality today. This new kind of transit isn't just viable; it is the essential connective tissue that will ensure communities are *thriving* without *driving*.

# Reimagining Public Transportation:
## Today's Innovations and Experimentation

-       Redesigned bus networks are providing a new foundation for mobility in today's metro-economies, with more frequent, connecting, and efficient service.

-       More rapid bus service – in a variety of forms including BRT – is helping to maintain and even increase ridership by adding station amenities, improving route frequency and capacity, and in some cases providing dedicated lanes for buses to avoid traffic.

-       Microtransit, an on-demand service for all that is being embraced by a growing number of public transit systems, offers flexible routes and schedules as an alternative to conventional fixed-route bus service. It is increasing transit's efficiency and accessibility, particularly in low-density areas, during late night hours, and for special needs customers.

-       Public transportation agencies and private sponsors are planning, piloting, and deploying low-speed autonomous vehicles that complement and are integrated with traditional bus and rail services. In 2019, there were more than 60 longer-term pilot projects underway and hundreds of shorter-term demonstrations.

-       Major urban centers like New York City and Los Angeles are exploring congestion pricing – charging people a fee to drive in certain areas during rush hours

167

– in ways that would be workable and equitable. Fees would prompt more people to use public transit and the funds could be used to eliminate transit fares, and for new transportation infrastructure.

-      "No fare" transit service is an idea that is attracting big interest in some smaller communities. Several transit agencies are experimenting with the concept as a way to combat inequality, reduce carbon emissions, and redefine public transportation as a pure public service, much like police and fire services.

-      Both vehicles and stations embody cutting edge technologies. For passenger convenience, there is Wi-Fi, mobile fare payment, bike racks, and real-time signage and trip planning data that tell customers the best travel route and mode. To advance safety, there are onboard cameras and collision avoidance systems.

-      Passenger rail systems are improving safety for their workers, customers, and communities. By leveraging advancements in technology and automation, they are providing greater protection for roadway workers and installing state-of-the-art accident avoidance systems, such as Positive Train Control.

-      The use of low- or zero-emissions buses and electric-powered trains, as well as predictive maintenance systems and connected/automated features are making it possible for public transit agencies to reduce their carbon footprint and to deliver more benefits to the communities they serve.

-      Public transit systems are creating alliances with rideshare, bikeshare and other transportation services that connect customers with transit, alleviate "first-mile / last mile" hurdles, and in some cases, provide affordable mobility where transit is not available.

## Connecting to What's "Next":

What is the future of public transit in the new mobility landscape?

**Demographics** are our destiny. The U.S. population is projected to reach nearly 400 million (up from 328 million today) by 2050. The percentage of people age 18 and under and of people age 65 and older will be roughly the same: 21 percent. Both of these cohorts will be more inclined to rely on public transit and other mobility services than to own a private vehicle.

A different segment of the population – Millennials – will continue to demand more multimodal transportation choices. Today, 70 percent of this age group prefer to live in a community that features a variety of flexible transportation options that include public transportation.

The ability to be more responsive to shifts in customer preferences and needs will allow the transit industry to reach new users. For example, an APTA study found there is a growing demand for transit services for late-shift workers. These individuals, which are disproportionately people of color and at lower income levels, earn $28 billion in wages annually and account for $84 billion in sales per year.

In addition to demographics, **technology** is transforming transportation – with artificial intelligence, high-tech propulsion systems, and smart vehicles connected to smartphones. We want what's modern, cool, and different. As such, some may be tempted to perceive buses, subways, and rail systems as large, lumbering, soon-to-be-extinct dinosaurs of the public transit world. Yet, nearly all global thought leaders predict the opposite.

Public transportation is the only feasible solution to the challenges presented by population growth and demographic changes. There is simply no more cost-efficient or time-efficient way to serve all citizens, regardless of their socio-economic standing in society, and to move large numbers of people through densely-populated areas.

A single commuter bus has seating capacity for almost 80 people; one passenger railcar can carry 100 – 180 riders. If private cars, taxis, and rideshare vehicles attempted to take the place of public transit, the consequences would be catastrophic: more congestion, more time in traffic, more accidents, and more pollution and fuel consumption.

As our cities grow denser and an increasing number of residents choose to forego or limit car ownership, public transit will take on even greater importance.

Here are the four trends that will shape our industry's successful future:

## 1) The Need for More Investment and Pro-Transit Policies

Robust funding and transit-friendly government policies are essential for advancing public transportation's essential role in the new mobility era.

Despite our many recent advancements and achievements, the public transportation industry has not received an adequate share of investment and support. This general trend must be reversed.

Federal funding is critical to help local and state transit agencies address the backlog of nearly $100 $99 billion in repair and replacement work needed to bring America's public transportation infrastructure back into a state of good repair. Unfortunately, the Highway Trust Fund already faces an enormous deficit — $176 billion over the next 10 years — to finance current highway and transit funding levels.

Preserving – and strengthening – the historically successful federal-state-local funding partnership is the bedrock of an effective and efficient public transportation network.

APTA continues to advocate for significant increases in federal funding for public transit and passenger rail programs, a sustainable fix to the Highway Trust Fund, policies that help transit agencies better serve their communities' evolving needs, and federal support that encourage more innovative experimentation.

## 2) A Highly-Skilled, Knowledge-Based, Future-Ready Workforce

Every industry is competing for the best and brightest workers. A skilled and educated workforce is the foundation of public transportation's future. No other investment yields as great a return as the investment in our employees.

According to a Transit Cooperative Research Program report, our industry is facing a critical shortage of experienced, skilled workers as thousands of employees near retirement over the next 5 - 10 years. The federal government agrees: The U.S. Departments of Education, Labor, and Transportation say 4.6 million new workers will be needed in the transportation sector to meet new demands caused by growth, turnover, and retirement.

Our public transit agencies, businesses, and partners will need to be more agile and adaptable. In today's environment, knowledge and skills can become obsolete within months. What's required is a culture that values life-long learning and emphasizes communications skills, strategic thinking, creative problem-solving, and collaborative teamwork.

Additionally, advancing greater diversity and inclusion throughout our industry is both a social and economic imperative. It needs to be woven into our organizations' business plans because our success is linked to making public transportation a more welcoming career choice for all ages, work styles, cultures, beliefs and sexual orientations.

APTA is committed to providing the tools and knowledge needed to fill skills gaps, develop the next generation of transit leaders, encourage lifelong learning, and position public transportation as an attractive, dynamic, and innovative career.

## 3) Public Transit's Expanding Influence in Society

From cybersecurity to climate change, from homelessness to evolving community needs, public transit agencies are increasingly expected to address complex societal, environmental and economic issues far beyond the scope of managing the movement of people and vehicles. This is a trend that has major implications for our industry's resources and identity in the communities we serve.

Below are three relatively new or emerging issues that public transit will need to embrace and own.

### ➢ Who Owns the Curb … and the Road:

City and county governments will be working with public transit agencies and other entities to improve transit speed, curb access, and ridership. Innovative methods – such as car-free street, signal technology, and bus-only lanes – are making us more mobile at a fraction of the cost and time of conventional government projects.

- Some cities and public transit agencies are already partnering to make some streets car-free to reduce traffic and give priority status to public transit and emergency vehicles.

- Using wireless technology, buses and trains can signal traffic signals to extend a green light so they avoid delays. This type of "Transit Signal Priority" technology will make public transit service faster and more reliable.

- Creating more dedicated "transit only" lanes will speed up trips, boost ridership, and save agencies money. By the end of 2019, residents in at least 12 U.S. cities will see red-painted, bus-only, lanes on their streets.

- Our ongoing fascination with automation will lead to a common set of standards, policies, and vocabulary for public transit agencies, other types of mobility service providers, and automakers. After all, even with "transit only" lanes, we will need to share many of the same roads.

➢ **Affordable Housing Near Transit:**

Research shows that public transportation hubs and busy routes attract investment and growth. In turn, this can lead to increased demand for housing and higher residential property values.

The lack of affordability of housing near transit stations and hubs is an issue that calls for public transit's involvement in supporting local and national solutions. Decades of under building and a lack of investment in housing for those with the lowest incomes have led to two crises: 1) a dearth of housing options for nearly all income levels; and 2) an increasing homeless population that at times impacts public transportation operations.

> **Investment in Smarter, Sustainable, and More Resilient Infrastructure:**

When transit systems slow down due to natural disaster, aging infrastructure, maintenance, or repairs, customers become frustrated and begin looking for alternatives. Operators, designers, manufacturers, and technicians will need to continue to seek creative solutions, model a spirit of continuous improvement, prepare for new challenges, and invent ways to delight their customers.

- As more cities focus on challenges associated with climate change, public transit operators play an important role in reducing greenhouse gas emissions. Sustainability, preserving the environment, being socially responsible, maintaining economic viability, and contributing to the quality of life are all integral to what we do. Many transit agencies have already made sustainability a strategic objective. The trend is to become more resource efficient and to engage and educate transit employees and customers.

- Public transportation depends on public support. A significant factor in earning and maintaining that support is in the effective use of public funds. Future infrastructure investments will require balancing long-term reliability and resilience with the flexibility to adapt to innovations in technology and operations, new competitors, and changing ridership preferences.

- High-speed rail investment in the U.S. has lagged behind Japan, France, China and more than a dozen other countries. However, there is growing evidence – and support for – new projects, financed with private and public funds. High-speed rail can be an environmentally-friendly alternative to air travel. Currently, California's High-Speed Rail project, a result of a successful ballot measure, is currently under construction; Virgin Trains USA (formerly known as Brightline) operates a line in Florida that will eventually connect Tampa to Miami; Texas Central is seeking to link Houston and Dallas, TX, in under 90 minutes by rail, and Virgin Trains USA has unveiled plans to build a fully electric, high-speed train that would connect Southern California to Las Vegas by 2023.

## 4) Technology and the New Mobility Network

Finally – and most important – is the power of technology to redefine mobility and the future of public transportation. The trend to experiment and innovate will grow in next decade.

More public transit and mobility services will be built around the smartphone, particularly as 5G technology becomes more common. Watch for new fare collection apps, customizable travel options, and universal access to the Internet to change the way the public thinks about mobility.

Today's transit customers will continue to expect more from our industry. "Mobility as a Service" (MaaS) – as a concept and a business model – is likely to become a defining theme for our systems. Through an APTA-sponsored study mission, our members saw first-hand how European transit systems are taking different approaches to integrating various new and existing mobility options. In the U.S., we also need to explore how MaaS can complement U.S. public transportation, attract new customers, and increase revenue.

As shared, self-navigating, autonomous train, minibus, and bus services become more widespread in the coming years, the cost of travel will decrease and the benefits to riders, the environment, and public health and safety will grow. We're already seeing this kind of potential in pilot programs that carry riders to specific work locations or health care facilities.

Technology is crucial, but what matters most is quality of service to all types of transit customers, not the devices that deliver it. We need to continue to deliver great services and ensure our services are seamlessly and conveniently connecting our customers to what they want and need: 1) real-time information; 2) a range of options / personal choices; and 3) greater ease of use, including automatic fare payments.

It will be increasingly important to create new alliances with transportation service providers, vehicle manufacturers, technology companies, community leaders, and policymakers to enhance our industry's ability to connect and strengthen communities – in an equitable and efficient manner.

The bottom line: Technology is more of an "enhancer" than a "disruptor" for our industry. The key is connectivity – making public transportation the essential, integral element of the ever-expanding mobility mosaic, regardless of how that mosaic evolves.

We are entering a new era of American mobility that includes the renaissance of public transportation. Our industry has successfully reinvented itself several times over the past 200 years. As technologies, geography, lifestyles, and the economy changed, so too did transit agencies and the services they provided.

Today, we stand ready to meet any future challenge and to continue transforming mobility across the U.S. Public transportation's role and responsibilities will be more varied and vital than at any other time in our history. We have the knowledge, experience, and character to lead change, not simply respond to it.

The services that we design, provide, and manage will continue to evolve and become more advanced, as will our vehicles, operating systems, and the skills of our workforce.

Our passion and purpose, however, remain steadfast and strong: to improve the quality of all people's lives by providing convenient, dependable, and desirable access to opportunities.

# Chapter 20

# Scott Bogren

## Executive Director
## Community Transportation Association of America (CTAA)

*I've known Scott Bogren for 30 years. When I ran smaller transit systems, I was actively involved as a State Delegate from Maryland to the Community Transportation Association of America (CTAA). Scott ran the association magazine on staff at CTAA and we would hang out at conferences and discuss articles and industry trends.*

*In 1991 the system I oversaw (County Ride) won CTAA's top national award. David Raphael was the CTAA Executive Director then and was somewhat of a mentor to both Scott and me. Now Scott heads this important association representing America's mid-size and smaller public transportation systems. Scott is a dynamic leader for our industry (and somehow stayed skinny and handsome.)*

*Anyway, I spoke at CTAA's Small Urban Network Conference for mid-size transit executives in Athens, GA this past year and asked Scott to share the direction of this part of the industry for our book and he does so here - thanks Scott:*

# The Community Association of America (CTAA)

Though often overlooked when it comes to service and technological innovation in the public transportation space, our nation's small cities and rural communities, too, are in the midst of a period of dramatic change when it comes to mobility. The Community Transportation Association of America (CTAA) has more than 1,400 members and represents the operators in these rural and small-urban areas. What I'll share in this chapter derives largely from my vantage point as CTAA's executive director and the important work we're doing to both inspire and understand exactly how our members are forging the future of public transportation.

Driven by economic regionalism and demographics, our nation's rural communities (those with less than 50,000 population) are seeing soaring demand for on-demand mobility across large regions of the country where traditional fixed-route public transit operations simply are not economically viable. The average rural resident is older, more likely to have a disability and slightly poorer than their urban counterpart. Rural populations are declining with the most mobile segments of the population decamping to urban areas — leading to the dynamic of simultaneous population decline and transit demand growth. Trip distances in the past decade have increased for core transit trips like employment, health care, education and retail. The future for effective rural public transportation is, no doubt, some combination of such emerging transit concepts like Mobility as a Service (MaaS), on-demand mobility and mobility management.

For the nation's more than 300 small-urban (cities with populations between 50,000 and 200,000) transit operators, scalable deployments of new technologies and the on-boarding of new theories in the cost-effective provision of public transit are emerging everywhere, from fare integration models to service re-designs to limited testing of automated vehicle shuttles to MaaS deployments.

Since CTAA's inception in 1988, we've worked to instill a more person-centric approach to providing public transportation, one that asks the system to flex to meet the needs of the customer rather than the customer forced to meet the rigidity of an unyielding system. For the nation's urban operators, that rely heavily on fixed-route operations, this person-centric approach may seem revolutionary — but to rural transit operators it's always been the only way to effectively move a dispersed population.

So the core tenants of MaaS, on-demand transportation and mobility management are well established in rural public transportation. What's changed, and what will continue to influence the future of public transportation in rural America is the smart phone, data and analytics, and the realization that the value of a trip is far more than just counting how many are provided. For small-urban operators that typically operate fixed-routes, a more passenger-centric approach is leading to vital service re-design efforts as well as the integration of on-demand operations that network with traditional operations and not separate and apart like complimentary paratransit services (mandated by the Americans with Disabilities Act for fixed-route operators).

The future of public transportation must focus on customers, and traditional public transit systems are arriving to that realization a little late. The Transportation Network Companies (TNCs — primarily Uber and Lyft) have exploded into the public transportation ecosystem precisely because they understood this dynamic, as well as the potential of an internet-enabled smart phone to book trips and pay fares. Brilliant, easy-to-use technology hasn't hurt, either.

Volumes have already been written about the impact of the TNCs on public transportation, much of it speculation. It seems clear that the TNCs have done the following:

• Created a high level of (often unrealistic) expectations on the part of the transit riding public that all transit providers provide personalized, timely service;

• Reduced transit ridership in areas with high concentrations of TNC drivers;

• Increased congestion in many major metropolitan areas;

• Lost a lot of money because the pricing dynamics of providing the trips exceeds what current TNC customers are willing to pay.

Some in the transit industry choose to focus on the TNC's failing business model, the staggering congestion they create and their refusal to serve people with disabilities; while others point to the millions of rides they provide, their nascent partnerships with transit and their fantastically easy-to-use app. The reality is they are both right. And further, the reality is that the niche the TNCs have carved is a vital one that is unlikely to go away.

The future of public transportation is a blended approach to mobility that incorporates all of a community's assets together in a seamless, easy-to-use collection of interfaces (app, web, phone, kiosk, paper, etc.). Fixed routes, paratransit, volunteer driver networks, taxis and TNCs, bike/scooter share, pedestrian, micro-transit, on-demand and whatever other sources that reside in the region, all in one place. Yes, this is the very definition of MaaS!

In large metropolitan areas, these collections of mobility assets will be available to the general public for whatever purpose a passenger needs. Population densities in large cities are typically sufficient enough to create the necessary demand on this type of MaaS arrangement. A version of the "build it and they will come" theory.

In smaller cities and rural communities, these assemblages of mobility assets — which will likely be less diverse — must be purpose built; that is, created with a specific outcome in mind. We believe this distinction is critical. In smaller cities and rural communities, deploying the same "build it and they will come" approach that works in major metropolitan areas is a guarantee for failure. But by focusing the MaaS approach on specific outcomes, for example:

connecting rural veterans with health care; improving specific, measurable human service outcomes; or reducing health care network no-shows, the approach makes sense in smaller communities.

CTAA is currently engaged across the country in a number of projects piloting the development of MaaS concepts in smaller cities and rural America. These concepts are bringing together all available forms of mobility into cohesive networks to improve outcomes in the foster care system, with local drug courts, with no-shows at rural hospitals and in enhanced access to opioid treatment and recovery programs. Simply put, we want to translate theory into practice and the Association is excited about the initial results in these pilots, and the opportunity to do more of them in the near future.

We believe that the future vision of public transportation must be tied to measurable, data-driven economic improvements that move evaluative discussions away from focusing merely on ridership and the cost of transit and into a more thorough understanding of the value of all forms of public transit. Because the value of networked mobility in a community has always accrued to the private sector (think employers, developers, retail/entertainment, etc), it's future clearly lies in right-sized public-private partnerships that share in both the investment and the benefit.

The history of the United States is one of distinct transportation eras. From trails to waterways, railroads to interstate highways, the country's economy, land use and population demographics have been inalterably impacted by transportation. Here in 2020, the nation stands at the precipice of the next great transportation era — one that will be characterized by all that I've discussed in this brief chapter; and one that will no doubt profoundly influence how we live and work. It's an era that all of us at CTAA are excited to help build.

# Chapter 21

# Marco D'Angelo

## President & CEO
## Canadian Urban Transit Association (CUTA)

*As head of CUTA and prior to that the Ontario Traffic Council, Marco D'Angelo has raised the profile and influence of these important associations. It has been a pleasure getting to know and work with him over the past couple years in my new role as Trapeze's industry ambassador.*

*We worked together this past year on the CUTA Annual Conference in Calgary where I led a Transit Unplugged CEO Roundtable of some of Canada's top transit CEOs. He is a wonderful advocate for our industry and shares what the future looks like for transit in Canada and around the world in this insightful chapter:*

# Innovating with microtransit pilots in Canada

Unlike flying cars, Hyperloop and SpaceX, microtransit is much more than a futuristic concept. In fact, various types of microtransit (also known as on-demand, demand-responsive, or flexible transit) have been with us for quite a long time: think airport and hotel shuttles, school buses, accessible transit, transport networking companies (TNCs) like Uber and Lyft, and even good old-fashioned taxis. The key difference between micro and conventional transit is that microtransit is flexible – that means no fixed routes or schedules.

## Trend towards convenience

One thing that has changed quite dramatically in recent years is customer expectation – a shift that was flagged 10 years ago in CUTA's Transit Vision 2040 document: "Consumer trends factor large and include moves to individualism, comfort and convenience and personal connectivity. Demand for customized or personalized lifestyles and a drive for greater personal connectivity blends altruistic lifestyles, strong relationships, ethics, and connective technology."

The most significant words in the Transit Vision 2040 excerpt are convenience and technology. Today's consumers increasingly want and expect ultra-convenience, along with more choice in their day-to-day lives. Services you can access from your phone, like Amazon, Uber, Netflix, Foodora and online banking have become the norm so that now people expect services to come to them rather than the other way around. On the contrary, this kind of on-demand convenience in Canadian transit has been much slower to take off.

**Canadian pilots**

Things are beginning to change though. Several small and mid-sized Canadian cities have taken steps toward microtransit, offering customers apps for hailing, navigation and payment (rather than reserving their ride well in advance, as is often the case with accessible/specialized transit). In contrast to big cities with large grid networks, it may be less daunting for smaller cities to pilot microtransit for a few reasons: there's more flexibility to try new things; it could be easier to get customer input; there's less road traffic to slow things down; managers can take ownership of the project; and transit system directors are more likely to be involved in daily operations. It remains to be seen whether microtransit can also be cost effective for small to medium-sized communities.

In 2018, the Réseau de transport de Longueuil (RTL) was the first transit system in the province of Quebec to pilot an on-demand microtransit service. Using the "RTL à la demande" app, users in Saint-Bruno-de-Montarville (a suburb of Montreal) living in a delimited residential neighbourhood have access to an on-demand taxi service during rush hours. The app automatically groups trip requests to optimize the use of taxis. Residents can use the service to get around within their own neighbourhood, reach two local commuter train stations, transfer to local and intercity bus stops at a park-and-ride stop and get to downtown Saint-Bruno-de-Montarville.

The pilot was made permanent in December 2019 and Longueuil (population about 430,000) is planning to expand the service to other sectors in 2020.

The city of Belleville, Ontario, started operating a pilot service in 2018 in off-peak hours, in partnership with Toronto-based technology company Pantonium, to let riders order buses on demand to take them to and from any bus stop. The technology works with the help of connected mobile apps that allow the software to communicate with riders and drivers in real time.

By all accounts, the Belleville pilot was a huge success. In its first month, ridership increased by 300%, per-vehicle mileage dropped by 30%, and the number of bus stops covered by the service is 70% greater than the previous bus service, while using the same number of vehicles and service hours. On-demand transit buses are now a permanent fixture in Belleville.

In Western Canada, Calgary Transit began a one-year on-demand pilot in August 2019 in new communities under development where the population density is low. The pilot offers shared-ride transportation to a central transit hub in communities that don't have access to traditional bus service. Residents book trips using an app on their smartphone, it costs the same as regular transit, uses the same passes or tickets, and drivers provide transfers to those connecting to regular transit. The demand has been strong: in the first four months, the service averaged 125 rides per weekday and 1,000 customer accounts were created.

The pilot has also allowed Calgary Transit to respond fast to changes in demand. For example, when students returned to school in September there was a large increase in customers, so an extra 9-passenger vehicle was quickly added to the fleet. Pick-up locations can also be adjusted to increase efficiency and service by grouping more customers together.

Calgary Transit will continue to monitor progress over the remainder of the pilot project before making further plans, but early success indicates it could be a solution for providing transit to areas with low population density.

Most recently, in December, 2019, the town of Okotoks (population under 30,000) just south of Calgary became the first community in Canada to offer a "curb-to-curb" on-demand transit system for the general public, operating 8-seater shuttles from 6 a.m. to 11 p.m., Monday to Saturday. The service is partly funded by the province of Alberta's GreenTRIP program, which contributed 67% of the capital expenditures.

**Risks and rewards, ridership versus coverage**

These Canadian cities are setting the stage for others to pilot microtransit. But before they head down that path, they will have to ask themselves some important questions. Is microtransit a practical solution for your community? Is it affordable for the existing transit system to provide, or would subsidies or perhaps public-private partnerships be needed? What is the main goal in providing microtransit, e.g. bridging the first mile/last mile gap, improving customer service, increasing ridership, reducing wait times, replacing

191

underused existing transit, increasing coverage, or just wanting to try something new? Do you have drivers who can adapt to flexible routes and schedules? Do you have the IT resources required?

Transit systems embarking on microtransit should engage their IT departments early to ensure they ask the right questions when looking to sign on with a transit app provider. Among the considerations: will customer and agency data be private and secure (not easily hackable)? Also, some users (for example, seniors and those with visual impairments) may not be able to use a smartphone app so integration with other services like Alexa and OK Google might be necessary to increase uptake among these groups.

Since the risks inherent in microtransit are high, starting with a pilot is probably the way to go – a trial-and-error approach that's relatively low cost, low commitment, and time-limited. The pilot should deliver metrics and insights such as riders per revenue-vehicle hour, average wait time, customer satisfaction and so on. And whenever possible, systems should learn from the successes and failures of others who have gone before them.

Jarrett Walker, a U.S.-based international consultant in public transit planning and policy, points out that flexible transit only makes sense for transit systems to undertake if ridership is not their primary goal. "If you want ridership, you run big buses and trains offering frequent services in places with high demand. If you want coverage, you spread service out so that everyone gets a little bit." Microtransit is, he says, "by definition, a way to serve very few people at very high cost, compared to fixed routes."

**Outside Canada**

Looking to Europe and the US, Germany is showing a trend toward shared, on-demand shuttles being developed by private companies but funded and operated by local communities – an interesting hybrid.

One of the things that differentiates European cities is that the concept of integrated urban mobility is more prevalent, with bicycles, scooters and e-bikes being much more popular than in North America, especially Canada, perhaps because of cultural and historical differences, not to mention inclement weather. In Europe, the combination of public transit and bicycles is proving to be a feasible first mile/last mile solution and, as a bonus, gets people out exercising and frees up all that space previously used for parking.

In the U.S., cities like Sacramento, Kansas City, Columbus and Denver are experimenting with microtransit shuttles – some charging passengers by distance travelled, like a taxi, and others integrating the service into existing accessible or specialized transit.

**Rapid bus transit**

An alternative to microtransit being explored by some Canadian municipalities is rapid bus transit.

Kingston Transit in eastern Ontario has moved away from a "pulse" system where all buses arrive and depart at the same time and at low frequencies. Their express bus service provides buses every 8 minutes or less during weekday peak periods. The success of the express service has created a launching pad for additional improvements and over five years, Kingston Transit has cut peak service frequency in half.

In York Region, a sprawling area north of Toronto, they are using both a conventional and a bus rapid transit service called Viva where buses travel on dedicated bus lanes (dubbed Rapidways) in the centre of the road. They are also piloting a ride-on-request app for both specialized and standard travelers to customize and book their trip by smartphone. Viva routes connect to the Toronto subway as well as GO Transit railway stations and bus terminals. Further expansion of the Rapidways is underway.

In the city of Brampton, Ontario, Brampton Transit launched the Züm bus rapid transit system in 2010, which has contributed to an overall increase in the system's ridership of 154% between 2009 and 2018, compared to the city's population growth of 24% in the same period. Expansion of the express bus service has continued since then to include connections to other transport systems, such as GO Transit, York Region and Mississauga routes. Recent growth includes an extension to York University and Vaughan Metropolitan Centre featuring direct links to Toronto Transit Commission subway stations. Buses continue to be added to existing routes to meet growing demand – 19 buses in 2018 and 12 more in 2019.

## The future is flexible

All these examples, whether Canadian, European or American, indicate that agencies are trying to listen to their customers more and meet their expectations better. Customers want a lot – choice, convenience, low cost, safety and sustainability – and there will have to be compromise and flexibility on both sides as transit grows and evolves.

Will microtransit ever take over from traditional, fixed-route transit? Not likely. But we will see a greater diversity of modes that will include trains, standard and rapid express buses, streetcars and shuttles – with or without drivers – and first and last-mile options like ridesharing, scooters and others that we haven't even thought of yet. Some systems may choose to partner with accessible transit, other types of private shuttles or TNCs. Each agency will have to weigh the pros and cons of flexible versus fixed routes and schedules, ridership versus coverage goals, different types of funding models and partnerships, and how to evolve towards greener, more sustainable fuel sources.

The combination of new technology and entrepreneurship is creating the conditions for transit to fill gaps that have long existed within a fixed-route, fixed-schedule service. Using a pilot approach to microtransit, listening to customers, a willingness to be flexible and innovative, and learning from other systems' experiences could prove to be a win-win for both agencies and customers.

# Chapter 22

# Rob Puentes

President & CEO

Eno Center for Transportation

*Rob Puentes is one of the most respected leaders in our transportation industry. He leads the think tank most known for transit, aviation and all modes of transportation, the ENO Center for Transportation. Over the past few years I've been able to write articles for their publications, lead a webinar and speak to upcoming transit leaders and academicians at training sessions ENO offers.*

*Eno really is unlike any other institution I am aware of in that it is totally focused on improving our leaders and thought leadership for mobility in our era. With his 20 year background at another respected Washington Think Tank, the Brookings Institution, Rob brings gravitas and a sense of purpose to his mission.*

*Take a look at his fascinating view of some of the most interesting new innovations impacting public transport here:*

## ENO CENTER For Transportation

We're the only think tank in the country focused on all modes of transportation. We work on everything from aviation to electric scooters and everything in between. We're based here in Washington, so we pay close attention to everything federal but our work informs all levels of government—federal, state, metropolitan, local—and we work with the public, private, and nonprofit sectors.

However, we obviously don't do all that at the same time. We're only about a dozen people here at our office in Washington. So our precise areas of work at any given time has to be on that which is the most relevant, timely, and potentially impactful. That philosophy governs everything we do. Eno is able to have such an extensive reach because we are the hub of a network of people and organizations all around the country and, increasingly, across the globe with whom we work. Partnerships, relationships, collaboration is in the DNA of this organization, and we are going to continue to do that for years to come.

There are several discrete, but totally interrelated, parts of what we do here at Eno. We have a policy shop that works on a range of different issues. Right now, we have major projects related to public transit, automation (including both surface vehicles and unmanned aerial systems), mobility on demand, pricing, and more. A lot of Eno's policy work is informed by active working groups in freight, aviation, finance, and technology.

We also have a stellar set of programs where we deliver state-of-the-art classes to provide leadership and professional development for the public transit industry. Our annual Leadership Development Conference occurs every spring, where we bring in 25 of the nation's top graduate students to be immersed in all things transportation. We also run a wonderful 5-day course several times a year intended for second-level managers at transit properties, the federal government, and vendors to transit operators. It provides an introduction to leadership and management skills. It's a wonderful class and those folks go on to do amazing things. They stay connected to us. Our long running Transit Senior Executive program is an intensive 6-day course tailored specifically for individuals in the top 2-3 layers of the organizational chart with a strong commitment to the public transportation industry and serve in a senior leadership capacity.

We also pay a lot of attention to our communications and outreach function. Of course, we have Jeff Davis' Eno Transportation Weekly, which we refer to as a newsletter but it's more like a journal. It's indispensable reading for anybody in transportation. But because we want to get all of our information and everything out there, we have a major communications function - just trying to make sure that people are consuming the work that we produce here, as well as other important and relevant information across the transportation landscape.

## Autonomous Vehicles

One area where we continue to be present is at the intersection of public policy and automated vehicles. There is certainly a lot of hype around AV's but the hype is understandable since the promise of AVs top address a range of transportation challenges is enormous.

About 40,000 people die on our roadways each year. In terms of people, that's the equivalent of three big jet airliners crashing every day. Since about 90 percent of car crashes are result of human error, there is potential for AVs to reduce crashes. We also waster billions each year sitting in traffic. Because AVs continuously optimize routes and travel close together, we could finally make a dent in certain types of congestion. Transportation is also the #2 household expense for most American families mostly due to the costs of car ownership. If fleets of AVs are shared and one could call one up a car on your phone and subscribe to a service, it could be cheaper.

So what we are looking at here is what analysts call the "heaven" and "hell" scenarios (or "utopia" and "dystopia" visions) for AVs. In the former, vehicles are parts of shared fleets like we're seeing today (bike share/car share). Traffic crashes are virtually eliminated, and carbon emissions are much lower due to the proliferation of electric vehicles. There are fewer parking lots, roadways, traffic congestion, and broadly shared general economic growth and prosperity.

But there is also the possibility for the latter scenario where vehicles are all individually and privately owned.

There is a decline in infrastructure quality due to no gas tax or tolls being collected. Carbon emissions skyrocket if vehicles have internal combustion engines. And roadways become parking lots as vehicle miles travelled explode and cars roam around with no driver.

Of course, it probably won't be that binary and the reality is that we're probably looking at a combination of the two scenarios.

Fortunately, cities and metro areas across the country are wrestling right now with this issue. As we travel around and talk to officials we tell them, "Well, you don't have to have one or the other. You can choose what you want the future to look like." And then you start talking to them, and they think, well, if we do AVs, we can have smaller road widths, and we can manage the curb space better, and we can do all these different innovations. But when we tell them they don't have to wait to do that you can almost see the light bulbs going on. The message is that they are empowered to do things today. They don't have to wait until level five vehicles land on them from outer space.

The trucking industry is very interested in this AV technology for obvious reasons. Maybe not fully automated trucks that are moving through the city of Chicago. But once they get out onto I-80, and they're facing a long trip out to the West Coast, there might be some clear applications for where autonomy might result in more efficient vehicles by increased safety and might be better on the drivers and the workers. And the workforce piece is super important because we all know the trucking industry is facing enormous challenges when it comes to the workforce. If there is someplace where it might pop first, that seems like there are some clear applications. Perhaps not level five vehicles the way that we're talking about them or they're popularly described, but I think there are some clear applications in trucking.

I do think there are also some in public transit as well, with low-speed autonomous shuttles (LSAV) that operate on predictable routes running in high-capacity corridors. It's not clear what it means for drivers of those vehicles. it may change the role of what the drivers are. They may be more of a concierge-type service than the public bus drivers we see today. But we do think there are some examples of that and there's a ton of testing that's going on right now. The team here at Eno was working on a report for the Transportation Research Board with several other partners that are looking at where all these LSAVs are being tested, and it's quite a few around the country.

But I do think the industry is starting to recognize that its taking longer than expected to get AVs into our modern city network. How long will it take? Exactly when is hard to say—30, 40 years, who knows? Whenever there's a safety challenge that's going to set it back, so they've got to make sure that safety is paramount. If they keep doing that, it might move along faster, and there is a ton of investment that's going into all of it, so it's not from lack of trying. But it's just hard to imagine it happening anytime soon, just given how complex we know cities and metropolitan areas are.

## Microtransit & MaaS

On another topic, there were several experiments with so-called microtransit a few years ago. And the good thing about this time in transportation is that there are lots of tests and pilots and things going on and some of them are successful, and some of them are not. And I think we learned a lot from some of those microtransit pilots.

Kansas City is the most prominent one of how challenging this can be. While I think there is an opportunity for traditional public transit agencies to leverage the potential of flexible route, on-demand microtransit, it is critical to keep in mind that technology cannot solve all of public transportation's challenges. Regardless of the technology available, the customer should remain in the forefront when considering service adjustments and new service models. Agencies should be intentional and deliberate in identifying the problem they are looking to solve or the question they seek to answer when testing microtransit.

We also cannot expect the private sector to come in and provide these services in lieu of public services. The private sector is there to make money. And there's nothing wrong with that. But that's why they're there. To find and generate some profit for them or their shareholders, or to get into markets. They're not doing it for the same altruistic reasons that a public company, a public agency, might be doing it. We have to make sure that we understand those public and private roles together when we think about where a microtransit application might be useful.

In Los Angeles, LA Metro is right now trying to figure out, well, is this something that we can figure out ourselves as a public entity? Can we figure out a microtransit application that's dynamic, that's on-demand? It has all those features from a private company but also doing it on the public side while adhering to other public policy goals they want to achieve. That's the kind of discussion going on in many places right now.

These experiments are flourishing, private sector, public sector. We're not going to nail it anytime soon. Not in the next year or two. But I think we will. I think we're going to start to figure out what works, what doesn't work. There's an insatiable demand for places to learn from one another and to keep on experimenting, especially when federal Washington doesn't seem to be helping them do anything right now.

Nat Ford, runs the Jacksonville Transportation Authority and was recently the chair of APTA where he helped lead the industry into what he said was the new mobility paradigm. And people have talked about the role of mobility aggregators being the transit agency. You've got cities like Denver where they are letting Uber put the mobility as a service app together. Then you got places like Dallas where they're putting it out themselves. And then you have a third model, which is private companies like Whim in Helsinki or other private software companies, putting out apps.

This is why it is a dynamic time in transportation. So many interesting things are happening, and all of it relates to what the purpose of transportation is in the first place, and that's to provide access. It's about getting people to access jobs, economic mobility, economic activity, education. All the things that we travel for. That's not super insightful, but the shift from mobility to accessibility is very important. It's not just moving people around but that's how we've engineered our transportation network for years. We've made sure that intersections move vehicles through as fast as they can. But it hasn't worked to serve the people in those places.

But when you shift to an accessibility model and you're thinking about, well, how are we trying to get people to do the things they want to do? That changes everything. And transit agencies have a great role to play in that because they obviously have public transit in most cities and metros and they probably have a great role to play in managing these micro-mobility options, the scooters, the bikes, car-sharing, everything else. Because people generally don't seem to care about the mode they're taking. They're trying to figure out what's going to get me to the thing that I want to do fastest, cheapest, most predictable.

Of course, there are climate concerns and concerns about costs, but what most people are trying to do is accomplish something. A transit agency, a metropolitan entity like that, is probably a really good manager for those accessibility/mobility options. And I love examples that you just mentioned, it's really interesting to see how it plays out because it's a big country and what's happening in Dallas and Denver is different from what's happening in Detroit and Philadelphia. There's going to be different flavors around the country, and different agencies have different capacities for being that mobility manager. But I think all that's going to shake out in the next year or two as well.

We all know that public transit is facing severe challenges in many places. Huge drops in ridership that don't seem to be just little blips. What's the result? What's the cause of that? It's not entirely clear. Some would point to micro-mobility and these new options as being the culprit. Others will point to the growing economy and folks buying cars and sprawling metros. All this stuff is still going on at the same time.

But while we are trying to answer that question, we also need to think about what the transit agency of the future looks like? How do they adapt? And I think it's great what's going on now, and some folks, like Nat Ford, are starting to think very differently about it. There are lots of different roles for public agencies. There's still a public policy reason to run transit services, but it's probably not going to look the same as it did 10, 15, 20 years ago, and it probably shouldn't because transportation is changing.

**Now onto congestion pricing.**

There is no silver bullet to fix the woes of urban mobility and access, but there is consensus among transportation experts that congestion pricing strategies are among the most viable and effective. Charging a fee for the parts of the roadway network used the most at the busiest times of day reduces demand and incentivizes travelers to seek alternative routes or shared and active modes of transportation. It can also provide much-needed support for more sustainable modes of travel—such as transit, carpooling, biking, and walking—and can serve as a powerful tool to address the deeply regressive nature of traditional transportation fees. The idea has been around since ever there have been transportation economists.

And we do know it works with evidence internationally in cities like Singapore, Stockholm, Milan, and London which all adopted cordon pricing schemes. There are no examples of cordon-style congestion pricing in the United States because we don't have the same kind of super-dense urban cores as they do in other places. We don't have the tremendously expansive public transit networks as they do in those places with a couple of exceptions.

New York is a big exception. They have a dense core, and they have tremendous congestion. They have a robust transit network, so it's, it's a no brainer for New York. You have the bridges, you have the tunnels, and we're excited about this experiment that they're going to roll out in 2021. The focus there is on plugging the hole in the gap of the MTA, and some people will tell you that it's probably not a good idea to just put congestion pricing in to fix a budget hole, but in this case, it's actually very related. There's a rational nexus between the charge being collected and where the revenue is going, right into the MTA, which is going to provide alternatives to using the charge. It makes perfect sense.

What they need to watch out for is that they're not going to give away too many exemptions to folks to outer-borough commuters, New Jersey commuters, TNCs, or whatever it's going to be. In places like that, maybe it's naive to say, if you have an exemption in New York, it's going to be hard to imagine putting it back on after a number of years. They've got to get that right from the very, very start.

There's different models too. There's cordon pricing, which is London, Stockholm, New York, Singapore, places like that where there's an area that's defined, and you have to pay to go in and out of the area. There are electronic devices, different models in different places. But basically you go through a gantry or some camera takes a picture of your license tag or pass device and you're assessed a fee for the privilege of driving at that time. Sometimes they're dynamically priced. The more congestion there is, the higher the charge - all that makes sense to an economist.

But what's happening here in the United States, because we don't have that same kind of city infrastructure and transit infrastructure, but we are doing a lot of things around tolling and dynamic pricing. The Washington DC area is a great example. Northern Virginia, we have a very expansive network of tolled facilities on major interstates. But they're dynamically priced by time, by real-time conditions. The bigger the congestion, the more revenue is collected. On Interstate 66, that money goes right back into the corridor, paying for a lot of transit and pedestrian infrastructure in that corridor.

And it depends on what you do with that revenue. If that revenue was being collected and going into general state coffers and being spent for who knows what else, that would be untenable. But that money is going right back into the corridor to pay for transit investments. If you're in a transit vehicle, you're not paying the toll at all. If you're on a bike adjacent to the corridor, you're not paying the toll at all. But you're benefiting from those who are doing it.

In Los Angeles, LA Metro CEO Phil Washington is firmly committed to congestion pricing as a way not just to solve congestion in Los Angeles, which is a perennial problem, but to use that revenue to subsidize public transit, which has, once again, they have big ridership declines over there. A way to beef that up and to have a symbiotic relationship between the tolls collected and the money being spent. I am worried that in Chicago they're talking about it as a way to fix general budgetary problems but, again, if those three places can get it right, you might see a North American style in other places.

On the flip side there is another trend in places like Kansas City to make riding transit "fare-free" at no cost to the passenger. I think it is an exciting proposition because especially in places where agencies are facing big declines, free transit is very attractive especially for low income riders. When free transit experiments are tried, we see transit ridership increase. If it costs you more to collect the fares than you're bringing in revenue, it kind of makes a little bit economic sense.

It's a bold idea for obvious reasons, and there are some expenses go along with it. You've got to beef up security, you've got to beef up enforcement and all kinds of different things. But I think it's a really interesting trend that's going on across the country. And then tying it back to what you said, if in Los Angeles, if they can use congestion pricing and bold and aggressive public policy to pay for free or reduced-cost transit, I think that's tremendous. I'd love to see it happen in more places.

These are the top three mega trends – Autonomous Vehicles, Mobility as a Service and Congestion Pricing that will continue to move forward over the next 2-5 years in the USA.

# Part IV

# TOP TRANSIT TRENDS

## Chapter 23

### Top Transit Trends Into the Future

By **Paul Comfort**

Transit Evangelist

This past year I was in London speaking with Simon Reed, Head of Tech & Data: Surface Transport at Transport for London (TfL) and we were discussing how technology is evolving so quickly that it's important not to "overdrive your headlights" as it were. To me, government "innovation" always seems to be a lagging rather than a leading indicator and so while many transit agencies are just putting out their own smart phone apps, Simon says, "Apps have been around now for nearly ten years and for every fabulous one that exactly matches the your needs, there are literally hundreds that do not. As we end the decade, the only business case for investing in a transport app is as a gateway to a better service and not just another way of accessing your timetable."

Over the past couple years, I've had the privilege of traveling the globe interviewing over 70 top transit executives like Simon for my award-winning podcast, Transit Unplugged (www.transitunplugged.com). On this program, I spend about a half hour interviewing mostly CEOs of public and private transit systems and companies about their careers, their current project and future endeavors. I always conduct the interviews in person (not over the phone/computer) and usually on site at their administrative or operations facilities. I often get a tour of their offices and garages and sometimes get a chance to meet with staff and maybe teach a class on The Five Hidden Flaws of Most Transit Systems or Global Transit Trends.

That's what led to my idea to write this book. After meeting with so many leaders I felt I had a decent handle on what's happening now in the public transportation industry but even more importantly what's going to happen next. I've heard it straight from the proverbial "horse's mouth" – a lot of them in fact.

### So, what are the trends that are leading our industry now?

We all know the focus over the past couple years has been how to increase ridership on public transit. But what if I told you, that there are agencies that are not just staying consistent, they're actually increasing ridership? And that there are a few things they're doing that you could do too, to see the effect in your agency?

As you know, we've had a multi-year downward trend in ridership. A major story on this topic in the Washington Post newspaper noted that "Transit ridership fell in 31 of 35 major metropolitan areas in the

211

U.S. in 2017, including each of the seven cities that serve the majority of riders, with losses largely stemming from buses."
https://www.washingtonpost.com/local/trafficandcommuting/fallin g-transit-ridership-poses-an-emergency-for-cities-experts-fear/2018/03/20/ffb67c28-2865-11e8-874b-d517e912f125_story.html?utm_term=.42b725cbb589

The American Public Transportation Association (APTA) data showed that from 2014-2016, nearly every major transit system in America saw a decline in ridership. The national average was a loss of 4.5% of transit ridership over that time. Lower fuel costs, the uptick of new transportation options from companies like Lyft/Uber and an increase in telecommuting were often cited as reasons for this decline. An ENO Transportation Center article noted the National Transit Database (NTD) showed an actual decline of 5.2% in the number of miles traveled by the nation's public bus systems from 2009-2014, so this certainly contributed to the overall ridership decline.

But all that started to change in 2018. Houston and Seattle bucked the trend in 2017 by re-booting their bus route network and/or making other improvements like adding bus only lanes to their system and they began to see ridership increase. Then other city transit executives started reviewing their systems and evaluating how they could make changes to attract riders. You see, nearly all public transit systems rely on public subsidies and the elected officials who dole out the dollars had wanted to know why they should be giving more money to transit systems each year if they were providing services to fewer riders/taxpayers.

So, transportation leaders in the spirit of Einstein's comment that "Insanity is doing the same thing over and over again and expecting different results" began to look to do something different. I remember being at an APTA CEOs Conference in 2017 where this was the major topic of conversation and presentations – what could we do differently to stop the ridership losses and turn this industry around.

So new approaches began to develop and take root at numerous transit systems. And it has started to work. In the United States, in 2018 of the top 35 regions for transit usage, ridership rose in 7 cities - Seattle, Pittsburgh, Houston, Austin, San Antonio, Detroit, and Las Vegas. (2018 NTD Data). What did they do (along with other some other smaller cities who have seen an increase in ridership)? I'll tell you.

## The "Silver Bullet" to Increase Public Transit Ridership

I talked to transit executives in all these seven cities about what they did to increase ridership. I also spoke with transit leaders in other cities where ridership has begun to grow - both in America and in other countries like Canada and the United Kingdom. I've also studied their stats, their materials produced about their new programs and scholarly publications that have studied their results. Then I distilled these impact producing actions down to what I call the three "Silver Bullets" that have produced the greatest results in terms of increasing ridership. Here they are:

## 1.Reconfigure the entire bus route network to take people to where they want to go today.

This trend was started by Houston and then followed by Columbus, Baltimore and other cities to great aplomb. My good friend Tom Lambert, CEO of Houston Metro actually took a day from his senior team's schedule to meet with me and our Maryland Transit Administration team to give us a symposium on what worked well in their approach to a bus network reconfiguration.  We took their lessons learned and applied them to our plan in Baltimore. Now many major cities in North America have already done this or are in the process of re-booting their routes. Most cities' core bus route networks were laid out decades ago with a majority of routes leading to their central business districts in the most congested parts of their downtown. These routes haven't been comprehensively updated to take into account new rail networks (light rail, subways and commuter trains) or new commuting patterns of potential passengers to jobs and services in the suburbs.

## 2. Add frequency (10-15 minute headways) to the most heavily used routes.

As one transit expert put it – "there are three ways to increase ridership today – frequency, frequency, and frequency." That's because no one wants to wait anymore for a bus that may or may not be on time every thirty or even sixty minutes. Plus as Gary Rosenfeld, CEO of Memphis Area Transit Authority (MATA) told me, his county leads the state of Tennessee in the rate of poverty and many riders with low income have to spend up to four hours in commute time for an eight hour shift at a job that pays little more than minimum wage, when bus routes on are one hour headways. It's an unsustainable mode of mobility under these circumstances for employment purposes.

With Uber/Lyft and other mobility options now available for most choice riders, transit systems need to provide fast, efficient buses often to compete. Most reboots of the bus network include this added frequency feature for major routes. An additional benefit is that passengers don't need to use a bus schedule anymore during peak periods. They simply can wait briefly at a bus stop (just like they do now for a subway) and a bus will be there within 10-15 minutes.

Adding frequency to routes requires a shift from timepoint management to headway management and some systems are still grappling with effective means to do so. Here is a story of one city (Honolulu, Hawaii) who has done this effectively and how: https://busride.com/oahus-thebus-and-trapeze-develop-headway-management-system/

**3. Reducing the friction that slows buses and makes routes too long by adding bus only lanes, transit signal priority and new quicker faring options.**

215

One of the bad side effects of bus routes that go through the Central Business District (CBD) of most cities is that they get caught in the congestion there and their average speed is no better or even worse than the cars around them. This leads to passengers thinking there is not much benefit to them personally to ride the bus vs. their car. In Baltimore, 2/3 of our bus routes went to the downtown CBD and some route speeds there in "rush hour" were often slower than you could walk it before we revamped the route structure. One of the biggest concerns of passengers about riding public transit expressed in a recent major study by the VISA credit card company was time to reach a destination: 80% of Baby Boomers, 81% of Generation X and 67% of Generation Z respondents noted this issue.
https://www.visa.co.uk/content/dam/VCOM/regional/ve/unite dkingdom/PDF/blog/future-of-transportation-mobility-in-the-age-of-the-megacity.pdf

Adding bus only lanes and transit signal priority speeds up the buses and allows for que jumping to increase the average mph of the bus and its efficiency. This attracts riders to get out of their cars and ride the bus.

Another improvement to speed up the bus is the addition of contactless credit cards to pay fare and e-faring with apps on the passengers' smart phones. In late 2019, Visa announced that 100 partners had enrolled in its global transit partner program, Visa Ready for Transit, giving transit agencies access to an expanded network of technology solutions and expertise to make it easier to get around.

Many transit agencies are recognizing the benefits of enabling contactless payments at turnstiles and on buses. Tapping to ride with a contactless card or digital wallet helps riders save valuable time by avoiding the need to pre-purchase a ticket, manage a standalone transit card, or stand in line to reload their fare card. Projects that are live currently are seeing positive adoption with a 40% year-over-year rise in contactless transit transactions. Contactless transit solutions have been shown to streamline fare collection and reduce operational costs while helping to boost ridership through an improved customer experience.

The addition of bus tracking apps also allows passengers a sense of comfort knowing exactly where the bus is now and when it will be arriving at the bus stop.

**Results**

All these changes are bringing passengers back to the bus and the downward ridership trend seems to have bottomed out in 2017 with a rebound now firmly afoot. Nationally, ridership increased by 2.20% in the third quarter of 2019 compared to the third quarter of 2018, according to the quarterly "Transit Ridership Report" released by the American Public Transportation Association (APTA). This includes a rise of 5.46% for heavy rail, 4.38% for commuter rail systems, and 0.59% for all bus systems.

Riders in the third quarter of 2019 took 2.5 billion trips. This is the second quarter in a row with an increase, and the first consecutive quarters with an increase since the third and fourth quarters of 2014. This added up to 54 million more trips in the third quarter of 2019 compared to the third quarter of 2018.

Look for these trends to continue into 2020 and beyond as more systems reconfigure their routes, add frequency and reduce the friction that slows their bus routes. New route planning and business intelligence tools that even use artificial intelligence are coming onto the scene to assist agencies in ensuring their routes will be most productive. Ridership is on a rebound as transit becomes more customer-centric.

As BC Transit CEO Erinn Pinkerton told me, "One thing that I'm confident on is that fixed route, high-capacity transit will never fail. Regardless of the other mobility entrants into the market, public transit will continue to lead the market with the ability to carry the most amount of passengers, with high frequency and reliability. A rideshare vehicle is still in congestion with the rest of the rideshare vehicles, and so we in the transit industry need to make sure that we focus our investment on where we know we're going to be relevant."

She continued that we need to "Focus on our strengths, and then recognize that our customers, their travel experience is going to change, and their demand or expectations is going to grow. And so how do we keep up with that and stay relevant?

I'm the first to admit that we need to be able to pay for fares with our phone, our app, our credit card or debit card. Why can't customers see where their bus is and almost hail it? What draws our customers to rideshare and how can we mirror that? For example, let our customers rate their experience when they get off and say, "My driver was great" or report a concern or give any immediate real-time feedback. We should consider the use of family accounts. I want to be able to let my 12 year old nephew ride, know where he is, and know he's safe. How do we take what the private industry is doing and make sure that we're staying relevant in that market?"

## What else?

I believe three other big trends from the past couple years will continue to be influential on our transit executives as they grow their systems:

1. Zero Emission Buses – This is a big trend as agencies move to transform their fleets away from diesel fuel to ZEB options, either through political pressure or operational considerations. The largest market share is moving toward electric buses with others adopting Compressed Natural Gas (CNG) or even hydrogen fuels. We'll explore all three options in upcoming chapters of this book and see where they are headed.

2. Autonomous Vehicles – Many transit systems, colleges and cities are dipping their toe into this cool new arena. US DOT has issued new guidelines and funding to help agencies try it. Some are using these small, slow moving shuttle buses for last mile solutions to rail stations, others to boost tourism and still more

as campus shuttles. Look for this trend to continue to expand as driver shortages and safety considerations boost interest. There will be lots of discussion about this trend in the chapters of this section.

3. Mobility as a Service (MaaS) – This new trend has taken our industry by storm. Basically it involves using a smart phone app to combine trip planning and payment functions for mobility options in a given region. This may include traditional bus and rail options but also include our newer additions to the mobility landscape like TNCs (Uber/Lyft), E-bikes and E-scooters, traditional taxi, private microtransit and even rental cars and more. The APP can provide trip planning options to make the trip faster or less costly and the customer can pay for them all with one click on the phone. Fare Capping can be added as well.

Three basic models have emerged from this technology that got its big start in Helsinki, Finland:

| |
|---|
| A. Transit Agency Led APP Development: Cities like Dallas, Portland and Berlin, Germany have moved toward a Mobility Aggregator model and taken these other new mobility options "under their wing" so to speak and included their services as options for passengers. |

B. Private Company Led APP Development: Many cities have determined that they don't want to have to develop the APPs themselves so they have outsourced its development to private companies who "white label" the APP for the agency and handle all the upgrades and behind the scenes payment and mapping.

C. Private Provider Led APP Development: Denver RTD is the leading agency that has allowed Uber to take the lead in their approach to MaaS so that passengers can see transit options pop up on the Uber APP when they plug in their intended destination.

Some folks think that whole approach may be wrong headed. Transport for London's Head of Technology and Data for Surface Transport, Simon Reed told me that he believes many people today have "app fatigue" and would prefer that transit options appear on existing apps that they use to procure products and services. Under this approach, if a patron went online to a movie theater's app to purchase movie tickets, after they selected their theater and show time, transit/mobility times and locations would show up on that app to give options to get to and from the showing they chose.

Several of our industry leaders address MaaS as a whole and describe where they believe it is going and how it should develop. One question that many are asking now is will these developments lead to the end of smart fareboxes as we know them and will we see a shift to validators on board and cash only boxes or even a move away from cash altogether, as they have done in London. This seems to be the trend although some in the US see our Title VI requirements leaving cash fares as an option. Others like Robbie Makinen at KCATA see a fare-free future for their main transit systems, where other subsidies make up the difference in operating budgets and passengers can ride for free.

Now onto our other experts who will give you their take on our industry's top trends and how they may play out over the next decade. I start with a great quote from Industry Icon Nat Ford:

*"Today is a time of extraordinary change for the transportation industry, but we've been through big changes before and have come out on top. Each time, there are those who told us to resist the future; that change would divide us. But fears turned to strength. If we are to challenge the future, we challenge it by asking it to be bolder and greater."*

*Nathaniel P. Ford, APTA Chair (2017-18) and CEO, Jacksonville Transportation Authority*
*October 9, 2017 – APTA Annual Meeting & EXPO (Atlanta, GA)*

# Chapter 24

# Q&A with David Pickeral
## Mobility Futurist

*David Pickeral is one of the smartest guys in our business. He has a resume as long as my arm and speaks to audiences around the world about the future of mobility and smart cities. Not only does he focus on the technology but also how to make solid business models with it and the importance of regulatory compliance and clear governance.*

*I asked him to address some of the key components of today's top transit trends. I think you'll find his answers fascinating.*

## 1. What do you think is the future of MaaS for our cities?

Mobility-as-a-service (MaaS) has in recent years become in many circles yet another overused buzzword, as well as suffering from association with ban-the-car extremism or usurpation by sellers of discrete products or services. Entirely unnecessarily so!

In the often maddening Internet era habit of having to distill everything down and create catchy labels in attempt to the capture the decreasing attention spans of an increasingly distracted audience, pundits, politicians and productizers have often left behind (pun intended) what government-industry-academia in communities around the world are now actively trying to do at the most basic level:

"How do we, with the resources we have or can reasonably obtain, best use transportation technology (and commonsense) to deploy them now and going forward to provide revenues for business, cut cost for government, and serve the needs of our citizens / constituents / customers?"

Significantly it should NEVER be about eliminating personal vehicles, fixed route mass transit, or any other element of the value chain versus ensuring a seamless mix of options for each journey whilst avoiding the extremes of people either having to purchase vehicles to get around or spend their lives waiting for slow and inefficient scheduled route services to show up.

In trying to talk about the next evolution of Mobility — whether or not it is ultimately termed MaaS especially here in the US—in simple terms I am inclined towards no less than a perhaps blasphemous inversion of our national motto: "Out of One, Many."

What exactly I mean by this is that I believe that it is fundamentally important that even as planning, selection and payment functions are consolidated (perhaps in the cloud, again like the MaaS issue a dialogue for another time) it will be fundamental that end users are able to reach them via their choice of a single point of access.

But, then—it will be reciprocally important to be able to deconstruct all of them when needed in an environment of neutrality allowing rapid, uncomplicated and reliable selection and payment for one or more modes to cover each specific journey portal-to-portal.

Mobility-as-a-service will not be so much a service as it will a movement— Although the automotive world is finally shifting beyond the centennial mindset of Everything-as-a-Product—recalling some of the most frustrating conversations of my entire career to that effect with OEMs on multiple continents—even the concept of a service does not entirely cover the landscape.

No one entity no matter how diverse can enable this new Mobility itself. Rather it will take collective agreement followed by active collaboration across open standards converging the optimal public and private resources for each community. This was—and still is—how the Internet has scaled across global ICT infrastructure and how transportation itself incrementally evolved with local services networked with those beyond.

MaaS by in every community needs to start locally and be done with direct engagement by state / provincial transportation authorities and national governments providing high level funding and even more importantly standardization, and with industry and academia involved at every level.

## 2. What do you think is the future role of Hyperloop?

There is no exact answer to that question yet, which is exactly the problem.

The world is due for a new mode of transportation, and I do not think there will be any doubt that hyperloop, maglev, flying cars or some other substantially new system of travel will emerge before the end of the 21<sup>st</sup> Century. However there is an open question of what critical need will be served in doing so even as there is a need to maintain existing assets and equipment and to gather and analyze data to optimize what we already have.

In the past four years I have engaged directly and substantively with three of the Hyperloop companies in relation to this challenge and here are some of the conclusions made, mostly around what will not work.

High speed passenger operations seems the most logical and popular solution, but as with any other mode throughout history the ability to provide these services competitively and show ROI is extremely challenging—noting of course that both mass transit, commuter and intercity rail operations, and even airlines have large public subsidies, tax concessions or other government support to stay in business in order to serve the public. Right now there really isn't political or public support for that, again in light of all the other transportation and other infrastructure challenges facing the country. And how many passengers at least in current generations will be willing to shoot themselves thousands of miles through a tube, especially running what would be miles deep under the ocean even if such infrastructure could be built—with of course the issues of emergency egress and even routine maintenance likely being also beyond current capability or cost effectiveness.

In contrast, commercial freight / logistics operations are invariably more profitable than passenger operations and always have been. However existing assets, especially heavy rail and maritime, are able to move a great deal of freight long distances at low cost— including and especially bulk cargoes like iron ore, petroleum and grain— and it will be unlikely that a Hyperloop system could duplicate that. Moreover the speed advantage of a Hyperloop really would not come into play in moving most loads which are effectively fungible commodities that rely on a steady but not necessarily fast pipeline.

This would effectively leave a freight Hyperloop to focus on high value cargoes such as mail and package delivery. As far as mail, with instantaneous options like email or secure electronic documents transmission worldwide, there is less and less use for moving paper. As far as cargo, at this point multimodal logistics using technologies such as IoT and analytics are already so highly refined along with such things as regional distribution centers that it would be hard to justify construction of a Hyperloop system for what would be only minimal improvement.

Where I think Hyperloop or similar assets are likely to first appear will be in intermediate distance travel, such as between New York and Washington DC, Los Angeles and San Francisco or Dallas and Houston (where a new high speed rail system continues to move forward). I continue to support these efforts myself to the extent that they do not conflict with some of the other more pressing issues that we will need to focus on in our careers and lifetimes.

### 3. What do you think is the future of autonomous vehicles for public transportation agencies?

As concerned as I've been in recent Posts about overly aggressive predictions re. <u>self-driving</u> and <u>AV</u> deployment for light duty consumer use, in I hope understandable contrast I see intra-urban mass transit as well as <u>OTR</u> commercial freight as the best early adopters of this technology.

This is for a number of reasons including the fact that transit properties like all common carriers are usually better oriented towards compliance and liability issues, use set routes and terminals, have centralized service and maintenance, and invariably have standard operational and training procedures. Furthermore despite a great deal of social science rumination about job displacement, the practical reality is that there is tangible need for change—now—given a chronic and growing shortage of drivers to replace those retiring or going into other lines or work en masse.

Beyond that the sort of last mile / km services that AVs will fill and as are being demonstrated around the world are critical because no one is doing them in a profitable and/or cost effective manner. TNC drivers universally dislike servicing transit stops because the waits are often long, parking is often a challenge, and the fares low compared to picking up people from bars, at airports, etc. Transit fixed route loop service through neighborhoods is very expensive in terms of both labor and equipment costs and usually involves long headways such that few people use them in favor of park and ride, calling someone to pick them up, or using TNC services.

I think a combination of autonomous vehicles as well as human-driven microtransit will be essential for evolving mobility, consistent with the cost-takeout metrics I discuss in the next section.

## 4. The Question you didn't Ask—"How do we resolve the conflict between private on-demand services and mass transit?"

The transportation technology world and indeed the mainstream media were ablaze with news that Uber has incinerated another USD $5.2 BN investment (in 2Q 2019) with as yet no turnaround of profitability.

In practical reality there have been two fires burning for some time— Half a century of data affirms that taxis make little ROI and mass transit none at all, indeed quite the reverse. Fanned by the TNC phenomenon every US MTA except Seattle and Houston faces progressively lower transit ridership and commensurately reduced farebox return year-by-year—a slow burn collectively costing taxpayers an order of magnitude more than the individual loss here.

Eventually the mobility market will believe those of us who have suggested for decades that ondemand services can monetize cost takeout over many low density fixed route operations. Let me explain again how this works:

If there is a 10% farebox return on a route (equating to a 90% loss), if it is possible to substitute publicly funded

TNC, microtransit or shared mobility from one or more private operators to reduce that loss to 80%, that differential can be monetized as both government savings and industry profit.

This sounds simple, but in practical reality it isn't.

The real artifice—and complexity—will come using transportation technology including IoT, analytics, AI, CAV and digital twin to gather and analyze ridership, VMT, Passenger Seat Miles and other data to deploy the right mix of services not only for each individual community but each demographic within it. In so doing the ability to Pareto-optimally adjust G2B subsidies versus B2C recoupment to ensure all populations are served and all providers compensated is eminently achievable.

# Chapter 25

# AI, Machine Learning

## And the Next Chapter of Transportation

## Alex Ni
## Chief Technology Officer
## Trapeze Group

*Talk about smart guys, I've got two of them back to back in these chapters. Alex is Trapeze's Chief Technology Officer with a wide background of innovation with numerous tech companies. I'm thrilled to have him share here how artificial intelligence can impact mobility for millions of passengers.*

*Take a look at what he says and see how you can adopt some of what he projects will be important ways AI can impact autonomous vehicles, traffic management systems and On-Time Performance and Real Time Predictions in the coming years.*

# What is AI and why is it important?

*"The AI conversation is important in terms of both urgency and impact."*

- *Max Tegmark (Life 3.0., 2017)*

No matter what field of work you are in these days, it is getting hard to go one day without hearing about AI and machine learning.

So what is AI? AI stands for artificial intelligence. To understand AI, it is better to come back to the fundamental question of "what is intelligence". Throughout history, there had been much debate on how to define the concept of intelligence. For the purpose of having a functional definition we can extend, we consider intelligence to be *the ability to accomplish a complex set of goals*. Artificial intelligence, by extension, means an artificial entity – a system or program that possesses such an ability.

This means any system, endowed with logic and can solve a class of problems or achieve well-defined goals reasonably well compared to their human counterparts can be classified as AI. In a lot of cases, AI applications can match if not outperform their human counterparts.

## A Brief History of AI

If you read science fiction, or have been to the movies in the past ten years, you would recall that one of the most well-known blockbusters on AI – titled "I, Robot" was based on a novel with the same title written by Isaac Asimov in the winter of 1950. Coincidentally the same year when Alan Turing published his seminal work "Can Machines Think", in which he coined the original concept of the "Turing Test" as the first proposed means to examine whether a system can be considered artificially intelligent.

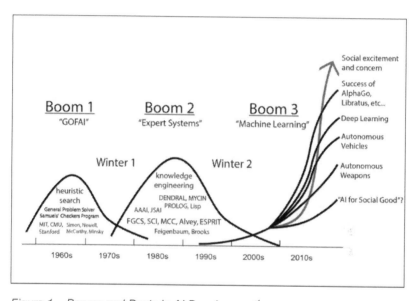

*Figure 1 – Booms and Busts in AI Development[1]*

The above chart depicts the booms as well as "winters" of AI dating back to its first emergence in science as well as in pop culture. The pivotal moment when AI became a concept known today was during the Dartmouth Summer Research Project in 1956, when

---

[1] Matsuo, Yutaka. "Does artificial intelligence go beyond humans: beyond deep learning, 2015"

scientists boldly hypothesized that "significant advance [on one or more problems related to machine intelligence] can be made with a selected group of scientists working together." While the workshop did yield limited practical advancement, it sparked wide academic interest in the field. In 1970, Minsky famously (and exuberantly) claimed "from 3-8 years, we will have a machine with general intelligence of a human being". The "GOFAI" approach – Good Old Fashioned AI leverage brute-force and heuristic search algorithms was predominate in the 60's and 70's.

When GOFAI failed deliver on the hyped expectations, the field of AI went into its first winter. In the early 80's, a new concept of "expert systems" – a system to represent knowledge and make expert-like decision was introduced by Edward Feigenbaum. This ultimately enabled IBM to build its famous chess-playing AI running on the powerful Deep Blue supercomputer that defeated then-reigning chess world champion Gary Kasparov. Though this was impressive and helped boosting IBM's share price, the industry application of this approach is still limited due to the amount of effort required to manually construct such immense database of knowledge required for each application domain. The AI market fell into another "winter" from the 90's to the mid 2000's.

However, research in another domain of AI – machine learning went on despite the AI "winter". In the late 2000's, the advancement in a special branch of machine learning called deep learning had drastically catapulted the potential of AI far beyond that of the traditional AI paradigms before. Different from traditional AI approaches (heuristic search and expert systems), machine learning uses highly mathematically sophisticated concepts called backpropagation. The use of backpropagation, or backward propagation of errors, seeks to determine the conditions under which errors are removed from networks built to resemble the human neurons by changing the weights (how much a particular input figures into the result) and biases (which features are selected) of the network. The goal is to continue changing the weights and biases until such time as the actual output matches the target output. At this point, the artificial neuron fires and passes its solution along to the next neuron in line. This is a much closer mimicry to how the human brain actually works in terms of learning and acquiring new skill sets.

The applications enabled by deep learning have become so prevalent that most of us are not even aware that we are using them in our everyday lives. From making appointments by conversing with our smartphones to getting movie recommendations, from investing to fighting identity theft, AI powered applications have become omnipresent. It suffices to say that the advent of deep learning and its applications has brought the field of AI out of its second winter.


**The Impact – Hype and Reality**

According to PwC and CB Insights, the venture capital funding of AI companies hit a record $9.3 billion high in

2018 – a 72% increase from the previous year[2]. The largest American venture deal in AI for all 2018 was the $500 million funding round to self-driving car start-up Zoox Inc, dwarfed only by a $600 million round to a Beijing-based AI company SenseTime Group Ltd, which produces AI-enabled software to recognize people and objects. It suffices to say that 7 out of 10 of world's most valued brands powers their primary product offering with AI[3]. The other 3 all have strong presence of AI embedded in their service offerings to help recommend and protect consumers. In the image

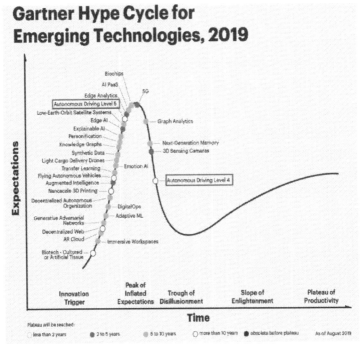

**Gartner Hype Cycle for Emerging Technologies, 2019**

---

[2] Venture Capital Funding Report, 2018
(https://www.cbinsights.com/research/report/venture-capital-q4-2018/)

[3] BrandZ, 2018 (https://www.wpp.com/news/2018/05/brandz-top-100-most-valuable-global-brands-2018)

236

here, you can see where Gartner ranks most of well-known AI enabled technologies in its famous "hype curve".

*Figure 2 - Gartner Hype Cycle for Emerging Technologies[4]*

## Key AI Interests in Transportation

Transportation is one of the most important areas where modern AI demonstrates its compelling advantage over conventional algorithm used in classic AI paradigms. In order to demonstrate the effectiveness and promises of AI-based solutions in the space of transit, we will be looking at some of the most well-known problems in transit. The implication of AI to transportation is interesting as transportation is one of the oldest industries known to humanity. It was estimated that the history of transportation started back to 60,000 to 40,000 years ago when human beings first crossed the ocean with boats and colonized Oceania.

## Self-Driving Vehicles

Self-driven cars have been a topic of high interest in the transportation and transit industry. It is hard to not notice autonomous vehicles on every headline in the second half of 2010's when we read tech news. With the maturing of AI technology, the development of autonomous vehicles has accelerated drastically from concept and early prototypes to reality. Deep learning

---

[4] Gartner, Inc. 2019 (https://www.gartner.com/smarterwithgartner/5-trends-appear-on-the-gartner-hype-cycle-for-emerging-technologies-2019/

research and affordable, powerful GPU's (graphic processing units) enabled real-time decision making based on image recognition and obstacle recognition systems built with LiDar technology and large array of cameras. Pioneered by innovative companies such as Waymo, Google, Tesla and Drive.ai, self-driving cars leverage the learning algorithms and GPU to process a blinding amount of information fed by sensors, extract key intelligence from these streams of data and make just-in-time decisions based on this intelligence. Self-driving cars have the ability to learn the road conditions as well and improve upon its own driving. It is worthwhile to point out that in 2018, the largest sums of venture capital invested in AI was invested in companies that are working on self-driving cars and related technologies (image analysis and object recognition technology).

We have all heard about the promises of self-driving cars by now. So just how exactly powerful are they and when can we expect them? Based on the IEEE definition, there are five levels of autonomous driving vehicles:

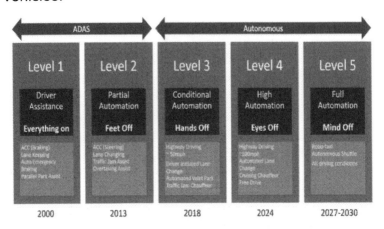

*Figure 3 - Five Levels of Autonomous Driving Vehicles*[5]

- Level 1 – driver assistance: Control is still in the hands of the driver, yet the car can perform simple activities such as controlling the speed. We already have this.

- Level 2 – partial automation: The driver's responsibility is to remain alert and maintain control of the car. This level has been available on commercial cars since 2013.

- Level 3 – conditional automation: Conditional automation means that a car can drive by itself in certain contexts under speed limits, and under vigilant human control. The automation could prompt the human to resume driving control. This has been available since 2015.

- Level 4 – high automation: The car performs all the driving tasks (steering, throttle, and brake) and monitors any changes in road conditions from departure to destination. This level of automation doesn't require human intervention to operate, but it's accessible only in certain locations and situations, so the driver must be available to take over as required. Vendors expect to introduce this level of automation around 2020. Tesla has claimed to have

---

[5] IEEE Spectrum, Accelerating Autonomous Driving Technology, 2019

achieved this level of automation with its auto-pilot.[6]

- Level 5 – full automation: The car can drive from departure to destination with no human intervention, with a level of ability comparable or superior to a human driver. Level-5 automated cars won't have a steering wheel. This level of automation is expected by 2025. Waymo has demonstrated that the full automation has been achieved in limited cities.

When the age of full autonomous vehicles comes, massive economic benefits will be realized in form of fewer accidents, lower insurance costs, fewer jobs in driving to reduce more time to do other productive tasks. Self-driving vehicles is poised to disrupt public

---

[6] https://www.tesla.com/support/autopilot

transit as well. Driverless buses can be seen in the streets of Europe. The world's first driverless bus was introduced in the French city of Lyon back in 2016, and there has been great progress ever since. In 2018, Stockholm also introduced driverless buses which could travel at 20 mph. Using sensors, cameras, GPS technology, and AI, these buses are capable of carrying passengers to their destination. This will have deep and far reaching implications to many aspects in transit in the long run as more transportation modes will start becoming automated.

**Traffic Management Systems**

The other equally prominent area of AI application in transit and transportation is traffic management. The quality of transit and transportation is greatly affected by the traffic flow patterns, understanding these patterns better can result in greatly improved traffic flow.

With the help of machine learning, AI systems can predict and prevent traffic jams. AI algorithms have been developed which could beat the world's worst traffic jams. Traffic congestion cost $87 billion to Americans in 2018[7]. AI could allow streamlined traffic flow and will reduce congestion. Smart traffic light systems can manage the traffic more efficiently which can save a lot of money. With artificial intelligence in place, you are less likely to get stuck in a traffic jam. AI

---

[7] http://inrix.com/press-releases/scorecard-2018-us/

can also process complex data and suggest the best route to the drivers real-time based on traffic condition.

Thanks to its immense processing power, the GPU's have been used in various of IoT devices deployed on the "edge" to accomplish the heavy lifting of real-time image recognition and prediction. The recognition algorithms can provide better information on the mix of traffic, density and rate of flow. The optimization algorithms can aggregate these data points by region to produce the optimized control pattern to reduce traffic jams and distribute flow optimally. This architecture allows for much more rapid decision making and gives the control system a significant higher degree of failure tolerance and redundancy compared to the traditional hub-and-spoke model.

*Smart cameras at junctions can automatically identify different road users, allowing the traffic management system to adapt according to their needs*

There are innovative companies such as Vivacity, NoTraffic, and Siemens Mobility to experiment with intelligent camera systems integrating with traffic light to change how traffic management is done today. Intelligent traffic management systems driven by machine learning can advise transit agency to dynamically change the routes to reduce inefficiencies and time in traffic. The implications for this reduction will be significantly positive in terms of reduction of environmentally harmful emission, reduction of cost and increase of rider experience.

## On-Time Performance and Real Time Predictions

The most important aspect of transit is quality of its service. A big component of ridership satisfaction is real-time prediction of bus arrival time. This applies to both fixed route transit and on-demand transit. The end user experience is closely associated with how accurately the system can predict arrival times with so many different factors involved such as distance between stops, geography, traffic, weather, and timing.

Traditional algorithms typically use a fixed time segment between stops. The issue is that if one bus starts to deviate from the planned arrival time, the prediction gets thrown off and the inaccuracy cascades through all subsequent buses after. This approach also does not take in consideration of times of day, historical trends for certain stops during certain times of the day, the weather, and a few other modalities of information that can affect the prediction.

- Leveraging a rich set of data accumulated from over 20 years of operation, Trapeze Group is developing a data lake and building a set of predictive features to increase the accuracy of prediction in order to offer exceptional service to our customers and passengers' wait times and enhance their experience. This service will leverage not only historical data set on fixed schedule for arrival, but also other modalities of information such as weather patterns, rider count information (obtained from our CAD / AVL system), geography, time of day to create a data model using all these relevant features. Machine learning will help filter and predict the arrival time based on selected "features" and greatly boost accuracy by cross examining multiple seemingly discrete factors that impact travel time. The accuracy will be similar to that of industry-leading solutions such as Google Maps and Tom Tom based on multitude of information and advanced machine learning techniques. Once complete, this will elevate average prediction accuracy up to the mid 90% range.

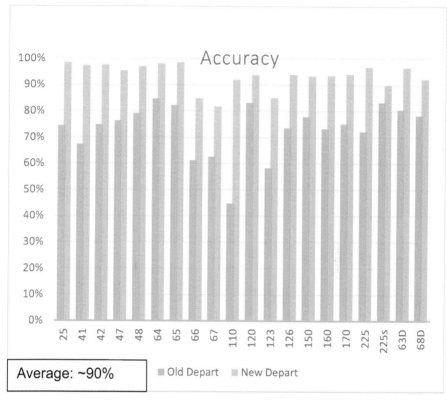

Accuracy

Average: ~90%    ■ Old Depart   ■ New Depart

## New Algorithm using scaled prediction time

Our sister company, TripSpark has utilized a simplistic yet ingenious algorithm that dynamically adjusted the predictive time based on time delays scaled to the distance, as well as historical arrival times on each stop in all the routes for a particular city combined with a Kalman filter[8] to take a composite prediction. This

---

[8] An algorithm that uses a series of measurements observed over time, containing statistical noise and other inaccuracies, and produces estimates of unknown variables that tend to be more accurate than those based on a single measurement alone, by estimating a joint probability distribution over the variables for each timeframe.

elevated the prediction accuracy to the 90% from 60% average using a naïve algorithm.

These advances will greatly improve the satisfaction of the ridership by shortening the wait for transit and reducing the total travel time.

There are many exciting discoveries and applications of AI in transit and transportation. The superior predictions and just-in-time decision making of AI, combined with IoT devices and sensors will fundamentally change how transit operates. Overall, we will be looking at a much more cost effective, user-friendly and overall pleasant experience.

# Chapter 26

# Embracing the Death Spiral

## Charting a new path for US transit agencies in the next decade

By **Mark I. Joseph**, CEO Mobitas Advisors and former CEO Transdev North America and

**Tim Kennedy**, MBA Candidate, MIT Sloan School of Management, former Deputy GM Transdev New Orleans

*Mark Joseph recruited me to his company Yellow Transportation in the late 1990s to help take the company national. First in my role as VP of National Contracts and then as General Manager of ten operations in the mid-Atlantic area, I enjoyed my five years working with him. I left to pursue a position in local government and Mark's company was acquired by what became Veolia and now Transdev. Mark went on to become CEO of this major international corporation and one of the top leaders in our public transportation industry.*

*He now consults and invests in tech start-ups, mostly in our mobility arena. He is a visionary and*

*inspirational leader that I count as one of my mentors. So happy he has shared his vision of what's coming next for our industry in this next chapter.*

*Many transit systems are moving toward zero emission solutions. Be it electric, CNG or even hydrogen powered systems. Sasha is an expert in this topic sitting on the Zero Emission Bus Task Force for the California Transit Association and helping numerous transit agencies in North America adopt their strategies to move toward this goal.*

*I think you'll enjoy his balanced and thorough approach toward where this trend is going and how you can prepare to transition your fleet.*

The 2010s were a tale of contradictions for urban transportation in the US. First, the good news: new apps built on a nationwide 4G network allowed for fundamental changes in how we get around, providing job opportunities and cheap, convenient rides for millions of people. We're talking not just about ride-hailing companies such as Uber and Lyft, but also about shared bikes and scooters, not to mention passenger-information and ticketing systems that make public transit easier to use.

On the flip side, transit agencies themselves, the backbone of mobility for our cities, have struggled. Most importantly, ridership has dropped. Nationally, despite increased service levels and more spending, rides on our nation's transit systems are lowest since

2006,[9] and bus ridership has dipped 13 percent since 2010[10]. Some macro trends – new options, plus cheap gas and a good economy – are part of the cause, but part is also internal.

Transit agencies' operational efficiency is also eroding, and new technology has caught them flat-footed. Nationally, we spent $22.3 billion in 2018 on operating costs for buses. We get less for that than we ever have, with operational costs per bus-passenger up 40% since 2010.[11] Antiquated infrastructure, underinvestment, and static, rigid relationships with organized labor make innovation difficult for transit agencies. Political priorities, especially the need to maintain "coverage routes"[12], can muddle agencies' priorities. Coverage routes provide service in low-ridership areas; they aim to cover a geography, rather than maximize ridership. That is a perfectly acceptable goal, but too often low-ridership routes are legacy lines or the result of narrow political interests, rather than a result of clear thinking on how to use transit agency resources.

Falling ridership and fare revenues can push transit agencies into a tough spot. Agencies typically have two main levers to make up budget shortfalls: hike up fares

---

[9] Compared to 2018 ridership as reported by the National Transit Database.
[10] 2010 to 2018 change, using NTD. Bus service has increased 4% over this period. Rail ridership is up 7% over the same period, though bus and rail combined ridership is still down 2%.
[11] This is partly due to the drop in ridership. But operating costs per vehicle-revenue hour are also outpacing inflation; they are up 17% since 2010 and 129% since 1991.
[12] A term for which we give full credit to Jarrett Walker.

or cut service. Either path can further reduce ridership and revenue, necessitating even higher fares or less service – this is the dreaded death spiral. Even where elected officials identify low farebox recovery as a purposeful policy choice, very low recovery rates make political coalitions for continued operating subsidies, let alone increased investment, tough to keep together.

Take San Jose's Valley Transit Authority as an example. With bus farebox recovery just over 10%[13] in recent years, officials have prioritized recouping a higher portion of operating costs from customers, with plans to push the number up to 25% or more[14]. This was part of the impetus for a recent bus-network redesign aimed at increasing ridership, but also led to the shuttering of one segment on the light rail system – the first-ever closure of a portion of a modern light rail network. Overall, it's hard to imagine meeting those re-vamped farebox recovery goals while expanding service.

Despite these struggles, we believe that well-run transit agencies remain essential for national prosperity and a just society. Transit allows our densest, most productive cities to move, driving the innovation that will make 2030 a different world from 2020. Public transit is also an essential resource for those without

---

[13]
http://www.scscourt.org/court_divisions/civil/cgj/2019/CGJ%20VTA%20Final%20Report%20-%2006.18.19.pdf

[14]
https://www.vta.org/sites/default/files/documents/Chapter08%2520-%2520Financial%2520Considerations.pdf

cars, or those who cannot or choose not to drive. So how to fix these essential agencies?

**Back to Basics**

We believe that transit agencies can thrive in the next decade and beyond by focusing on three core functions that they can do better than anyone. We call these the three Ps:

- Procurement – buying and managing transit services.
- Platforms – agencies have a key role in making sure that technology continues to make our cities better places to live, work, and get around. That will mean setting rules for platforms, or in some cases managing them directly, to encourage a level playing field.
- Policy – this means setting goals, setting and monitoring standards (especially for safety) and planning services. Planning includes identifying service needs, where those services should go, and how services should be integrated with each other and with the city as a whole (especially land-use planning).

These are complex tasks, with real agency expertise needed to do them well.

**Buying Things is Hard (and Important)**

Something so seemingly simple as procurement is really hard, and there's lots of evidence that US transit agencies have room for improvement. It's now well-documented that US agencies pay many times more for transit investments than other developed countries.

Alon Levy, a blogger who has developed the best estimates available, reckons the *cheapest* costs for new US new rail lines are double European costs, but the US premium can run to 7 times European costs.[15]

Differences in procurement processes are likely an important contributing factor. In Madrid, for example, the local government invested in a highly competent procurement and construction management team to build out 131km of new rail lines from 1995-2003. The government team got into the weeds, specifying details of sizes for tunnel boring at the outset, then managing the project directly; they also weighted most of the bid evaluation to technical merit and construction time, rather than only cost, as US transit agencies often do.[16]

Contrast that with the typical US approach, which often involves lump-sum design-build contracts that motivate contractors to underbid, then find "surprises" in the ground as they begin construction, leading to cost overruns and delays. Too often those costs are pushed to transit agencies, which lack the expertise to evaluate contractor claims – agencies are instead represented by consultants.

Procurement processes for operations contracts suffer from similar ailments. Much of US transit is contracted to private operators. With just a few exceptions, agencies run bids for these contracts that allow no imagination on the part of the private operator. Operators are often evaluated solely on the basis of

[15] https://www.citylab.com/transportation/2018/01/why-its-so-expensive-to-build-urban-rail-in-the-us/551408/
[16] Manuel Melis Maynar, 2003.

cost per-operating hour. In Europe, transit agencies commonly require private operators to suggest route changes or other improvements to drive up ridership, and then to back up those proposals by taking on revenue risk. In other words, part of the operator's payment comes from encouraging city residents to ride transit, and poor service delivery that reduces ridership leads directly to a financial squeeze for the private operator.

## Building Platforms

For procurement, there is good, global evidence from decades of experience on what works well – the trick is applying those lessons. For our second P, building and managing platforms, there is very little global experience. We know that consumers now expect transparency and high-quality service, and smartphones give them options. The number of true transit-dependent people is falling, since even low-income transit riders can jump in a Lyft Line or Uber POOL. Agencies have to compete with those services, but cannot sacrifice efficiency, since budgets won't stretch to allow for on-demand rides for every transit rider.

It's therefore still unclear what the "killer app" will be. What is clear is that transit agencies have a key role to play in getting there. Transit agencies also clearly have the right to play this role, since many third-party apps rely on government-provided data, such as real-time bus locations and maps of transit networks.

One option is for agencies to get into the game themselves. In New Orleans, the transit agency has contracted to build a tailored app that integrates trip planning, real-time vehicle locations, and ticketing. Passengers buy tickets on the app, then scan the QR code on the on-board scanners – a similar passenger experience to boarding a flight. This approach is complex and requires close agency management, but aims to give passengers a seamless experience.

Another option is for agencies to let third-party apps do the work. This is cheaper for agencies, but still requires expert management. Denver's transit agency now allows ticket sales through Uber, where of course passengers can also hail a ride, or grab a scooter or bike. Several cities have partnered with Transit App, another third-party, as the official trip-planning app – saving transit agencies time and money to develop their own proprietary apps. One city in Ontario has expanded that partnership to offering mobile ticketing through Transit App. Finally, there are third-parties that offer full mobility integration, from transit to bikes to car rental, with various subscriber tiers.

More agencies should push these types of experiments, and they shouldn't be afraid to try several at once. Regardless of the solution, agencies need to hire true experts in transit technology and planning to set out a local vision and manage solutions. A real danger is that some third-parties build walls by scraping public data and hoarding their own private data, to the detriment of competition and the public. This might be okay (at least in the short term), as it could allow third-parties to build out new services we haven't even thought of yet. But there are real tradeoffs, and agencies must make the tough decisions on standards that encourage competition while maintaining passenger privacy and incentives to enter the markets.

**Policy as an Enabler, Not as a Cudgel**

We see three broad policy choices for transit agencies as they consider the death spiral:

1. The regulatory cudgel – that is, banning many of the new services that are changing urban public transportation. Vancouver and Barcelona, for example, prohibit ride-hailing and allow only city-sponsored bike-sharing. To be clear, this can work, at least in building a short-term moat around transit agencies.

   Yet depending on the regulatory moat is short-sighted and bad for cities. Mark, one of our co-authors, built his career in the taxi industry, and saw the limits of relying on regulatory protection first-hand, as Uber and Lyft gritted their way into cities, quickly breaking down a century of restrictions on ride-hailing, and gutting taxi profits in the process. Worse, these moats are bad for residents, who are deprived on new ways of getting around – often ways that particularly benefit historically disadvantaged communities. Ride-hailing dramatically expands access to cars for communities where car ownership is low, and it appears to reduce racial bias compared to taxi services.[17] In

---

[17] One recent study is here, among others that come to similar conclusions: https://transfersmagazine.org/the-equalizer-could-ride-hailing-extend-equitable-car-access/

Washington, DC, dockless bikes and scooters quickly ramped up access for people of color.[18]

2. The business-as-usual route. Transit agencies could stay the course, making few or incremental improvements in operational efficiency while letting others cannibalize their ridership (as Lyft and Uber are too often doing now).

3. Embrace the change. We think there's a third path in which agencies double down on expertise in core areas. To start, that means building expertise in procurement and guiding development of smartphone-based mobility apps – the two Ps above. But transit agencies are well placed for many other areas of policy expertise. Safety is the most important example. In addition to strict oversight on safety performance for transit operations, agencies should develop requirements about data that third-parties must provide on safety incidents, to allow consumers to make informed decisions.

Cities appear to be catching up to ride-hailing companies, and are now requiring more disclosures of safety information and trip data, an essential tool for transit planning. That is a welcome trend. Continuing it will require more large investments in talent and technology to set standards, then collect and use data.

---

[18] https://www.citylab.com/transportation/2018/01/can-dockless-bikeshare-pump-up-cyclings-diversity/549629/

The corollary to embracing the change is spinning off functions where transit agencies don't have any special advantage. In particular, this means contracting operations to third-parties – through top-notch, well-funded procurement departments. Third-party contracting brings some well-known benefits. On average, private operators are 28% cheaper than direct public operations.[19] This suggests that just by switching to private operations, even under existing procurement models, many agencies could save a lot of money, which could in turn be used for service expansion.

Of course, counter-examples abound, and spinning off operations isn't the right approach for every single agency. But for the many agencies shedding ridership and struggling with operational efficiency, we suggest a bold new direction, focused on transit needs of the future.

There are real concerns with this approach, with worker protections high on the list. Our approach will often mean more jobs, such as when transit agencies hire many more employees in the procurement departments to directly manage contractors – tasks that are today too-often outsourced to consultants.

The real social risk is preserving opportunities for drivers; driving is perhaps the most important job for male workers in the US. The business-as-usual route puts those jobs at risks, since a true transit agency

---

[19] In 2018, average bus operating costs were $102 for privately contracted operations, compared to $141 for directly operated public operations (National Transit Database).

death spiral would be the worst-possible outcome for drivers. By focusing on the three Ps, agencies can preserve those jobs, even if they are no longer in the public sector.

Happily, the federal government recognizes the need to protect transit workers. The existing federal labor protection for transit workers, known as 13(c), was developed with the right intent, such as in protecting pay and benefits for transit workers whose jobs would be eliminated. Yet many aspects of it are outdated, entrenching workers in jobs where they are undervalued and hamstringing agencies' budding efforts to modernize. Among other restrictions, protections mandate six years of unemployment pay.

Now is a particularly good time for reform. With very low unemployment and shortages of transit drivers, there is an opportunity to shift resources from protecting jobs – many of which are unfilled – to protect workers. Federally supported training efforts can equip workers with the skills they need for the future.

**Foresight 2020s**

Over the last decade, transit agencies have abdicated leadership in moving our cities. Private-sector innovation has brought new possibilities, but a poorly resourced public sector has proven slow to harness (or in some cases, constrain) new technologies for a well-functioning transit system. The status quo risks a creeping increase in congestion – endangering economic prosperity and climate goals.

We'd like to see a bold national re-commitment to public transit, with transit agencies leading the way. In many ways, agencies must stake out an increased role. They need to attract and train talented staff to build standard setting, data management, and second-to-none expertise in procurement.


*You can contact Mark at:*
*mark@mobitasadvisors.com Website -*
*www.mobitasadvisors.com*

# Chapter 27
# The Road

## From "Transit on Demand" to "Mobility on Demand"

## By Andrea L. Potter
### General Manager of TripSpark Technologies

*I first met Andrea Potter in the early 2000s while I was GM at Yellow Transportation and she was helping our company with our software. She has risen through the ranks and now oversees a major transportation software company.*

*She also is an industry leader who "gets it" with a deep understanding of what makes a public transportation system tick and how to improve it.*

*In this chapter Andrea addresses what's coming next to the mobility on demand part of our business and how to get there.*

While everyone agrees on the definition of Mobility on Demand (MOD) and the philosophical arguments for it, few can agree on what implementation looks like or how to get there. And that's OK.

## Current Challenges Facing Smaller Urban and Rural Agencies

As a multi-modal software company providing fixed route, paratransit, non-emergency medical, K-12 school and rideshare solutions to smaller urban and rural agencies (including campuses), our customers typically serve large geographic areas with a high percentage of non-drivers: such as older adults, students, veterans and low-income families living in suburbs. Low density and increasing demand for transit in rural areas make for a unique set of challenges.

The goal of transit agencies in rural communities is to provide equitable, efficient and convenient transportation. They often must be more creative than large urban agencies in how they offer these services due to limitations in funding and resources. Some agencies use disparate software to manage their disparate services and are looking for ways to consolidate and use their vehicles and drivers more flexibly to fill empty seats, make better use of resources and provide better service to riders. They want a solution that can meet their basic needs and will scale up as their demands grow.

261

Our customers offer a range of services including fixed route, flex route, specialized or paratransit, regional integrated service, commuter service, contracted service for universities, subsidized taxi, carpools, vanpools, integration with TNCs and even volunteer drivers. They offer transportation services within their communities, between communities and connect communities with employment hubs. These services will continue to exist in the future but may be blended or expanded.

**What is Mobility on Demand?**

The concise definition of Mobility on Demand is "complete trips for all". It's traveler-centric, mode-agnostic, technology-enabled and partnership-driven.

Putting all these buzzwords aside, it's a concept that says connected travelers can access mobility whenever needed, choosing from whatever combination of modes meets their needs best. Transit will be one component in the larger network of service offerings. MOD provides more options for a broader scope of riders, allowing them to choose whatever is most efficient for them – be it shortest travel time, lowest cost, fewest transfers, or limited walking.

There are many ways to implement MOD, and to varying degrees. Agencies around the world are currently working through what exactly it means in practice.

Transit agencies are well-positioned to become the central Mobility on Demand broker, meaning "the centralized entity connecting modes being offered by providers". The broker will need to standardize the offerings and look after the maintenance of different components (like payments). However, MOD will never be one-size-fits-all. It must be adaptable so agencies can do what they need to for their communities.

## The First Small Step: Transit on Demand

Transit on Demand is the first step on the long road to Mobility on Demand. Quinte Access Transportation is currently offering this as a three-year pilot project, offering on-demand, shared-ride transportation to connect select communities without traditional bus service with a local transit hub.

We support these new types of services that agencies want to offer, like first mile/last mile, flex route, off-peak, and being able to offer service into new subdivisions with low density or areas with physical constraints.

## The Large Leap: Mobility on Demand

TripSpark's goal is to facilitate the integration of multiple transportation modes and allow agencies to efficiently offer more choices to their riders through an integrated mobility platform. We position transit agencies at the center of MOD in their geographic area. We believe that we can help make transportation more accessible by bringing it closer to people's doorstep and by getting riders to inter-modal hubs so they can continue their journeys.

## How TripSpark Is Getting There

One key aspect to achieving Mobility on Demand will be successfully partnering with agencies and industry to build agreements related to standards, data sharing, partnerships, and proprietary information. We need to understand all the interfaces that other service providers are making available. No single partner will be able to provide it "all" in the changing world. However, the technology needs to accommodate for the future of transportation by putting the rider first.

## Lego Blocks of MOD

Another key aspect is building the mobility platform. In order to give agencies the flexibility and features they need, the solution is structured like Lego blocks – allowing agencies to pick what they need, when they need it and to build their own customized system.

## Innovating Together

We believe that smaller urban and rural agencies will be at the forefront of adopting Mobility on Demand because they are more willing to adopt and adapt new services if they can find options that meet their budgets while improving service provided to their community. Necessity is the mother of invention. Mobility on Demand won't be dictated by a vendor but will be driven by agencies' creativity and riders' demands.


*You can contact Andrea Potter through her company website: www.tripspark.com*

# Chapter 28
## Smoothly Shifting Transit Gears:

## How to Prepare for Your Transition to Zero-Emissions Buses

### Sasha Pejcic
Principal, Transit Advisory Lead at Stantec

*Many transit systems are moving toward zero emission solutions. Be it electric, CNG or even hydrogen powered systems. Sasha Pajcic is an expert in this topic sitting on the Zero Emission Bus Task Force for the California Transit Association and helping numerous transit agencies in North America adopt their strategies to move toward this goal.*

*I think you'll enjoy his balanced and thorough approach toward where this trend is going and how you can prepare to transition your fleet.*

As part of the effort to fight climate change and improve quality of life, many communities are actively pursuing sustainable transit options. Zero-emissions buses (ZEBs) are one very attractive solution—but transitioning from traditional fossil-fueled buses to ZEBs requires careful planning.

## Why ZEBs?

A quieter, smoother ride. Lower operating costs. A healthier city, thanks to reduced pollution from diesel fumes. And zero carbon emissions. All excellent reasons for cities to replace their aging bus fleets with ZEBs.

But it's not as simple as buying new buses. Transitioning to a ZEB fleet means considering procurement, schedules, infrastructure support, repair and maintenance, capital expenditures, and labor. At first, the amount of work may seem daunting—but thorough research and solid planning will get you on track.

### The Route to Success

There are already thousands of ZEBs operating across North America. Most are battery-electric buses (BEBs), which require charging at the depot or along the route; the remainder are hydrogen fuel cell electric buses (FCEBs), which have onboard hydrogen fuel cells that generate power for the bus and recharge its batteries, delivering up to 18 hours (approximately 300 miles/450 km) of continuous use. On average, BEBs cost twice as much as a diesel bus; given their greater range,

FCEBs cost about four times as much. In either case, long-term operational and maintenance savings should compensate for the higher up-front cost of your initial investment.

No matter which type of ZEB you choose (or if you choose a mix of both), there are procurement factors to evaluate: choosing a supplier (charging standards & methods for BEBs are still in flux, while FCEBs have been more standardized); maintenance and service needs (battery changes and range capacity); and availability of replacement parts.

Up-front financial impacts must be handled before agencies can enjoy the long-term operational savings offered by ZEBs. In addition to the higher price of ZEBs, your insurance providers may raise their premiums, since the assets are more expensive. The ZEBs will have to be licenced, and new safety training provided. And there will be new infrastructure needs, including charging stations, higher electricity consumption, and possibly larger garages to handle a larger fleet. On the other hand, ZEBs have fewer moving parts than diesel buses and therefore lower maintenance and inventory costs. Financial planning should use the Total Cost of Ownership (TCO) model throughout the lifetime of the vehicles to truly capture the value proposition.

Agencies will also need to face regulatory impacts of the ZEB transition, examining local laws carefully to ensure compliance with inspection rules and labor regulations.

Maintenance and operations during the transition period—which could take a decade or more, considering the lifespan of buses—will require adjustment. Agencies will need to retain or acquire technicians familiar with both the old and the new buses. Drivers will also need to be trained to operate both types of buses. Your parts inventory will expand during the transition to handle old and new buses, but decrease as older buses are phased out. Maintenance tasks will change over time; for example, you'll see fewer and fewer fluid and filter changes as diesel buses are phased out of service. Dispatch and vehicle storage will become a little more complex to accommodate range factors and charging requirements. Scheduling will become critical so that buses are being charged at periods of lowest ridership.

**Garage/Depot Design**

Depending on your procurement choices, your garages will need to accommodate BEBs, FCEBs, or both. Whether constructing new garages or retrofitting existing infrastructure, the following must be considered:

•   Charging system

o   Overhead—a stationary ceiling-mounted charger or a bus roof-mounted charger?

o   Floor-mounted—pedestal, or inductive pad for charging while being serviced?

o    3-phase AC or DC charging?

•    Charging location

o    Depot charging—requires facilities with charging solutions

o    Route charging—fast charging on bus routes, can disrupt public space and increase rider wait times

•    Number of chargers needed

o    Consider number of buses, size of depot, number of service lanes, type of charging system

•    Circulation and logistics

o    Assuming vehicle size remains roughly the same as pre-transition, existing circulation should work—but consider buses are out of service while charging, which may require reassessment of how many spare buses and drivers are required to meet service needs

•    Power infrastructure

o    ZEBs require charging cabinets and upgraded transformers, switchgear, backup power generation, and reworked, upsized conduits to the grid

o    Concurrent fleet charging may also require stationary battery storage to buffer power demand

o    A significant transformer or utility service upgrade may be necessary

•    Timetable

o    Between procurement, design, construction, and turnover, a new depot may take three years to build new, or 18-24 months for a retrofit

## A Smooth Shift

Successfully transitioning to a ZEB transit system will take most transit agencies years of planning, procurement, and construction. But the rewards—happier, healthier riders, reduced operational costs, and, most importantly, no emissions—are worth the effort. Plan to succeed: develop a transition and implementation strategy with a built-in definition of what success means to you; ensure your plan leads to designs that incorporate lessons learned from successful ZEB experiences in other communities; understand the risks, but press on; and remember to start early and be patient. ZEB technology is constantly improving, and the issues you face today will be solved during the transition.

The result? A better, cleaner transit solution for your community. And a greener, healthier world.

*You can reach Sasha Pejcic, Principal, Transportation, Transit Advisory Lead, Mobile: 416 276-7057*
*Sasha.Pejcic@stantec.com*

# Chapter 29

# Mobility as a Service (Maas)

## Roger Helmy

## VP Product
## Trapeze Group

*Roger takes on the topic of Mobility as a Service (MaaS) head on in this chapter. This important trend is affecting much of what public transit systems are doing to adapt to today's riders. With the advent of smart phones now being used to manage most of our lives, MaaS pulls together all the mobility options in a city and allows you to create your own path toward mobility simply and elegantly.*

*Where should it go? Hear this important take on how MaaS can be used to really improve our world.*

The mobility landscape is changing faster than it ever has before. We can see it happening right before our eyes. Every time we call an Uber, pay for ride with a mobile phone, or take one of those thrilling scooter rides. Commuters have more options today than ever before. Competition has created higher quality experiences such as the ones offered by rideshare companies. That's great for riders, but it has certainly proven to impact public transit as most North American agencies have seen declines in ridership the last number of years. This is leading us to a critical juncture for our industry. As you likely guessed, it is the adoption and deployment of Mobility-as-a-Service (MaaS).

The future of public transit, really the future of mobility, will be incredibly bright. The opportunity to transform our communities and way of living in a positive way is right in front of us. As cities work to evaluate and select MaaS models, one consideration remains paramount: the rider experience. Populations are rapidly rising in urban cities. If we don't act now, this will lead to more congestion and diminishing quality of life. If we wish to improve the rider experience, we must first understand riders and their decision-making process. This isn't as easy as one might think. Riders will focus on four (4) paramount factors when making their decision: safety, convenience, reliability, and affordability. Safety, of course, is the most essential consideration. It really doesn't matter how reliable or affordable the mobility mode may be. If it's not safe, it just won't work. The other three factors will be more important to some than others, but really, if your service checks all the boxes relative to a personal car, more people will take public transit.

Therein lies the beauty of what is ahead of us. Mobility-as-a-service offers us the opportunity to understand the rider and their decision-making process better than ever before. That, in turn, allows us to create integrated mobility solutions that can make a profound impact for our communities. At Trapeze, we describe the 'pinnacle of MaaS' as the ideal state where the factors that drive the rider's decision become so compelling that it causes major shift from personal cars to public mobility. This becomes possible as long as transit is at the epicenter. We use the following term to reflect this:

## The backbone of MaaS is Mass

Living in Toronto, the best way for me to get downtown is the train. Public transit is still the best way to move people efficiently. Don't get me wrong, personal vehicles will always have their place, but the most critical piece to achieving the pinnacle of MaaS is a great transit system. At Trapeze, we focus on delivering solutions that help transit agencies improve the rider decision-making considerations I mentioned above. I lead Product at Trapeze. At times I've been asked what our product is. Is it software? Hardware? Both? Nope. Our product is every single interaction between us and our customers. The buying process, project implementation work, production support, and of course our technology is all part of our product. What is Amazon's product? Is it the new set of headphones you just purchased? No. Their product is the ease of purchasing, quick shipping to your door, and if necessary, returning. They have created a new experience for shopping, and that is their product. Likewise, we need to think about mobility in the same manner. The integration of public transit with private mobility options in a MaaS system needs to be viewed as an end-to-end experience; from the point of intent to travel, through arriving at one's destination. It doesn't matter if a train was running on schedule if the on-demand ride doesn't get to the station on time. If not planned and implemented carefully, MaaS can become a mess. However, if approached with diligence, MaaS can be a game-changer for our communities.

Most define MaaS as multi-modal trip planning that spans both public and private providers, with one step for electronic payment. While that creates a better rider experience, it is only the beginning. Through adoption of MaaS, transit agencies will be able to understand their customers like never before. Agencies will be able to segment rider demographics and determine preferred modes of mobility, walking times, waiting times, and begin to anticipate needs. Deep customer engagement can be created by personalizing the rider experience. Through partnerships with private mobility providers, unique payment structures can be created. Loyalty programs can drive further adoption. Imagine getting a free coffee as you get off your bus and walk to the office in the morning. Remember, that walk to the office is still part of the product, and an aspect of the rider experience that needs to be considered.

The single most important aspect to achieving the pinnacle of MaaS will result from advancing planning practices. Today, transit is still fundamentally based on providing supply to a defined system. Automatic passenger counters and faring data provide us insights on ridership, but this is all based on the existing transit network. With additional mobility modes available today, how do we optimize the entire network? How do we do that while providing preferred mobility options for each of our riders?  This is where things will become very exciting. On-demand mobility solutions are here, but are they viable for transit agencies to offer?  If so, where?  These are tough questions to answer.

Ultimately, we will need technology to figure it all out. Through adoption of MaaS, we can also begin to leverage machine learning to predict mobility demand. That will allow cities to allocate their resources and create more optimized mobility networks which will lead to more efficient and convenient options. Today, transit agencies still operate schedules based on 'sign up' periods that define the service that will be provided. Over the last decade we've witnessed the number of sign ups increase steadily per year. Why? We need to provide more dynamic mobility solutions to customers. Rider needs change, and much more often than a quarterly basis. When I first started in transit many years ago, transit agencies defined 'exceptions' to define a variance from a standard schedule. Today, exceptions are the standard.  Although unions and pick processes can pose obstacles for us, we can see how the industry is trending. I anticipate that the role of the planner and scheduler will transform over the next decade, and it will be critical to creating a rider experience that delights.

At the end of the day, we have an opportunity to radically elevate the rider experience, leading to more sustainable and livable cities. Through MaaS we can decrease congestion, waiting times, travel times, and truly optimize and personalize the mobility experience. The factors that drive the rider decision can now become much more compelling, and this can transform a city. Whether it's connecting someone to more employment or allowing someone to spend an extra ten minutes with their families each day, we all have an opportunity to make our communities a better place for generations to come. After all, isn't that why we do what we do?

*www.trapezegroup.com*

# Chapter 30

# It's Time to Open the Loop

## Matt Cole

### Past President
### Cubic Transportation Systems

*Matt Cole, until very recently, led one of the largest technology companies in our industry. Here are just some of his accolades - MaaS Influencer of the Year by Business MaaS (2018) | Top 10 Private Sector Disruptors in Transportation by the Eno Center for Transportation (2016) | Mass Transit magazine's Top 40 Under 40 (2016).*

*But not only that, Matt is a good friend. Several years ago, he arranged for me to meet with Shashi Verma, CTO of Transport for London, who led the contactless card revolution for transit in the western world. After meeting with him, I completely changed the strategy of the MTA to move toward using credit cards and e-ticketing as our future faring strategy.*

*In this chapter Matt shares where this whole "open loop" payment methodology is headed and how you can get on board.*

On my recent trip home to London, which enjoys one of the world's largest open payment fare collection system, I took the underground from Heathrow to the city center. As I tapped my phone at the underground station turnstile and passed through the gate without slowing, I remember reminiscing over that time, many years ago, when I had to fish for coins in my pocket to buy a paper travel ticket before I could travel.

Times have certainly changed. Today, many transit networks around the world boast modern, integrated and customer-friendly fare systems that can be accessed through our smartphones at the touch of a button. They offer passengers a plethora of different payment options: from cash and paper tickets, to pre-paid transit cards, mobile ticketing and payments and contactless credit and debit cards. In some regions of the world, paying for travel is so simple it becomes an afterthought. Yet, it wasn't always that way. For years, transportation remained the domain of paper tickets and tokens, with each siloed mode of transit requiring its own separate ticket and fare.

The very first transit payment revolution came with the magnetic stripe card, which became broadly available in the 70s, after the successful trial of the technology at Chicago's O'Hare Airport. Magnetic stripe card systems became wildly popular in the United States, and elsewhere, and almost every large city had its own. While they required passengers to convert their money into transit-only funds and had to be periodically re-loaded, they offered quick access to the transit system, sparing travelers the need to stand in line to purchase a ticket for every ride.

Over the years, transit agencies implemented other fare payment innovations, most notably a transit-agency branded smartcard, and most recently contactless payments to complement or replace the existing payment options. Contactless payment systems work with physical smart cards and virtual smart cards saved on smart devices and use embedded radio-frequency identification or near-field communications technology to make secure payments. As we moved into the 21st Century transit-agency branded smartcards became the predominate form of transit payments. Later in London, the introduction and adoption of contactless exploded to such a degree that cash became nearly obsolete. For example, in 2014, only 0.7% of all bus journeys in London were paid for with cash. As a result, Transport for London (TfL) - one of Cubic's largest customers and a long-time partner - made the decision to make all bus travel cashless. Since then, Londoners make hundreds of millions of contactless journeys on the TfL network each year. 2019 is predicted to be the first year when that number surpasses a billion.

While early contactless smartcard systems relied on "closed-loop" payments: proprietary payment structures valid only within one system, hence "closed", modern tap and go "open-loop" systems take advantage of payment technology used in the retail industry. Open payment uses EMV, an open-standard set of specifications developed to create interoperability for credit and debit payment cards and devices. It allows pay-as-you-go travelers to use any contactless credit or debit payment card (such as Mastercard, Visa and American Express) to pay for transportation services, seamlessly integrating transportation into the mix of other goods and services that consumers are used to paying for directly with their cards or devices.

Open payment comes with many benefits to the end user: it offers travelers the same functionality as a transit card while bringing a whole new level of convenience. Travelers can use contactless credit or debit cards to tap and go and take advantage of any fare-capping or products that would have been otherwise available to transit card users, without having to worry about carrying a designated transit card, checking its balance or remembering to regularly top it up, as fares are charged directly to user's bank accounts. In addition, fare calculations happen automatically in the background, meaning travelers no longer have to shop around for the best available fare. For transit agencies who don't want to issue their own fare cards, moving to open payment reduces the need to procure, encode, distribute, and support literally millions of magnetic tickets or contactless smartcards, nor do they have to service the retail infrastructure required to sell and top-up those tickets. Transactions made through EMV cards are equally as quick as closed-loop smartcards - an important factor for transit agencies that need to maintain a high level of passenger throughput at stations and turnstiles.

As early adopters of EMV, many agencies in Europe, Canada and Australia were able to quickly transition legacy systems to open-loop contactless and I'm proud to say that Cubic has been at the forefront of this revolution since its very beginning. We became the first technology company in the world to bring open payment to the public transit system to scale, through that partnership with TfL. The contactless bankcard system, which first launched on London buses in 2012, and extended two years later to cover London's entire transit network, including underground, rail, bus and tram services, drove the consumer and retail adoption of contactless across the U.K. and Europe. In 2017, Cubic and Transport for New South Wales launched Australia's first open payment trial on the popular Manly Ferry Service and a year later, Cubic worked with TransLink to launch the very first open payments system to a public transit system in Canada.

By comparison, in the United States, the adoption of contactless was much slower and fraught by difficulties resulting from the lack of alignment between credit-card companies, technology companies and merchants. Despite this in 2013 Cubic and the Chicago Transit Authority launched Ventra this US's first major system capable of accepting open payment cards. EMV cards started gaining some traction in 2015, around the time of the so-called "EMV liability shift". While analysts estimate that in 2018, only 5% of point-of-sale transactions in the US were contactless-enabled, thankfully, things are starting to change here too. As I'm writing this, Cubic is working with some of the largest transit agencies in the US to bring open payment technology to travelers in numerous cities, including New York, Miami, , and of course, Chicago, and this is creating the incentive for banks to issue contactless cards in the US. Once again Cubic and our transit agency partners are changing the face of the payments industry, not only in transit but, just like in Europe, also in retail.

Yet, open payment is important not merely because it's a modern innovation but because it's one of the foundational elements of Mobility as a Service (MaaS), which Cubic defines as a "combination of public and private transportation services within a given regional environment that provides holistic, optimal and people-centered travel options, to enable end-to-end journeys paid for by the user as a single charge, and which aims to achieve key public policy objectives". This vision of future transportation starts with three key pillars: a true multi-modal journey planning platform that unbiasedly exposes all travel choices, a regional, centralized congestion management platform that provides a holistic view of all travel in the region and perhaps most importantly, a single account for the management and administration of travel fares and payments, which can be realized only through account-based transportation systems that accept open payment.

To truly fulfill the promise of MaaS, the centralized congestion management platform needs to encompass all forms of transportation, including road travel. By encouraging greater integration between public transit and private vehicles, cities will be able to make meaningful connections between millions of single occupancy cars traveling together, at similar times of day, between similar origins and destinations, and encourage drivers to consider alternative modes of travel that encourage a greater degree of sharing. This will not only help cities more effectively manage, control and forecast travel but it will also open up a wide array of travel choices to the public, allowing travelers to find one that most suits their needs - be it biking, carpooling, ride-sharing, using a "Park and Ride", a bus or any combination thereof. Full integration of road travel into the multimodal mix will enable greater integration of data, giving birth to a collaborative, centralized, multi-modal journey planning platform, which will prevent travelers from making decisions in a silo and empower them to consider and make travel choices that take into consideration factors such as convenience, cost, time of travel, walking distance, seat and parking availability, environmental impact etc.

This information will be accessible in real time, enabling transportation agencies and operators to directly influence travelers' behavior and optimize resource use, not only promoting more socially and environmentally friendly forms of transportation (e.g., trains over cars) but also providing incentives to riders to alter their regular journey plan to keep the flow of people through the network undisrupted. Dynamic or variable congestion pricing for road use will become possible, as will other incentives for shifting usage to specific transportation modes. Underpinned by a modern payment system with a single account, these platforms will enable true end-to-end journey management and ensure that whenever, wherever and however we travel, our fare is automatically calculated and paid for from a single account linked to our credit or debit card – all as part of a single trip.

While the adoption of open payments will be fundamental to make this vision a reality, the potential that MaaS offers goes beyond simply changing how we move people, data, goods, services and funds. MaaS will transform how people interact in their communities, and maximize the role of the government in maintaining the public good and optimizing the efficiency of how we move. Open-loop payments are not only making our transit experience seamless and frictionless, it will be the key to unlocking a future where all our travel options will be available to us at the push of a button.

*www.cubic.com/solutions/transportation*

# Chapter 31

# The Future of Electric Buses

## Ryan Popple

### Chief Executive Officer
### Proterra

*Ryan Popple is one of those guys that impresses you upon your first meeting. As former officer in the US Army he brings the bearing of a leader. One upon a time he helped Elon Musk as Senior Director of Finance for Tesla Motors and now has a passion to make North America a clean energy beacon for the world.*

*I had the opportunity to interview him for our podcast Transit Unplugged and found him engaging, knowledgeable and passionate about the importance of electric buses for our industry. Hear his vision for what's next in this important part of the public transportation mosaic.*

# REVOLUTIONIZING TRANSPORTATION

A major shift is underway across North America. It is the complete transformation of transit. Communities are growing and evolving, and with that, our transportation needs are changing. Now more than ever, we need safer, more reliable and cleaner options.

Thanks to smart, connected, clean, efficient vehicles utilizing new technologies fueled by clean energy, advanced design and intelligent planning, we are seeing the future of transportation being deployed today.

More than a decade ago, Proterra set out to build a bus for the future of public transit, a vehicle free from the constraints of legacy fossil-fuel bus design. Recognizing that the right bus for a post-fossil fuel world wouldn't be a repurposed diesel bus, we started with a clean sheet of paper and an FTA innovation grant, and designed a bus that was optimized for performance as an electric vehicle. This vision required continued innovation, with the development of a lightweight, durable composite body, the industry's most advanced battery design, a drivetrain far more powerful than a diesel engine, and the vehicle control systems to make it all work seamlessly.

Public transit is vital to urban transit and is going to remain the backbone of how people get around in the city. We believe in making the transit bus better because, more than any other form of transportation, battery-electric buses are the cornerstone in addressing the future of mobility and sustainability for cities. Whether its addressing congestion, sustainability, or equity – investment in public transportation and zero-emission buses is a must for modern cities and communities.

Electric technology should be part of the strategy of every transit agency. Moving to electric buses has substantial environmental and public health benefits. Further, electric buses reduce greenhouse gas and diesel particulate matter without sacrificing vehicle performance or uptime.

The momentum of electric bus adoption has continued to grow around the world. Bloomberg says that there are over 400,000 electric buses on the road today globally and that number is expected to rise in the 2020s. In the next ten years, we will see about 50 percent of all buses utilize electric vehicle technology, according to their Electric Vehicle Outlook 2019.[20]

**Benefits**:

There are several reasons why transit operators are moving quickly to adopt and deploy electric vehicle technology. Unlike many other clean energy or clean technology categories, one of the primary reasons for this transition is the economics of a battery-electric bus fleet. Today when you look at the full ownership lifecycle, it is more cost effective to operate an electric bus compared to conventional technologies. Electric buses have low operational lifecycle costs primarily because, with significantly fewer parts, no liquid fuel and no oil changes needed, electric buses require less maintenance. Superior fuel efficiency also plays a

---

[20] https://about.bnef.com/electric-vehicle-outlook/

significant role in reducing the vehicle operating costs. The Proterra Catalyst® vehicle delivers fuel economies of up to 25 MPGe, compared to conventional diesel buses that typically only get about 3.6 MPG.

A recent report by the U.S. PIRG Education Fund notes that while the purchase price of an electric transit bus is more than that of a standard diesel bus, the lifetime fuel and maintenance savings of an electric bus can amount to around $400,000, well over the up-front price differential.[21]

Further, the performance of an electric bus is far superior to a typical diesel or CNG bus. Proterra's electric bus delivers nearly twice the horsepower of a standard diesel bus, and accelerates 1.5 times faster. Fleet managers are focused on providing excellent daily service to their riders, and electric buses provide them with the best technology and impressive performance features. In 2017, the Proterra 40-foot Catalyst E2 max bus broke the world record in test track conditions for the longest distance ever traveled by an electric vehicle on a single charge – a whopping 1,101 miles. Who would have thought that an electric bus would drive circles around any personal EV on the road?

Additionally, the health and environmental benefits from electric buses are outstanding. With zero tailpipe emissions or pollutants, a Proterra Catalyst vehicle eliminates curbside smoke and 230,000 pounds of $CO_2$ annually for every diesel vehicle replaced. Further, battery-electric buses produce less greenhouse gas emissions, even when taking into

---

[21] https://uspirg.org/reports/usp/paying-electric-buses

consideration the electricity generated to operate and charge the buses, according to a study by the Union of Concerned Scientists[22]. The study examined the source of electricity in all parts of the country and combined this with the lifecycle fuel efficiency and emissions of an electric bus. It found that electric buses are 2.5 times cleaner on average in terms of lifecycle emissions, vs. typical diesel buses.

Finally, we have an unprecedented opportunity to solve some of the greatest challenges facing us today while creating and preserving good-paying, quality manufacturing jobs within the United States. Electric vehicle technology is creating the manufacturing and engineering jobs of today and tomorrow, such as electricians, advanced manufacturing factory workers, EV service and maintenance workers, and battery technicians. Proterra is proud to help the United States be a global leader in electric vehicles and bring the next wave of transit innovation directly to communities across North America.

**Meeting Today's Challenges**

The big challenge today is helping transit agencies scale from pilot programs to full fleet electrification. We see two big hurdles: designing future-proof infrastructure and upfront costs. We have worked really hard to identify the hurdles and create solutions for transit agencies of any size to overcome them.

---

[22] https://www.ucsusa.org/about/news/study-finds-electric-buses-are-cleaner-all-parts-country

Beginning with a high-fidelity route simulation, fleet modeling and a detailed total cost of ownership analysis, Proterra helps agencies choose the right vehicle battery and charging configurations to meet their route requirements now and as they scale their electric vehicle fleet for the future.

In order to provide the best cost analysis and charging infrastructure planning for our customers, we have to start with data. We use data from our current vehicle fleets on the road, combined with sophisticated fleet modeling tools and high-fidelity route simulations to learn not only how electric vehicles will perform during their daily block schedules and how to optimally scale an EV fleet, but also what charging infrastructure is needed, where it should be placed and when to charge.

When we engage with a customer and share this information, often times they turn to us and ask if we could design and implement their charging infrastructure. To meet this request, we recently launched our Proterra Energy™ fleet solutions that enable turnkey delivery of a complete energy ecosystem for heavy-duty electric fleets, including design, build, financing, operations, maintenance and energy optimization, and ultimately help our customers build out the energy ecosystem needed to power a fleet of vehicles.

In addition to infrastructure, the upfront cost of an electric bus remains a barrier for many transit agencies looking to implement zero-emission vehicles into their fleet. To address this challenge, Proterra offers a battery leasing program which lowers the upfront cost of a Proterra electric bus to be roughly the same as a standard diesel or natural gas-powered bus.

Customers can utilize operating funds previously earmarked for fuel to pay for the battery lease.

Battery leasing enables a faster transition to electric buses for public transit agencies, universities, airports and other commercial fleets. By decoupling the batteries from the sale of its buses, Proterra enables fleet operators to purchase the electric bus for a similar price as a standard fossil-fueled bus and lease the batteries over the 12-year lifetime of the bus. Because electric buses typically cost less to maintain and fuel, this savings in operating expenses can be applied toward the battery lease.

**What's Next**

There are a couple of big trends that are going to continue to ripple through the industry and create lasting change. First, battery technology is going to improve. We will continue to see a decrease in the cost of batteries and an increase in energy density. A recent report "Electric Buses in Cities", which was commissioned by the C40 Cities Climate Leadership Group, [23] predicts that costs should fall sufficiently for electric buses to reach unsubsidized upfront cost parity with diesel buses in this next decade of the 2020s. By that time, the battery costs will have fallen to only 8% of the total electric bus price, down from around 26% of the total price in 2016.

There will also be more energy density improvements for batteries. Soon, nearly every route in North America will be able to be serviced by an electric bus with just one overnight charge. High speed and wireless

---

[23] https://www.c40.org/networks/zero-emission-vehicles

charging of buses will also continue to advance along with vehicle automation features to improve safety.

More cities and states will commit to reducing greenhouse gas emissions and pollution in their communities. Today, many major cities across North America have already made pledges to go 100% electric with their fleets. For example, Los Angeles has doubled down on its commitments to full fleet electrification by 2030. New York City's MTA has committed to all electric buses by 2040, as has the state of California for all of its bus fleets. Elected and appointed officials are driving this trend, as they push for improved community health and a reduction of their carbon footprint.

We started with a clear vision: to deliver clean, quiet transportation to all communities. Today, that vision is being realized. Battery-electric buses are no longer a concept – they are being deployed all around the world. In North America, we are proud to serve more than 120 customers in almost every state across the U.S. as well as several Canadian provinces, including transit agencies, universities, airports and national parks.

*You can contact Ryan Popple through his company website www.proterra.com.*

# Chapter 32
# The Future of Public Transportation

**Thomas A. Egan**
Chief Executive Officer
MV Transportation, Inc.

*MV Transportation is the largest privately held passenger transportation services contractor in North America, employing more than 20,000 dedicated transit professionals in 153 locations. It's also somewhat of a home for me as I spent five years working directly for MV and many other years working with folks on their senior leadership team at other companies and as a consultant. Tom Egan is MV's Chief Executive Officer. Prior to being named CEO in April 2019, Tom served as MV's President and Chief Operating Officer where he was responsible for overseeing MV's customer relationships and service delivery. In this role he led a significant transformation of operations including overseeing a regional restructure of the organization, strengthening division leadership, implementing companywide best practices, and leveraging advanced technology and analytics – collectively resulting in increased operational efficiency and improved customer satisfaction. Tom has an extensive background and track record for success in leading large and complex global operations at companies including Electronic Data Systems, Hewlett-Packard, and DXC Technology.*

When I think about how much transit systems of the past century have evolved, I know that communities have as well – and not always in the same direction. Rising real estate costs, suburban outgrowth, and business migration from city centers have led to congested roadways and underused transit routes – while unmet transportation needs still exist. Moreover, these changes, along with our aging population, mandate new transportation options for those who are elderly and those who have disabilities beyond the ADA-required ¾ mile corridor.

The transportation industry is on the precipice of change, and I am proud to lead an organization that committed to remaining an agent of change.

Today we are seeing the influence of green initiatives, on-demand technologies, employee benefits, and a growing culture of personalization on passengers' expectations of transit. Meanwhile, constrained budgets, regulatory requirements, record unemployment, and rising costs of running service all affect how agencies deliver transit. As the pace of technology change continues to accelerate with the faster and cheaper computing power available to transit agencies and an always-connected passenger population, we are ready to face this challenge.

Together, we must and can reshape the role of transit, and contracted service providers like MV must find ways to deliver higher value on behalf of customers and their passengers. Our team is making great strides in transforming our role in the industry to unite our operational expertise and scale with the right technologies and strategic partnerships to deliver unique transit service model designs as a systems integrator.

This positioning will enable transit systems to create data-driven environments in which we can build small, disadvantaged businesses while leveraging existing mobility modes to deliver scalable, flexible systems that fit within our customers' budgets and our riders' specific mobility needs.

Big data will become the force multiplier in the future to further improve safety, efficiency, and the overall passenger experience. Replacing unmet needs surveys, analysis of populations, ridership patterns, and route transfers will drive reimagined transit networks, help provision optimally sized vehicles and environmentally sustainable fleets, and provide a personalized approach to meeting the needs and preferences of each rider.

Machine learning will eliminate the need for pilot programs, number-crunching, and route testing. When coupled with environmental factors such as route length, elevation, and weather, this technology can develop predictive models that tell us what vehicle is best suited for a route and will supplement OEM maintenance recommendations to further mitigate costs. Beyond the bus, we will leverage this same technology to develop predictive accident models that consider both human and environmental factors.

Ideally, the level of information sharing and open systems will expand, enabling a seamless experience across public-private networks accessible to all.

I am excited for a future where transportation contractors are no longer just managing operations on behalf of their customers but instead collaborating to develop transit networks that mobilize communities in a new and meaningful way.

Tom Egan is the CEO of MV Transportation, a company founded on meeting unmet transit needs. Twenty years before our government passed the Americans with Disabilities Act, MV's owners were transporting people with disabilities using two vans in San Francisco. MV often states that it is "in their DNA to do their part to mobilize communities and improve the lives of their riders."

*www.mvtransit.com*

# Chapter 33

# The Role of TNCs

## Bridgette Beato
Chief Executive Officer
Lumenor Consulting Group

*I consider Bridgette Beato a good friend. She heads up an important consulting firm and was just on the cover of American DBE Magazine! She also is active as a Board Member for Women's Transportation Seminar (WTS) International and helps transit agencies integrate new technology and techniques to stay on the cutting edge.*

*She writes an insightful chapter here on the role that Transportation Networking Companies (TNCs) are playing and will play in our mobility mosaic.*

As the founder of a management consulting firm that helps public transit agencies optimize their systems and services, and a Board member of WTS International, I participate in dozens of customer meetings, trade shows and industry events each year. Most of these events take place in cities like Los Angeles, New York and Chicago, where you'd expect robust, well-thought-out public transit systems capable of seamlessly handling a wide range of use cases.

And while that's usually true, getting from the airport to downtown in Any City USA still typically means hopping on a shuttle or a bus to a rail station and catching the subway. And then probably transferring mid-route somewhere. And possibly getting on a bus to finish the journey.

Most of the time it's very economical and in some ways a fairly seamless trip. But to execute it correctly, you will first have to buy the local system's fare products. Then you'll have to load the right fare amount on it for the route you want to take. Then you've got to figure out where your transfers are and be prepared to wait for your connections.

Or you could just tap your phone and take an Uber. That's what I end up doing a lot of the time. And based on the conversations I have with my peers at these events, I'm far from the only one. In fact, it's a grim standing joke at this point: We're industry professionals who believe in the value and utility of public transit. But when our schedules are tight and we want one less thing to think about, we opt for the convenience that transportation network companies (TNCs) like Uber and Lyft provide.

So what does that say about the future of public transit?

According to American Public Transit Association statistics, public transit ridership numbers across the U.S. have been declining since 2015. Researchers cite a number of reasons why – including both the rising popularity of TNCs and, perhaps more surprisingly, increasing private car ownership.

In fact, TransitCenter, a non-profit organization that advocates for better public transit options, cites "greater to access to private cars" as the primary cause of the recent decline in public transit usage in its 2019 report, "Who's on Board." A 2018 report from UCLA's Institute of Transportation Studies found that public transit ridership decline in Southern California was best explained by the dramatic growth in vehicle access "among subsets of the population that are among the heaviest users of transit."

Simply put, people for whom public transportation was once the only option now have more options. Time is money and convenience over cost is a major factor.

In the public transit industry, we often make the distinction between "captive" riders – i.e., people who can't afford car ownership or other private transportation options – and "choice" riders – i.e., people whose higher incomes give them more transportation alternatives from which to choose.

Amidst the overall decline in ridership numbers, many public transit industry professionals believe that focusing on the captive riders represents the best path forward: By primarily positioning public transit as a safety net service for a demographic that would otherwise go unserved, public transit retains its utility.

Others contend that aggressively targeting affluent choice riders with upscale amenities like on-board Wi-Fi or retro-chic streetcar lines is the way to go.

What both perspectives overlook to varying degrees is that proliferating transportation options -- in the form of more affordable car ownership, TNCs, micro-mobility solutions like electric scooters and skateboards, and more – mean that everyone is evolving into a choice rider. And that "choice rider" shouldn't be synonymous with affluent urbanites looking for Instagram-worthy transportation to the latest downtown hotspot. Instead, it should mean anyone looking for the best option among many to serve their specific transportation needs.

In 2005, I was recruited by the Executive Sponsor/CIO to serve as the lead the Program Management Consultant on the Metropolitan Atlanta Rapid Transit Authority's (MARTA) $200 million overhaul of its fare collection system. That was my introduction to the public transportation industry, and my experience helping MARTA replace its magnetic ticketing and token-based system with North America's first 100 percent smart card system showed me how crucial ambitious technological innovation would be toward keeping public transit relevant and sustainable in the 21st century.

Fifteen years later, that's truer now than it was then – especially given how TNCs like Uber and Lyft, and on-demand service platforms in general, have changed how much responsiveness and personalization users expect during any transaction these days.

With Uber and Lyft, you decide when and where a trip starts, and where it ends. Tap your phone, and you immediately see what the trip will cost. You're told how many minutes it will take for a car to arrive, and how long your trip is projected to take. Payments happen automatically, with integrated, easy-to-sort receipts.

All told, TCNs are extremely responsive, user-driven systems. In contrast, public transit systems are operator-driven. Service commences in places the system operator chooses, on schedules the system operator sets.

Much of that won't ever change. Public transit's massive investments in physical infrastructure and equipment literally entrench certain business models and approaches. But that's precisely why public transit systems should aggressively pursue opportunities where they can make their systems more responsive

to users, instead of the other way around. If a system is not reliable and convenient, a potential rider will look for other options and it will be very difficult to get them back.

That's why adopting TNC-like apps and mobile ticketing and payment options sooner rather than later is key for keeping public transit viable in the face of growing transportation choices. These technologies create new possibilities that TNCs have already begun to pursue, like a single, seamless payment interfaces that enable multi-modal trips that incorporate ride-sharing, buses, bikes, and a cup of coffee. Or offering discounts and other loyalty incentives that increase customer usage.

Instead of competing against TNCs, I believe the most forward-looking public transit agencies will look for opportunities to collaborate with them. That's because companies like Uber and Lyft are already operating in hundreds of cities. So every dollar they invest in software development scales better than dollars that metropolitan or even regional public transit agencies invest toward the same ends. Every customer they sign up in one city becomes a potential customer in every city.

At the same time, it makes sense for TNCs to collaborate with public transit too, because of how public transit complements the services they offer. Thus, in partnership with the Denver Regional Transportation District, Uber now presents light rail or buses as an option alongside UberX and UberPool to Denver users – and if you pick public transit, you can purchase your tickets through the app. In Santa Monica, where Lyft now offers electric scooter rentals along with ridesharing, it has integrated a "Nearby Transit" feature into its app that shows route information and schedules for the city's bus and light rail options.

As these kinds of approaches become more widespread, with users mixing on-demand micro-mobility options with light rail, buses, and vans, not all of which are necessarily operated by the same company or agency, the ability to keep payments simple on the user side while simultaneously enabling revenue-sharing and the clearance of funds on the back end will become increasingly important.

And no doubt some public transit agencies, wary of sharing user data or losing the customer relationship altogether, will try to integrate TNCs into their own apps, rather than the other way around. But companies like Uber and Lyft are first and foremost technology companies. They've pioneered the app-based customer experiences that users have come to expect, and they have the expertise to maintain their dominant positions in software development for the foreseeable future.

At a time when customers empowered by choice have rising standards about both the quality and breadth of services it takes to win their business, I believe that all players in this domain should focus on their own core assets – and outsource or collaborating on everything else.

For public transit agencies, this means focusing on trains, buses, and tracks – and making sure that these assets are performing optimally. Even here, technology will play the defining role, as more agencies begin to implement Intelligent Transportation Systems (ITS) that instrumentize their assets in order to collect and analyze enormous quantities of data that can lead to new operational efficiencies while preserving the value of their equipment over time.

A well-designed ITS helps public transit agencies comply with federal regulations that arise out of the Moving Ahead for Progress in the 21st Century Act, or MAP-21, including provisions that require agencies to submit a "Transit Asset Management Plan" (TAMP) and to keep their assets in a "State of Good Repair" (SGR). A fully integrated system should be able to track and monitor the health of an agency's assets, manage work orders and the supply chain, and interface with financial and reporting systems to provide visibility into every aspect of their operations. This, in turn, can enable agencies to reduce their overall spend and prioritize maintenance instead of deferring it.

With new insights into which routes are seeing the highest levels of usage, and which equipment needs servicing, agencies can prevent breakdowns that cause delays or worse. A data-driven approach can also help agencies optimize their schedules by better understanding ridership patterns. Similarly, implementing Transit Signal Priority systems, which leverage Department of Transportation protocols to allow properly equipped buses to make red lights turn faster or hold green lights longer, can help transit operators keep to their schedules.

In the end, public transit can and should remain at the heart of the multi-modal transportation ecosystems that are starting to take shape in cities around the world. Its ability to move large numbers of people quickly, in spatially efficient fashion, is key to making increasingly congested cities more livable and environmentally sustainable. But the competition for riders will also continue to increase, as will rider expectations regarding ease of use, reliability, and efficiency.

To successfully adapt to these changing conditions, public transit agencies should move forward with a strategically collaborative mindset. Instead of trying to re-invent the wheel, they should seek out partnerships with software developers, system integrators, and other IT professionals who can help them deliver best-of-class experiences that it will take to succeed in an environment where every rider is a choice rider. Indeed, in the multi-modal transportation future, it's all about sharing the ride.

*You can contact Bridgette Beato through her company website www.LumenorConsulting.com*

# Chapter 34

# Strategic Partnerships

## The Future of Public Transportation

**James Chalmers**
Group President and CEO of
TACK10 Strategy, Inc.

*James Chalmers is a dynamic leader and strategist described as a growth and innovation agent. With and for the companies he has led, he has harnessed the power of strategic partnerships to produce incredible growth for those companies, which has in each case been sustained beyond his tenure. Now, through TACK10 Strategy, his focus is on educating and helping organizations leverage the Nine Core Value Drivers of Strategic Partnership™.*

Public transportation is under increasingly greater pressure to do more with less and to be all things to everyone. Public transportation is an ever-evolving service which caters to consumers whose behaviour is changing more rapidly than at any other point in history. Transit agencies are under funded and operate in a public ecosystem that is constraint oriented. For-profit businesses such as Uber, Lime,

Car2Go, Google and countless others have emerged to solve gaps in the system, and they are all vying for a stake and segment of the market. They operate in a private ecosystem which in the advent of venture funding is seemingly void of constraints. Both transit agencies and for-profit companies are looking to own the increasingly important channel of communication, data and relationship with the customer.

A comprehensive transportation ecosystem cannot be delivered by for-profit companies or public organizations alone. In order to grow ridership, loyalty and reliance on public transportation, there are three key challenges that need to be resolved:

1. First and Final Mile Service
2. Customer-Centric Experience
3. Sustainable Funding Models

The future of transportation and solving for these key challenges will be accomplished through identification, development, management and measurement of Strategic Partnerships. Leveraging the Nine Core Value Drivers of Strategic Partnership™ offers transit agencies and their private sector counterparts the ability to achieve their respective business objectives. Transit agencies need to lead the way in developing comprehensive transit ecosystems and it's clear that they will need to leverage Strategic Partnerships to get there.

Where It Begins

For Strategic Partnerships to deliver transformative impact for an organization, it is important to recognize that there is no one size fits all approach. This means understanding the value that your organization can deliver to a Strategic Partner, the types of organizations who will be able to extract the full value from what you can offer, the value that you expect to extract from a Strategic Partnership and the types of partners who will be able to deliver your organization with this expected value.

A valuable part of this process begins with understanding what business an organization is in and why the organization exists. This type of clarity provides the insight into the value proposition that an organization can provide to potential Strategic Partners. The business an organization is in is not always as clear as one might think. For instance, a transit agency is a resource management company in the human connection industry. It exists to connect people with places. Knowing what business an organization is in and why it exists is the cornerstone of a brand strategy, which creates the frame of reference through which every organizational decision should be made. A well articulated brand strategy ultimately drives an organization's mission, vision, values and every decision the organization makes. For organizations with a growth mindset as well as for those who are constrained by existing resources, Strategic Partnerships can be leveraged to deliver on a broad set of organizational objectives. For these models to be successful, it is imperative that an organization's leadership is prepared to challenge traditional business models and if the Nine Core Value Drivers of Strategic Partnership™ are to deliver on their full potential, the Strategic Partnerships sought must authentically align to and support the organization's brand strategy.

## The Nine Core Value Drivers of Strategic Partnership™

Strategic Partnerships go beyond advertising, sponsorship and traditional Public – Private Partnerships (P3s). A Strategic Partnership is an agreement between two or more organizations to create shared benefit of equal or similar value while equally sharing in the associated risks. This is done within a defined framework which is actively managed and measured to deliver against a minimum of three Core Value Drivers. The purpose of entering into these agreements is that alone, an organization's potential is limited by its internal constraints. Leveraging the Core Value Drivers of Strategic Partnerships, organizations dramatically reduce or eliminate these constraints.

The Nine Core Value Drivers of Strategic Partnership™ are:

- Cost Abatement
- Non-Traditional Revenue
- Advertising / Sponsorship Rev
- Audience Access
- Authority / Credibility / Trust
- Communication / Narrative
- Audience Experience
- Shared Expertise
- Competitive Advantage

'Above the line' Core Value Drivers deliver direct financial benefit for an organization which supplements primary operating revenue. 'Below the line' Core Value Drivers strengthen an organization's primary operating activities, creating incremental net revenue growth.

## Cost Abatement

The offsetting of budgeted line items, future expenses or investment, either in-part or in whole. Cost abatement is often accomplished by a partner creating efficiencies or as a result of a partner taking on that cost center. Most often, a partner takes on a cost center to open new business opportunities for their organization.

## Non-Traditional Revenue

Revenue generated through non-core operating activities, often through the introduction of a new product or service to an existing audience. While outside of the core business, value is created for the audience in the short term and the activity can be leveraged to grow core operating revenues over the long term.

## Advertising / Sponsorship Revenue

Advertising revenue is earned from displaying an organization's brand or message in a partner's communication channels and / or physical space. Sponsorship is the cash or in-kind rights fees paid to a partner in return for access to the exploitable commercial potential associated with the affiliation. It leverages the tangible and intangible assets of a property to create brand association.

## Audience Access

The ability to engage with new audience segments and/or grow existing audience segments. To ensure the most is made of the access opportunity, it is important to carefully tailor the message to align with the audience's expectations.

## Audience Experience

Consumers demand an experience economy. Key to creating and fostering loyalty from a customer base is delivering audience experiences that are relevant, add value and support the brand.

## Authority / Credibility / Trust
An affiliation between organizations creates an endorsement. It can be leveraged towards earning the perception of authority, the development of credibility and earned trust from an audience.

## Shared Expertise
All organizations have areas of specific expertise. The ability to leverage another organization's strengths to augment or strengthen areas that are weak or lacking. Most often this is a capacity building activity.

## Communication / Narrative
The ability to have a third party communicate a message that an organization does not have the permission to deliver on its own. Often this messaging is centered around audience sentiment.

## Competitive Advantage
The ability to creatively differentiate an organization from its competitors or those who provide similar products or services. This is a fundamental Core Value Driver that must be a part of every Strategic Partnership.

There are great examples of Strategic Partnership occurring around the world. Decades of experience, research, testing and measurement revealed that framework, process, creativity and innovation was missing to ensure ecosystems of Strategic Partnership could be developed and replicated. TACK10 Strategy developed and introduced proprietary framework and process through which organizations can formalize the value they look to extract and the value they can contribute to Strategic Partnerships. This allows organizations to identify, negotiate, manage and measure Strategic Partnerships.

## The Nine Core Value Drivers of Strategic Partnership™ At Work

Together, transit agencies and for-profit companies are bridging the gap around the three core challenges that stand in the way of a sustainable and comprehensive transportation ecosystem. The following case studies highlight a few best in class Strategic Partnerships that are delivering measurable value for all stakeholders within the transit ecosystem. Consistently across all examples, organizational leadership has demonstrated the perspective and willingness to challenge traditional business models and the Strategic Partnerships developed have supported the brand strategy in solving for the key business objectives. The primary case study which showcases shared value creation and shared risk comes from Metrolinx, an agency of the Government of Ontario, Canada. This has been done in order to highlight that a single agency can and should be leveraging all Nine Core Value Drivers of Strategic Partnership™.

## First and Final Mile Service

First and final mile service is a critical component in the future of public transportation. The ability to access transit service from point of origination through to final destination quickly and conveniently is an important consideration for travellers when selecting modes of transportation. As the number of options available for travellers increases, transit agencies are looking to

312

services that might otherwise be competitive to solve for first and final mile service through Strategic Partnerships.

One such example in Toronto, Canada is between UP Express, the dedicated air-rail link and Uber, the rideshare service. For UP Express, its value proposition for riders is a guaranteed 25-minute connection between the country's two busiest transportation hubs, downtown Toronto's Union Station and Toronto Pearson International Airport. With a strong value proposition around guaranteed travel time on a route that can take 1.5 hours+ to drive, the UP Express team recognized that the traveller's origin/destination is unlikely to be Union Station.

The challenge in solving for first and final mile service from Union Station is the congestion around the station, which sees 200,000 people pass through daily. By collaborating with Uber in the development of a Strategic Partnership, UP Express was able to create a dedicated pick-up/drop-off point at Union Station in close proximity to the UP Express platform. Uber is able to direct UP Express passengers to the designated pick-up/drop-off point through in-app wayfinding and additionally promotes the seamless two system service to travellers arriving at Toronto Pearson through in-app promotional messaging.

This First and Final Mile Strategic Partnership delivers on seven of the Nine Core Value Drivers of Strategic Partnership™.

- Cost Abatement
- Non-Traditional Revenue
- Advertising / Sponsorship Revenue

- Audience Access · Authority / Credibility / Trust · Communication / Narrative
- Audience Experience · Shared Expertise
- Competitive Advantage

Other examples of Strategic Partnerships focused on First and Final Mile Service include:

- Metro Transit and Hourcar in the Twin Cities, Minneapolis-Saint Paul, Minnesota which allows members of the car-sharing organization to use their Go-To transit cards to access Hourcar vehicles anywhere in its metro area network, making it possible to move seamlessly between transit and car-share modes of transportation. While integrated payment was not a component of the partnership initially, the possibility of paying for car-share service through Go-To cards opens the possibility for value to be created through **Cost Abatement** resulting from a volume discount on transaction fees.

- Uber has also partnered with the Town of Innisfil in Ontario, Canada to create Innisfil Transit. This service offers flat fare rides to popular civic destinations and major transit hubs and discounts for trips within city limits that range between $4 to $6. This partnership was developed because it offered the Town of Innisfil a **Cost Abatement** opportunity given that the subsidy for these rides was less costly than then establishment of an expanded public transit system with less coverage and no first and final mile service.

Ride sharing, Car sharing, Bike sharing, E-scooters - these are all forms of mobility and transportation. Businesses in these spaces are forming Strategic

314

Partnerships with transit agencies to solve for the first and final mile of the transit journey. Beyond these related services, there are opportunities to assess the specific needs of the first and final mile for each transit agency to create Strategic Partnerships in new categories that solve the respective needs of the agency and its customers.

## Customer-Centric Experience

Transit is not an isolated experience – transit experiences occur within a myriad of needs that people have in their daily lives. Eating meals, completing schoolwork, making work calls, doing household errands; it is a complex and layered ecosystem. The more that transit agencies can leverage Strategic Partnerships to create customer-centric experiences that help to directly alleviate pain points within the transit experience while meeting the ancillary needs of the consumer, the greater the likelihood that they will grow ridership and foster loyalty within the current customer base.

Metrolinx looked to its customer research to determine the needs of its current and prospective riders when building out programming and partnership concepts which would deliver on the daily needs of commuters. In reviewing the research, it was recognized that consumers who represented existing or potential GO Transit users desired additional product and service offerings which would add value to their transit experience. For example, commuters feel time starved and therefore anything GO Transit could offer which would give them time back in their day would be seen as beneficial and enhance the transit value proposition.

From the following insight a powerful program and Strategic Partnership was born; the last thing that commuters want to do after getting off a train at 7:30pm is go to the grocery store! Metrolinx partnered with Loblaws Companies Limited, the largest grocery chain in Canada, to launch the grocer's Click and Collect service at select GO Stations. Recognizing that traditional retailers are evolving their business models in light of increasing competition from online retailers and changing expectations of consumers, this Strategic Partnership provided a distinct competitive advantage to Loblaws by bringing groceries to customers, instead of expecting customers to come to their grocery stores.

This Customer-Centric Experience Strategic Partnership delivers on all nine of the Core Value Drivers of Strategic Partnership™.

- Cost Abatement   • Non-Traditional Revenue
- Advertising / Sponsorship Rev
- Audience Access   • Authority / Credibility / Trust • Communication / Narrative
- Audience Experience   • Shared Expertise
- Competitive Advantage

Other examples of Strategic Partnerships focused on Customer-Centric Experiences include:
- Tokyo Metro System's partnerships with private businesses to reduce ridership during peak periods when ridership is at 199 percent of capacity. About 1,000 businesses have partnered with the Tokyo Metropolitan Government on a pilot project by allowing employees to work from home or work different hours in order to reduce strain on the system during peak periods. Beyond this,

there is an innovative pilot partnership with food service providers to support behaviour change – transit riders have been offered free food items if they travel before peak transit hours. This is a brilliant example of a Strategic Partnership centered on **Audience Experience** driving behaviour change.

* Strategic Partnerships which deliver wi-fi in transit vehicles, reflect changing consumer behaviours and needs. A recent example is the partnership between Panasonic and Liverpool's Merseyrail system which will equip 52 four-car electric trains with wi-fi, enabling free connectivity for consumers along with seamless CCTV and voice links between the trains and control center. This type of **Competitive Advantage** will encourage consumers to select public transit over other forms of transportation.

The needs of each transit agency, its current and prospective consumer base are unique. Accordingly, the Strategic Partnerships that deliver Customer-Centric Experience need to reflect the needs of the audience. Consumer and ridership research is an ideal place to start when assessing the types of initiatives and by extension the Strategic Partnerships which are relevant and which will be successful.

Sustainable Funding Models
Perhaps most important of all, transit agencies must find ways to sustainably fund both operations and capital expenditures. Outside of the fare box and beyond Government investment in transit systems, Strategic Partnerships have the ability to generate new and non-traditional revenues as well as to offset costs.

317

Cost abatement through reduction in transaction fees was referenced earlier around the future of the Metro Transit and Hourcar Strategic Partnership. A primary example of this model in practice is again provided by Metrolinx, whose partnership with Loblaws Companies Limited includes an extensive retail program. The agency's fare media product, PRESTO, required an extensive physical retail network which would allow consumers to purchase and load funds onto a PRESTO card. A requirement of PRESTO's contract with a municipal transit agency was the delivery of an extensive brick and mortar distribution system.

Recognizing that brick and mortar retailers face increasing competition for customer foot traffic, there was natural alignment between PRESTO's needs and the interests of Shoppers Drug Mart, a banner of Loblaws Companies Limited with locations across the province of Ontario. As the Official Retail Distribution Partner of PRESTO, Shoppers Drug Mart was able to deliver on the distribution requirements of PRESTO and additionally, the volume of transactions driven through a single retail partner created efficiencies which drove transaction costs down.

This Sustainable Funding Model - Strategic Partnership, delivers on eight of the Nine Core Value Drivers of Strategic Partnership™.

- Cost Abatement  • Non-Traditional Revenue
- Advertising / Sponsorship Rev
- Audience Access  • Authority / Credibility / Trust • Communication / Narrative
- Audience Experience  • Shared Expertise
- Competitive Advantage

Other examples of Strategic Partnerships focused on Sustainable Funding Models include:

- The Strategic Partnership between Verizon and the City of Sacramento to develop smart city infrastructure is a fantastic example of a public-private partnership where there is shared risk and shared reward. Verizon is investing $100M into the project, including the provision of signal control software at road junctions to improve traffic flow and help reduce traffic injuries and deaths. The improvements which will come in light rail and bus services are expected to decrease congestion amongst other benefits.

- Uber and mobile ticketing developer Masabi announced a Strategic Partnership in 2018 which allows for the integration of public transit ticket purchase inside the Uber app. The first implementation of this relationship came in Denver in June 2019 when Uber announced it would begin selling bus and train tickets for the Regional Transportation District (RTD). In addition to the **Cost Abatement and Non-Traditional Revenue** opportunities for the partners, this evolving Strategic Partnership provides **Audience Access** to transit agencies and a strong **Narrative** for Uber, a company that has been criticized for competing with public transit.


The Final Bell

The Future of Public Transportation is Strategic Partnerships. Transit agencies and their for-profit counterparts are all under increasingly growing pressure to solve for changing consumer needs, to do more with less and to grow. Alone, neither can provide the comprehensive transportation ecosystem that riders are expecting. It is only through Strategic Partnerships with shared benefit and shared risk that we will see the three core challenges for public transportation solved.


*You can contact James by email at jchalmers@tack10.com or his company website http://www.tack10.com/*

# Chapter 35

# The Future of Public Transportation In Latin America

**Romano Garcia**
Commercial Director
Impresa 1

*I wanted to have a chapter focus on public transportation in Latin America and Romano Garcia was just the right guy to write it. Romano works from Brazil and has helped transit systems around the continent improve their technology and better serve their customers.*

*In this chapter he gives a comprehensive review of what's happening now in public transit among these twenty counties and what's coming next. I think you'll find it fascinating and informative.*

Public transport in Latin American countries has distinct operating features. Among these countries, Brazil is the only representative of the Portuguese language, with a public transport model based on large private operating companies. The other 19 countries are Spanish speaking and also use a private transport model, but with different stages of business maturity. Big cities like Bogota (Colombia), Santiago (Chile), and Buenos Aires (Argentina) already have systems operated by large private companies, while most cities in the region struggle to migrate from the individual carrier model to professional operating companies. In Latin America, except for Brazil, many cities still have public transport operated by individual bus owners (just like the cabs market). If a city has a fleet of 1.000 buses, for instance, there might be at least 1.000 individual operators in that city, each one owning a bus. Transit authorities all over Latin America are trying to get rid of this kind of operation, which is generally disorganized and dangerous, with very poor quality of service. One important action those authorities have taken is to launch new concession plans that accept only formal companies as concessionaires. This has led individual bus owners to come together and set up professional bus companies.

Both in Brazil and other Latin American countries, the main role of transit agencies is to grant the operation to the private sector and, on the other hand, to monitor and inspect the quality of the service provided by those private companies.

Currently, throughout Latin America, it´s possible to observe that public transport faces major challenges, such as:

- competition with other modals and transport services
- revenue fraud and evasion
- drastic drop in customers

- absence of government subsidies in most of the cities

- high operating costs

- lack of financial resources to invest in improvements

These challenges have led transit agencies, private operators and technology companies to focus their investments on developing new solutions that enable them to achieve operational efficiency, combat fraud, and improve customer (passenger) experience.

Among the most promising megatrends in technology, there has been strong elements in the market that lead us to believe that IoT (Internet of Things) , Big Data, Artificial Intelligence, APIs (Application Program Interface), 5G, and Facial Recognition will impact the sector in a short-term period.

With this feel, convergence and integration are keywords. Convergence enables transport operators to rely on multifunctional embedded equipment, with the ability to bring together different AFC (Automatic Fare Collection), FMS (Fleet Management Systems), Telemetry, CCTV, face recognition, Hot Spot and card recharge technologies. Integration is the element that enables all these technologies to coexist and operate in embedded environments and backoffice systems in the most harmonious and transparent way.

Mobility as a Service (MaaS) will bring significant changes for public transport. It represents a new concept that aims at different aspects such as integration, flexibility, security, intermodality and interoperability. Regarding payment methods, Latin

American cities are moving towards the adoption of QR Code, Near Field Communication (NFC), "Europay, Mastercard and Visa" (EMV) technologies. The Account Based Ticketing (ABT) model is also emerging in the region.

Micromobility is another aspect of MaaS that has played a prominent role among transportation agencies, operating companies and the final customer. Small regional displacements, referring to the first and last mile, have been the subject of extensive studies and debates for planning mobility. Convergence and integration, again, have become fundamental technological elements for the promotion and viability of micromobility.

Brazil was the first country in the world to develop a facial recognition solution for public transport, aiming to control the use of concessionary cards (anyone who is entitled to pay a reduced fare in public transport). In order to avoid fraud and evasion, the system checks if the person using the card is the same person who registered for this, by comparing the images (those taken onboard with the ones stored in the database). In 2013, this technology was awarded by UITP (International Union of Public Transport) as the most innovative initiative in public transport in Latin America. The benefits of applying facial recognition technology to public transport could be extended in the future, allowing previously registered customers to make fare payment through biometric validation of their faces.

The future of mobility in major urban centers in Brazil and Latin America depends on having flexible and dynamic solutions focused on improving customer experience and promoting life quality. Emerging models, such as Demand Response (DR), are major trends for the industry. Several Brazilian technology companies are already working with different transport operators to model this service and offer the market a solution based on DR technology.

Finally, Customer Experience is a term that the entire transit industry is learning to deal with in Latin America. With all the technology and connectivity available, the final customer has progressively had the power to decide how to get around in Latin American cities. Public and private investments in multimodal systems, passenger information generation, usage behavior analysis and segment-specific loyalty programs appear as trends to combat customer attrition. All the efforts being made are aiming to provide three elements that the typical Latin American customer values in transit: agility, safety and comfort.

*You can contact Romano at www.empresa1.com.br/en*

# Chapter 36

# Hyperloop

*Billionaire Elon Musk popularized the concept of hyperloop technology in which passengers or cargo are loaded into the hyperloop vehicle and accelerate gradually via electric propulsion through a low-pressure tube. The vehicle floats above the track using magnetic levitation and glides at airline speeds for long distances due to ultra-low aerodynamic drag.*

*Now there are two major companies working to implement it around the world. One of them is backed by Billionaire Sir Richard Branson – Virgin Hyperloop One.*

*I asked my friends at Virgin Hyperloop One to tell me about their technology and what's happening next. Here's what they told me:*

*******************************

Virgin Hyperloop One is the Company to Deliver on First New Mode of Mass Transport in over 100 Years

In 2014, hyperloop was an idea drawn on a whiteboard in a Los Angeles garage. A little over two years later, Virgin Hyperloop One (VHO) built the first, and only, full scale hyperloop prototype, attracting the attention of governments all over the world.

Since the summer of 2017, VHO has run hundreds of tests at its "DevLoop" test site in North Las Vegas – reaching historic test speeds of 240 mph – and integrating the knowledge that only comes from real world testing. VHO is now uniquely prepared to launch a commercial system.

VHO has attracted over $370 million in funding, a vote-of confidence for the company to deliver.

VHO is an American company employing more than 200 passionate experts across aerospace, energy, transportation, construction & more. The company is led by CEO Jay Walder, who has run some of the largest and most complex transportation systems in the world, including the MTA in New York, the MTR in Hong Kong, and Transport for London.

We are seeing incredible demand for this technology all over the U.S., with projects in nine states. At the federal level, USDOT Secretary Elaine Chao recently announced a landmark Non-Traditional and Emerging Transportation Technology (NETT) Council, which aims to explore the regulation and permitting of hyperloop technology to bring this new form of mass transportation to the United States.

The momentum isn't just in the United States; abroad, we have made significant progress as well. Our route in India connecting Mumbai and Pune would be the largest private infrastructure investment in the State of Maharashtra, creating 1.8 million new jobs and $36 billion in socio-economic benefits. Recently, the Government of Maharashtra deemed hyperloop a public infrastructure project and approved the Virgin

Hyperloop One-DP World Consortium as the Original Project Proponent. This is a landmark announcement, recognizing hyperloop technology alongside other more traditional forms of mass transit.

## How it Works

Hyperloop vehicles, called pods, accelerate gradually via electric propulsion through a low-pressure tube. The pod floats above the track using magnetic levitation and glides at airline speeds for long distances due to ultra-low aerodynamic drag.

Inherently Safe

Enclosed environment with no at-grade crossings, by far the leading risk posed by trains

Immune from weather elements

Fully autonomous, no human errors

Proprietary high-speed switching architecture eliminates unsafe track configurations, a failure point of traditional mechanical switches

High Capacity System that Accommodates Flexible Alignments

Accommodates 16,000+ passengers per hour per direction

Tolerates tighter curves and more flexible alignments than any other mode at the same speed

Accelerates and decelerates gradually for a comfortable ride, similar to a train

Above and below grade construction ensures less disruption to wildlife and people with minimal noise


Fast, Direct, and On-Demand Experience

Moves people and goods at speeds of up to 670 mph

Low pressure environment moves pods quickly and efficiently for long distances due to ultra-low aerodynamic drag

On-demand departures reduce waiting times and bring passengers directly to their destinations with no intermediate stops


Cost Efficient

Less than the cost of high-speed rail to build and operate

Tunnels are half the diameter of high speed rail tunnels, and thus half the cost

No wheel-on-rail wear and tear due to next-generation magnetic levitation technology, reducing pod maintenance

<u>Sustainable</u>

5-10X more energy efficient than air travel

100% electric with zero direct emissions

Potential to create a self-contained micro-grid, powering the system by solar panels that cover the tube or adjacent land


It remains to be seen where the first hyperloop will go into operation but the team here is planning on making it happen sometime in this decade of the 2020s.

*https://hyperloop-one.com/*

# Chapter 37

# Shared Mobility and Urban Transit Futures

**Dr Graham Currie FTSE**
Director, Public Transport Research Group
Monash University, Australia

*I met Dr. Graham Currie during my visit to Australia in 2019 to meet top transit leaders around the nation. We had coffee in Melbourne and exchanged ideas about our industry and its direction. I found his insights fascinating and wanted him to share them in this book.*

*Prof Currie has led numerous research projects in public transport in all states and territories of Australia as well as assignments in Europe, Asia and North America. Professor Currie has a unique range of experience in relation to the development of Public Transport strategies for Special Events. He developed the public transport plan for the successful 1996 Australian Grand Prix, led independent reviews of both the Atlanta and Sydney summer Olympic Games transport systems and was an advisor to both the Athens Olympic Committee and the London Olympic delivery Authority for the design of transport services for the 2004 and 2012 Olympic Games.*

*Since he commenced the chair in 2003 Professor Currie has published more papers in leading academic research journals on public transport planning than any other author. In 2017 Professor Currie was made a fellow of Academy of Technology Science and Engineering.*

*Dr. Currie's full-time gig is as a Professor of Public Transport at Monash University but he also is in demand as a speaker and futurist. Read this chapter and you'll find out why.*

# LIES, DAMN LIES, AV'S, SHARED MOBILITY AND URBAN TRANSIT FUTURES

"There are three kinds of lies: lies, damned lies, and statistics."
Mark Twain or Benjamin Disraeli (Velleman 2008)[24]

## INTRODUCTION

---

[24] I wanted to start this piece with the famous Benjamin Disraeli quote on 'lies, damn lies'; but in trying to find a source to cite the quote I found that there is no known attribution to Disraeli and indeed that many think Mark Twain might be the source. Either way I consider this confusion with ironic awe; what I thought was a foundation stone of thought about 'the truth' may indeed be a lie; perhaps this is a prophetic way start to this paper about transit futures?

I t seems to me there is a gigantic lot of nonsense being talked about the future of transport and the future of public transport in particular. As a researcher in the field I find my emotions boiling over; I get angry at blanket statements telling us public transport has no future and it seems to me much of what is talked about regarding transport futures flies in the face of facts and a long history of what knowledge has gleaned about the human condition, economics, cities and travel. My hope is that readers will see prevailing discourse differently as a result of this paper and get to share my feelings on the matter. Either way, debating the issues is worthwhile and new perspectives of much value to debate. Here are a few to be going on with.

This research paper aims to explore public transport futures but it also aims to challenge and "derail[25]" what current common thinking is on transport futures. It starts with an outline of a rather unusual approach which will use 'new words' as a novel medium to explain prevailing thinking. The paper then starts at 'THE END' since it is important that readers understand that prevailing thinking tends to believe that public transport has no future. The new word AUTO-NO-(E) MOTION is then presented so that readers can assess if a future of autonomous cars is really likely; or perhaps the 'emperor has no clothes'. The new word 'NON-O-SHARING' is then introduced to help readers understand what I shall term the 'shared mobility lie'. The paper then closes with a short outline of why public transport IS the future of cities and presents a new word' TRANSIT FUSION as a new way of explaining how developments in our past will act to enhance the future of public transport in cities.

---

[25] Apologies for the pun

## APPROACH

Thoughts about futures can be very trendy and often fickle. A key part of new trends in thinking is the creation and adoption of 'new words' which take on new meanings which are easier to conceptualise for a non-technical (public) audience. So autonomous vehicles (AV's) have been associated with 'automobility' and uber, lyft, bike share and car share linked to the word 'shared mobility'. All are widely currently associated with a highly positive and progressive image, where technological change is said to address the significant problems being faced by cities with a framework focussing on replacing the private car with a new, easier to use alternative. A major part of this common narrative is that public transport is old, doesn't work and its time an alternative mode is limited; AV's and shared mobility are said to be the progressive alternative and growth in them is said to be enormous implying they will soon take over. The author is highly sceptical about this prevailing thinking so is going to adopt the 'new word' approach in this paper to create new words to reinterpret current thinking. Along the way I shall highlight what I think are 'lies' and what I think are 'truths' with some technical support for these views.

## THE END

Its easy to find detractors of public transit services on planet earth not the least of which are day to day users having to cope with unreliable services, lack of investment and crowding. But more recently discussion around 'new mobility' (another new word) has often tended to see new approaches to transport as 'the end' of conventional public transport in cities;

- 'The End of Transit and the Beginning of New Mobility' (The Cato Institute 2014)
- 'The end of public transport' (Samuels 2016)

It is rare to see any solid factual assessment of the practical transport alternatives in this narrative. Rather it is assumed that public transport is old and not working and that new modes can cost effectively provide an alternative which is better and cheaper. There is also occasionally some implication that new modes are being 'held back' by old style thinking about public transport.

## AUTO-NO-(E)MOTION

DEFINITION: "Auto-no(e)motion" is the unscrupulous use of the concept of the autonomous car by technologists to assert that the driverless car will solve all the worlds mobility problems, so that we can get rid of urban public transport which is a bad and should have been got rid of anyway; good riddance!

There has been a tsunami of interest in popular culture about driverless cars. However a major thrust of this implies that this future is for the car, that it will make cities more efficient and even that this is the end of public transport (e.g. Ross 2016).

I think 'the emperor has no clothes' is an appropriate phrase to apply to current AV thinking; it is far too early to think these vehicles will dominate travel in cities; in 2016 there were only 180 experimental AV's in California (Stratforma undated) out of a population of cars of 35.3Million. So AV's in common use have some way to go. Indeed we have no actual working models in general use; rather trials and tests are the current version in implementation; my own work in Singapore, one of the worlds "AV capitals", has a driver in every AV car driving seat 'just in case'. Of course it is entirely possible that this technology will not work and not be adopted; this option doesn't seem to be discussed at present yet we have plenty of new technology failures adorning the history of transport research (e.g the Segway, Sinclair C5, the Flying Car, Hovercraft, Maglev amongst others). Indeed the failure of new technologies is actually common ;also the 'overselling' or 'hype' about the idea is also quite common and has now be enshrined in a theoretical framework called the 'hype cycle' (Gartner 2016). This is now a website which is updated with the current progress of new ideas through a progression from the oversold 'hype' phase past the 'peak of inflated expectation' and down to the 'trough of disillusionment'. Figure 1 shows a montage of the Hype Cycle for the last few years. AV's reached the 'peak of inflated expectations in 2015 and have commenced their path into the trough of disillusionment.

There are some important gaps in the rationale behind how AV's might assist transport problems in cities which point to how public transport might actually be a better solution. The first concerns the capacity problem; there is actually no clear consensus that fleets of AV's in cities will actually improve the significant congestion problem facing the worlds growing cities. Might they actually make the problem worse? Indeed most recent studies exploring AV futures have found it essential to recognise a role for urban rail in carrying mass volumes of people as part of any scenarios where AV's help cities to work effectively (International Transport Forum 2017). A key part of this discussion is that we need higher occupancy in vehicles to be space efficient in growing congested cities (an imperative I shall come back to);

this is clearly a major rationale and advantage of public transport.

**Figure 1 : Automated Vehicle Technologies and their Progress along the Hype Curve**

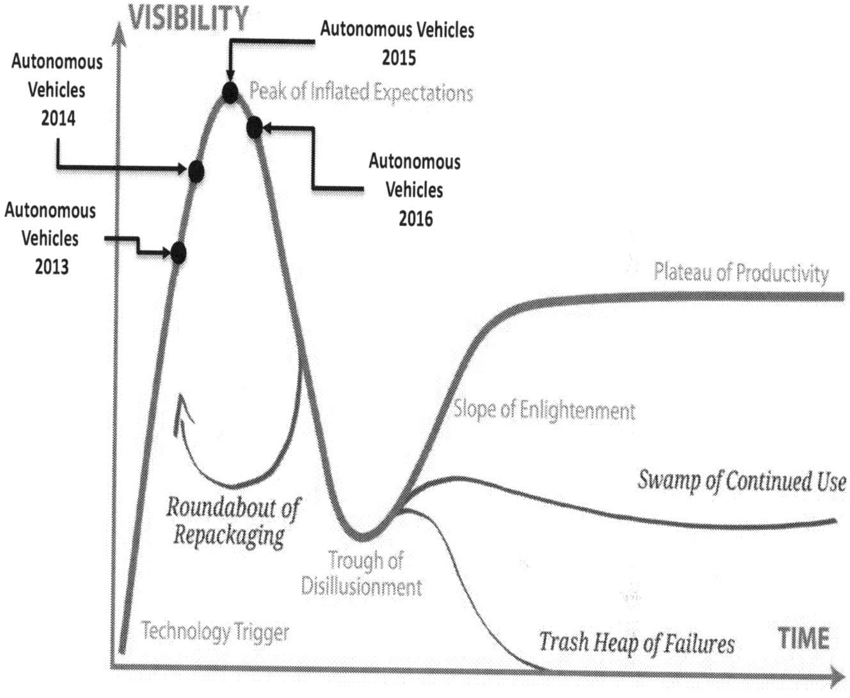

Source: (Authors edit based on Gartner 2016)

There is also an import **LIE** at the heart of the 'AV's will take over public transit' argument. That lie concerns the view that public transport is old, too old to be involved in the modern AV technology trend and hence car based AV's will take over. Here is a simple **truth**; **autonomous public transport vehicles dominate land based passenger travel on planet earth today and probably will for at the least the next decade** ;

one quarter of all railways in Asia have no drivers; autonomous trains operate today in Vancouver, Barcelona, London (Victoria Line), AirTrain (JFK NYC) and numerous other cities globally. Between 2006 and 2011 the number of automated train kms operated doubled; between 2011 and 2025 the volume of automated train kms is expected to increase by over 130% (UITP 2011). AV trains are not trials, they are not theoretical, they are full systems in passenger operation today. It seems these significant facts are forgotten in the AV car hype. Indeed ironically a high share of AV trials today involve AV buses; so how can AVs be the end of transit when they are transit?

**NON-O-SHARING**

DEFINITION: "Non-o-sharing" isn't sharing. Its using words to make it look like it is. It is the unscrupulous use of the word "sharing" by technologists to imply that new mobility modes are good and incorrectly asserts they involve lots of shared vehicle occupancy. This is to show they are much better than urban public transport which is not good and doesn't involve sharing in any good sort of way and which has to be got rid of as soon as possible.

'Shared mobility' is a term which is widely used now to refer to transport network companies such as Uber and Lyft, bike sharing and car sharing. Demand responsive transport systems related to these have also been widely said to challenge and even want to take over public transit (Free Enterprise 2014, Johnson and Moussako 2014, Brustein 2016).

'Shared mobility' has many fine features and its progressive, healthy image is in many ways well deserved since it demonstrates some of the best applications of new information and communications technologies as a means for making it easier to book and use a transport system. Bike use has many health and fitness advantages and car sharing can actively reduce car ownership in cities. However I argue that the term 'shared mobility' is a lie; I suggest it is used to imply that travel using these modes involves shared vehicle occupancy and is hence equitable and efficient. But to my mind the lie is that shared mobility doesn't involve sharing of travel within vehicles. In addition there is a view in current debate that the increasing the amount of shared mobility in our cities is providing new solutions to old problems. Yet I argue this is also a lie.

LIE ONE – Shared Mobility Involves Vehicle Sharing. The occupancy of a shared bike is almost always one; this means there is **no shared occupancy**. In data from California, the average occupancy of an Uber in traffic was found to be 1.66 (SFCTA 2017); accounting for the driver; this implies .66 of a passenger per trip or an empty car in traffic rate of 34%. In effect 34% of Ubers on the road are empty. **This is not shared occupancy.** Even with multiple occupancy of more than 1 passenger, the degree of sharing is hardly very high. In a study of car sharing also in California, average occupancy of vehicles was found to 1.44 (Cervero et al. 2007); here the driver is a valid passenger so there is some degree of occupancy but it's a long way from the shared occupancy of public transport vehicles; over 2,000 people can travel in one train; that's 'real' shared mobility! A bus with 50 people on it; that's shared mobility. In effect; most 'shared mobility' modes don't involve sharing yet its shared occupancy we need for the future of growing cities; that's what public transport provides.

LIE TWO – Shared Mobility is Growing Transforming Sharing in Cities   It is easy to look at the figures illustrated in Figure 2 and then to think shared mobility is the going to be 'the way of the future'.

However there are a few caveats worth considering before you come to this conclusion. Firstly the data shown suggests there are around 100,000 shared cars in the world in 2014 (possibly double that in 2017). There were 180,000 Uber drivers in the US in 2015 and 24,000 shared bikes. While these numbers look large they are actually a drop in the ocean of the 1.2 Billion cars registrations we have in the world (2014, Davis et al. 2014) and the 264M cars in the USA (2015, Statistica 2017). In effect these shared mobility modes are tiny and the private automobile dominates.

Then there is the other 'truth'; car occupancy has been falling dramatically and is still falling; Figure 3 illustrates this problem; it shows car occupancy data for Australian cities over the last 30 years; commuting is now close to 1 and is lowest for peak travel (where the need for higher occupancy is largest). World and US trends follow a similar pattern. **So the 'inconvenient truth' is that shared mobility is in decline and not growing**. This is a great tragedy which the world needs to do something about. Having us 'make-believe' that 'shared mobility' is increasing doesn't help.

**Figure 2 : Data Illustrating that Shared Mobility is Growth – but it is?**

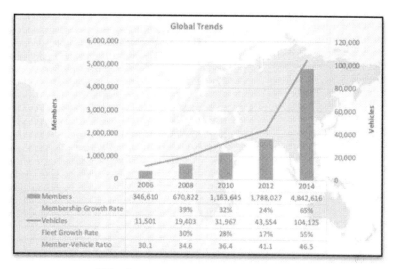

(Shaheen and Cohen 2016)

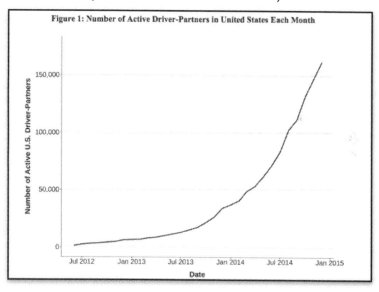

(Hall and Krueger 2015)

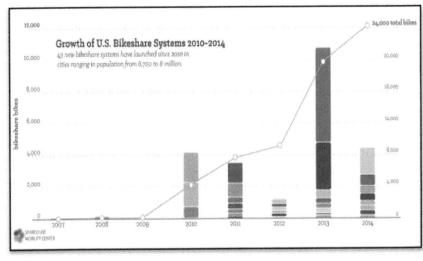

(Shared-Use Mobility Center 2015)

## Figure 3: Car Vehicle Occupancy Over Time (year) – Sharing is Declining NOT Growing

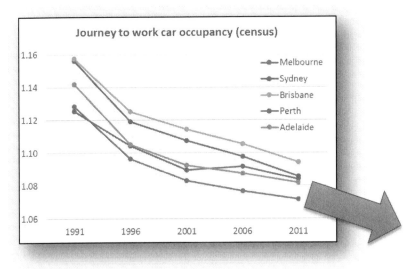

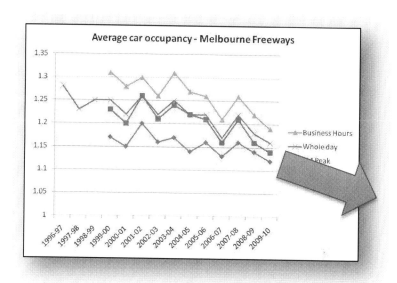

Source: Charting Transport https://chartingtransport.com/tag/car-occupancy/ (last accessed September 2017)

The arrows shown in Figure 3 also suggests a future forecast of car occupancy based on historical trends. This might suggest sharing goes below 1; not a likely scenario for current technologies which need a human driver. However with AV's this outcome becomes entirely feasible as repositioning trips, access and egress trips become feasible without anyone in the vehicle. Does this represent 'shared mobility'? Is a future with AV's including a proportion of vehicles not carrying anyone a realistic solution to high traffic volumes in congested areas?

There is a last point to be made about AV's and Shared Mobility in relation to the discourse regarding Public Transport. In general public transits detractors have implied a negative outcome will emerge for transit from these new modes. However there is quite a lot of evidence that this view is also wrong. In a review of the travel market profile of people who used new shared modes it was found that public transit was a major aspect of their mobility (Shared Use Mobility Centre 2016). Shared modes were also found to complement and actively act to increase public transport usage notably because 'super-sharers' had lower car ownership and car ownership reduction is highly related to transit use (Shared Use Mobility Centre 2016). Indeed a number of strategic reviews of the future of cities are emerging which confirm this view; In an international review of the future of cities new mobility services were forecast to either increase or maintain existing transit use in all city contexts explored (Bouton et al. 2015). A major feature of these arguments is that fact that new mobility modes might act to address the first/last mile problems faced in accessing public transport modes; thus acting to increase the coverage and attractiveness of transit services.

## WHY PUBLIC TRANSIT?

Cities now represent humanities home; in 2007, for the first time, more than half of the worlds' population were city dwellers (United Nations Population Fund 2007). Between 2000-2030 the worlds' urban population will double. City travel is dominated by the private car (Cosgrove et al. 2009) and is creating a substantial concern for the future of humanity:

- Traffic congestion is now widely recognized as a major and growing urban transportation problem (Cervero 1991, Downs 1992, Arnott and Small 1994). In Australia congestion costs $Aust 9.4 B p.a. (2005) and is expected to rise to $Aust 20.4 B by 2020 (Bureau of Transport and Regional Economics 2007). It is entirely likely based on our current conceptualisation of AV's that they will act to increase travel since those that cannot drive will be able to use AV's; in addition, declining vehicle occupancy and the fact that AV's can run empty suggest much potential for AV traffic to increase not decrease in cities of the future.

- There are significant social and community impacts which car traffic have on urban liveability (Vuchic 1999) including the separation of urban communities by busy roads and impacts on social disadvantage (Rosenbloom 2007). Av's increasing traffic volume will certainly act to exacerbate this issue affecting a larger urban population in growing cities.

- Research has established strong links between physical activity and health (British Medical Association 1997) (Dora and Phillips 2000). Public transport use involves more physical activity compared to car travel suggesting growing health concerns as car use increases (Woodcock et al. 2007). Door to door services, implied by AV's and Shared Mobility modes (other than bike) may act to reduce walking and physical activity.

Only public transit can address all these concerns since it has the highest vehicle occupancy and the largest capacity to carry large volumes of people in an efficient way in growing busy cities.

So what is transits future in this context? My view is that it is highly progressive and big; it is far from marginalised by new technologies; it is liberated by them. Growth in cities is continuing and is forecast into the future; there is a key imperative to make the future of humanity an efficient and effective one where humans share large capacity vehicles moving effectively through tunnels and on raised transitways and with priority on the streets where the majority of humans live.

## TRANSIT FUSION

DEFINITION: Transit fusion is the adaptation of transit vehicles, infrastructure and service design to integrate the best features of better performing modes into new transit modes and services to improve overall service performance, attractiveness and effectiveness outcomes.

Transit fusion is a trend which has been happening for some time; its just not been recognised before. The most obvious recent example is the Bus Rapid Transit movement where 'rail like' service features have created 'rubber tyred railways" including high frequency service, rail like station designs including platforms and turnstyles and rail like right of ways using bus vehicles. To some extent the light rail transit movement was an earlier incarnation of this trend bringing heavy/commuter rail like quality of service to suburban, local and street settings.

I predict Transit Fusion is a trend which will continue and develop to encompass new mobility modes to address the first/last mile access issue. Examples of this are already in trial today with several transit operators using Transport Network Companies to provide rail feeder functions. Shared bike schemes are the backbone of rail access in many cities in China today (and have been in the Netherlands for some time). Another more fundamental and potentially ground breaking variant emerging from Transit Fusion is how transit authorities might transform into shared mobility agencies. Already some German rail operators have started to operate car sharing schemes since they have found transit reliant passengers occasionally need cars and where better to provide them than at the stations they use every day. Also would transit agencies not be an obvious institution to run and maintain fleets of AVs should this type of future eventuate? They already operate and maintain large fleets covering all metropolitan geographies; who else is better placed, and have depots in place, to run AV's in these contexts into the future?

Overall my version of transit futures sees substantial growth in the scale and worldwide distribution of services as cities continue to grow and require greater efficiency and effectiveness from the shared occupancy of vehicles. There are some important lies implied in the prevailing discourse on AV's and Shared Mobility suggesting transit futures are limited as a result. The truth is that transit systems are the **only** option available for shared occupancy at the volume needed and the quality provided that can meet the needs of growing cities. New Shared Mobility and AV technologies act to enhance these transit futures reducing transit costs and increasing transit attractiveness. A critical failing of the contemporary narrative on AV's and 'Shared Mobility' is the lack of an understanding of the need to increase vehicle occupancy; there is a significant global trend towards reduced occupancy and 'personalised' sole person mobility driven by human behaviour and preferences. These are the intractable barriers to effective AV and shared mobility use but an area where public transit systems have shown much success.

So what form will public transit futures take? I would suggest mass transit using rail, and bus/light rapid transit will be a necessary requirement. Segregated rights of way for mass volume modes are a necessity; simple calculations on volume illustrate the need for mass transit shared occupancy of modes rather than privatised single person vehicles as a better use of limited space.

Transit fusion will ensure the most appropriate design but does require a move away from conventional transit single mode thinking.

So will this vision of transit futures happen in all contexts? Almost certainly not. Central downtowns and now inner and middle suburbs in growing cities will find mass transit compelling and essential. However small towns and outer suburban low density areas will struggle with low productivity bus services and the need for subsidy. Can new mobility modes act to replace transit in these contexts? Possibly but this may just be wishful thinking; there is a remarkably strong correlation between the availability of new mobility modes and higher density central areas. In effect these areas have low demand density, dispersed trip ends and long trip lengths. All modes struggle to provide quality service in these contexts and I have seen no evidence yet that new mobility services can do better in the long term than existing basic bus services. Perhaps here a bus based AV service can be more productive?; some 70% of bus costs are drivers so in theory costs can be reduced and potentially service levels enhanced with an automated vehicle bus service. What about demand responsive transit (DRT) bus services? Certainly DRT buses have been promoted in many new mobility services. One problem with this suggestion is the very very long history of almost complete failure we have seen in DRT based bus services for the last 50 years. Certainly we have seen no glowing long term survival of these schemes as an alternative to suburban buses to date. More recently, perhaps as expected, new mobility DRT's such as Bridj have failed.

The future is never fully known but the way we think about the future is often questionable. No one fully understands what will happen to our urban futures but as long as cities and urban densities grow, public transit is very likely to be at the heart of successful city futures forever.

## REFERENCES

Arnott, R. and K. Small (1994). "The economics of traffic congestion." American Scientist, **Vol. 82, No. 5,**: pp. 446-455.

Bouton, S., S. Knupfer, I. Mihov and S. Swartz (2015). Urban Mobility at a Tipping Point, McKinsey & Co.

British Medical Association (1997). Road Transport and Health. London, The Chameleon Press. .

Brustein, J. (2016) "Uber and Lyft want to replace public buses." Chicago Tribune.

Bureau of Transport and Regional Economics (2007). Estimating urban traffic and congestion cost trends for Australian cities - working paper 71. Canberra, Department of Transport and Regional Services.

Cervero, R. (1991). Congestion, growth and public choices. Berkeley, California., University of California Transportation Center. **Reprint No. 51.**

Cervero, R., A. Golub and B. Nee (2007). CarShare: Longer-Term Travel-Demand and Car Ownership Impacts, Institute of Urban and Regional Development University of California at Berkeley.

Cosgrove, D., D. Gargett and D. Mitchell (2009). Urban passenger transport:how people move about in Australian cities - Information Sheet 31. Canberra, Australia, Bureau of Infrastructure, Transport and Regional Economics. **ISSN 1440–9593**.

Davis, S., D. SW and R. Boundy (2014). "Transportation Energy Data Book: Edition 33" Office of Energy Efficiency and Renewable Energy, U.S. Department of Energy.

Dora, C. and M. Phillips, Eds. (2000). Transport, environment and health. WHO Regional Publications. European Series, World Health Organization (Regional Office for Europe).

Downs, A. (1992). Stuck in traffic: coping with peak-hour traffic congestion, . Washington, D.C., The

Brookings Institution.
Free Enterprise (2014) "BRIDJ: A BRIDGE TO A NEW KIND OF MASS TRANSIT." Free Enterprise.
Gartner. (2016). "Gartner's 2016 Hype Cycle for Emerging Technologies Identifies Three Key Trends That Organizations Must Track to Gain Competitive Advantage." Retrieved September 2017, from http://www.gartner.com/newsroom/id/3412017.
Hall, J. and A. Krueger (2015). An Analysis of the Labour Market for Uber's Driver-Partners in the United States. . IRS Working Papers. , Princeton University, United States. .
International Transport Forum (2017). Urban Mobility System Upgrade - How shared self-driving cars could change city traffic, International Transport Forum, OECD.
Johnson, B. and A. Moussako (2014) "Pop-up bus service looks to reinvent mass transit." Marketplace.
Rosenbloom, S. (2007). Lessons for Australia from the US: An Amercian looks at transportation and social exclusion. No Way to Go - Transport and Social Disadvantage in Australian Communities. Currie Graham, Stanley Janet and S. John. Melbourne, Australia, Monash University epress. 3.
Ross, D. (2016) "Driverless cars could make mass transit obsolete." myNorthWest.
Samuels, A. (2016) "The End of Public Transit? - Start-ups are proving more efficient than government in areas like transportation. Should some services be privatized?" The Atlantic.
SFCTA (2017). TNC's Today. San Fancisco California USA, San Francisco County Transportation Authority.
Shaheen, S. and A. Cohen (2016). Innovative Mobility Carsharing Outlook: Carsharing Market Overview, Analysis and Trends, Winter 2016, Transportation Sustainability Research Center, University of California, Berkeley, United States. .
Shared-Use Mobility Center (2015). Growth of U.S. Bikeshare Systems 2010-2014 What Bikesharing's Growth Means for Shared Mobility. Los Angeles, United States., Shared-Use Mobility Center, Los Angeles, USA.
Shared Use Mobility Centre (2016). Shared Mobility and the Transformation of Public Transit. TCRP J-11/TASK 21 Transit

350

Cooperative Research Program and American Public
Transportation Association.

Statistica. (2017). "Number of vehicles registered in the United States
from 1990 to 2015 (in 1,000s)." Retrieved September 2017,
from https://www.statista.com/statistics/183505/number-of-
vehicles-in-the-united-states-since-1990/.

Stratforma (undated) "The Digital Driving Age: A Bumpy Road
Ahead?".

The Cato Institute. (2014). "The End of Transit and the Beginning of
the New Mobility: Policy Implications of Self-Driving Cars."
Retrieved September 2017, from
https://www.cato.org/events/end-transit-beginning-new-
mobility-policy-implications-self-driving-cars.

UITP (2011). METRO AUTOMATION FACTS, FIGURES AND TRENDS. I. A.
o. P. Transport. Brussells, Belgium, Union International des
Transpoirts Publics.

United Nations Population Fund (2007). State of World Population
2007 - Unleashing the Potential of Urban Growth. New York,
U.S.A., United Nations Population Fund.

Velleman, P. (2008). ""Truth, Damn Truth, and Statistics"." Journal of
Statistics Education Volume 16, Number 2 (2008).

Vuchic, V. (1999). Transportation for Livable Cities. Rutgers, The State
University of New Jersey, New Brunswick, NJ, Center for
Urban Policy Research.

## Special Note of Thanks:

This paper was published in the Journal of
Public Transportation[26] for its special series on
the Future of Public Transportation. It is
reproduced in full for this chapter with kind
permission granted from publishers of this
journal, the Centre for Urban Transportation
Research at the University of South Florida
and also the author.

---

[26] Currie, Graham. 2018. Lies, Damned Lies, AVs, Shared
Mobility, and Urban Transit Futures. Journal of Public
Transportation, 21 (1): 19-30. DOI: http://doi.org/10.5038/2375-
0901.21.1.3
Available at: https://scholarcommons.usf.edu/jpt/vol21/iss1/3

*You can contact Professor Graham Currie at his*
*email: graham.currie@monash.edu*
*And at web site addresses; www.ptrg.info*
*www.worldtransitresearch.info*

# Chapter 38

# Transit Safety and Hazard Awareness

**Ed English**

Chief Executive Officer

ELERTS

*I first met Ed English at a Transit Conference where he was onstage discussing the serious issue of reducing human trafficking on transit. He has become a major advocate and sponsor of activities around this topic. Realizing people want to report safety & crime issues to authorities but don't like calling 911, Ed's company created a simple app to let them do so. Ed's previous tech company protected computers from spyware, this time he's protecting people from all sorts of dangers. Ed is a huge Batman fan and he programmed Frogger for the Atari in the 1980s.*

Safety is a top priority for public transportation agencies. The Federal Transportation Administration (FTA) requires transit employees be trained to recognize and report safety hazards, or risk losing grant funds. The million dollar question is, "how will hazards be reported?" Authorities can only mitigate hazards they know about.

Safety-minded transit agencies need employees <u>and</u> passengers to report hazards they observe. Often a phone number is provided to report hazards, but people dislike making phone calls.

> 📱 I have a concern about the of the track going east on the ▅▅ line in between ▅▅▅▅▅▅▅▅ station. I am on car ▅▅ and it was shaking hard at high speed on that segment. I have been riding for six years and have not felt the train rock so hard as it did today.
> Dave

Phone calls are inconvenient for the caller, expensive to process, and error prone to transcribe. Talking with a dispatcher leaves the caller feeling more involved than they want to be. As a result, they don't call. Employees and transit riders want to help but they are in a hurry. It's a lot easier to use a mobile app to

> ⚐ **Safety Issue**
> 📱 <u>Door is swinging open</u> between stations on ▅▅ train car ▅▅. There is also no train car number over the emergency intercom. A child could fall out of this door and it would be impossible for a rider to report.

discreetly report something to a transit agency.

Proactive transit agencies know how important it is to listen to their customers. Periodic surveys indicate what riders think about past experiences. There is no substitute for receiving real-time messages from passengers and employees who have a serious concern right now.

## Social Media is lousy for incident reporting

Riders want to vent when they see a problem. Complaints often end up on social media where they live forever, damaging the transit's reputation, and are often not actionable. One transit agency noticed a post with a photo of a discarded Christmas tree on its tracks, but with no location information. The agency learned exactly where the tree was when the train hit it!

## Human Hazards

People want to help. The fuel that drives ELERTS communication system is the person who reports a hazardous or quality of life condition. "Crowd-sourcing" safety concerns leverages the eyes and ears of employees and passengers to keep the system safe and comfortable for all. Transit agencies use ELERTS system to protect over 2 billion passengers annually.

---

⊕ Safety Issue

⚲ Bus

■ Route ▧▧▧, bus ▧▧ This driver had a attitude, and he was driving erratically at times. He would hit the brakes hard occasionally while driving very slow, and he almost ran another driver off the road on the highway near ▧▧▧▧ station. That other driver figuratively had to "lay" on the horn to get the bus driver's attention. Y'all might wanna have a manager or supervisor to check him out and make sure he's not falling asleep or DUI.

---

| | | | |
|---|---|---|---|
| Amtrak | Atlanta MARTA | Atlanta STREETCAR | Boston MBTA |
| Buffalo NFTA | Charlotte CATS | Northern Indiana SOUTH SHORE LINE | Chicago METRA |
| Contra Costa TRI DELTA | Columbia, SC THE COMET | Delaware DART | Delaware River Port Authority |
| Denver INTL. AIRPORT | Dallas DART | Jacksonville JTA | Los Angeles FOOTHILL TRANSIT |
| Louisville TARC | Petersburg Area Transit | Minnesota Valley MVTA | Orlando LYNX |
| Phoenix VALLEY METRO | Sacramento SACRT | San Francisco BART | Santa Clara VTA |
| SE Pennsylvania SEPTA | South Jersey & Philadelphia PATCO | Toronto TTC | Victor Valley VVTA |

## Human Sensors drive Situational Awareness

Transit riders make excellent sensors; when something looks suspicious or out of the ordinary they notice and report their concerns. Agencies have received over 500,000 incident reports from the ELERTS mobile app. An attached photo or video says a thousand words about what is going on. The GPS location tells where it is happening so a dispatcher can respond. These

early warnings make it possible to address a safety hazard promptly and sometimes save a life.

## Visualize the Situation at your Transit Agency

Analysis of hazard data reveals what is going on in a transit system, both, at the incident level and in aggregate over time, through charts and graphs. Trends become apparent. Passenger's real-life experiences provide actionable data for dispatchers and managers.

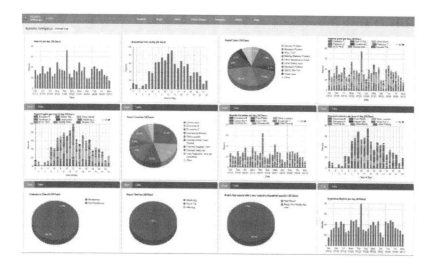

Data changes your perception. Agencies are making huge investments in Safety Management Systems. The value of these systems increases exponentially when fed a steady flow of hazard reports from employees and riders.

*You can contact Ed English at ede@elerts.com*
*877-256-1971; www.elerts.com*

# Chapter 39

# Beyond the Urban Mass Transportation Act

## Peter Varga

### American Public Transportation Association Chair (former)

*Peter Varga is a public transit industry legend. Not only did he lead The Rapid (Grand Rapid, Michigan's transit system) for over 20 years but he Chaired APTA at an important time in our nation's transit history. As such I thought he might be perfect to give us some historical perspective on where we've come from as it relates to US federal funding and regulation - so we can have context for where we are going. He does so here:*

Prior to the mid-1960s there was very little public funding of public transportation. This was certainly true of federal support for transit. With much lower ridership than existed at the end of World War II and mounting debts, Transit systems were losing revenue and going out of business as private businesses. Many of these were reorganized as public entities. One example I am familiar with is in Grand

Rapids Michigan, where until last year, I was the CEO of the Rapid for 21 years. The privately-operated public transit system was initially taken over by the City of Grand Rapids, and eventually evolved into a regional public transit system as the Grand Rapids Area Transit Authority (GRATA). Finally, during my tenure there, six cities created the Interurban Transit Partnership. Better known as The Rapid, the new authority was financially more stable and had increased operating funds as it was subsidized with local property tax and state gas taxes. Federal funds were need to recapitalize the system in Grand Rapids, much it had been necessary in other cities following the dissolution of the private transit operators. Today, the focus of the federal program is still on the capital side, but the program has evolved to support operational expenses in some circumstances, as well as safety oversight, planning, and research.

Major federal involvement in public transportation dates to the Urban Mass Transportation Act of 1964 (P.L. 88-365). In 1962, President Kennedy proposed capital assistance for mass transportation projects. Kennedy sent a major transportation message to Congress, that called for the establishment of a program of federal capital assistance for mass transportation. Said President Kennedy: "To conserve and enhance values in existing urban areas is essential. But at least as important are steps to promote economic efficiency and livability in areas of future development. Our national welfare therefore requires the provision of good urban transportation, with the properly balanced use of private vehicles and modern mass transport to help shape as well as serve urban growth." https://www.transit.dot.gov/about/brief-history-mass-transit

But President Kennedy did not live to see a bill funding his proposal into law. It was signed into law by President Lyndon Johnson on July 9, 1964. "We are a nation of travelers. You cannot write our history without devoting many chapters to the pony express, the stagecoach, the railroad, the automobile, the airplane. . . Yet, until 1964, the Federal Government did little or nothing to help the urban commuter." Said President Lyndon B. Johnson, in his remarks at the signing of the Urban Mass Transportation Act. The act created the Urban Mass Transportation Administration (UMTA). The agency was charged with providing federal assistance for mass transit projects, including an initial $375 million in capital assistance over three years as mandated by the act. In 1991, the agency was renamed the Federal Transit Administration (FTA).

Changes in federal assistance occurred over the next 55 years primarily in conjunction with each transportation reauthorization bill as the act eventually known as the Federal Transit Act was changed. The creation of UMTA and later the FTA stimulated a resurgence of transit investments in the United States. According to an FTA brochure - Transit services supported by FTA span many groups and provide wide-ranging benefits. Since 1964, FTA has partnered with state and local governments to create and enhance public transportation systems, investing more than $12 billion annually to support and expand public rail, bus, trolley, ferry and other transit services. That investment has helped modernize public transportation and extended service into small cities and rural communities that previously lacked transit options.

These investments gradually transformed America, as each transportation reauthorization bill was passed.

As stated in Wikipedia: "In the United States, the federal transportation bill refers to any of a number of multi-year funding bills for surface transportation programs. These have included:

- Surface Transportation and Uniform Relocation Assistance Act, 1987
- Intermodal Surface Transportation Efficiency Act (ISTEA), 1991
- The National Highway System Designation Act (NHS), 1995
- Transportation Equity Act for the 21st Century (TEA-21), 1998
- Safe, Accountable, Flexible, Efficient Transportation Equity Act: A Legacy for Users (SAFETEA-LU), 2005
- Moving Ahead for Progress in the 21st Century Act, (MAP-21) 2012
- Fixing America's Surface Transportation Act (FAST), 2015

Previous multi-year highway spending bills were known as Federal-Aid Highway Acts."

The following chart from Enotrans shows the historical trends over time.

*Federal Grants to State/Local Governments for Transportation and Water Infrastructure as a Percentage of US Gross Domestic Product, FY 1947-2016, By Mode*

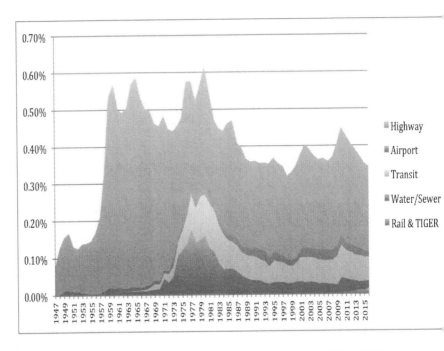

Source: Eno Transportation Weekly May 12, 2016, The 70-Year Trend in Federal Infrastructure Spending by Jeff Davis

In some years. Transportation reauthorization bills are more easily resolved. In other years failure to have a reauthorization bill causes interruptions in the funding process. In those years transportation funding could be only accomplished with continuing resolutions of a previous funding bill. This results in very little growth of the program.

What the chart clearly demonstrates is that, despite this larger federal investment in public transit throughout the years following the UMTA Act, there was not a proportionally greater growth of federal funding for transit as compared to other transportation programs in the federal-aid Highway acts.

*In 2015.* The House and Senate sent President Obama the largest transportation package in more than a decade, costing $305 billion over five years. The Fixing America Surface Transportation Act (FAST) is the last act that was passed that authorized funding for transit for the required five-year period. Ironically Congress has in the last few years actually increased the funding above the authorization levels.

This happened again in 2019. In February, Congress passed an appropriations act for FY 2019 which was signed by the President and provided more than $16 billion for public transportation and intercity passenger rail, including $13.4 billion for public transportation and $2.6 billion for intercity passenger rail grants. Although these total funding levels are slightly less than the historic FY 2018 funding levels (-$67 million for public transportation and -$218 million for intercity passenger rail), they are significant increases over funding in past years and are:

- $2.0 billion more than the FY 2017 enacted funding levels;
- $1.2 billion more than the FY 2019 FAST Act authorization levels; and
- $3.5 billion more than the FY 2019 President's Budget request.

Source: Congress Reaches Agreement on U.S. Department of Transportation Funding, February 15, 2019 APTA Legislative Alert.

The FY 2019 appropriations bill provided $2.6 billion for Capital Investment Grants (CIG) and required the Federal Transit Administration (FTA) to obligate 85 percent of these funds by December 31, 2020. Of the $2.6 billion, the bill provides $1.2 billion for New Starts, $635 million for Core Capacity projects, and $527 million for Small Starts. The bill also provides $100 million for the Expedited Project Delivery CIG Pilot Program, which is a pilot program with reduced regulatory requirements for projects supported by a public-private partnership and seeking a federal share of 25 percent or less. The reason why there was language requiring FTA to obligate the funds by a certain date was because in the previous year grants were delayed despite the projects having been approved by FTA in their review process.

In addition, the bill specifically required FTA to administer the CIG program in accordance with the procedural and substantive requirements of current law (49 U.S.C. 5309). Importantly, the bill prohibits FTA from implementing or furthering new policies detailed in FTA's June 29, 2018 "Dear Colleague" letter to CIG project sponsors. The Administration's Dear Colleague letter established geographic diversity as a factor in FTA funding allocation decisions; considered DOT loans "in the context of" all federal funding sources requested by the project sponsor, and not separate from the Federal funding sources; and included other Administration policy objectives.

*Of the $13.4 billion appropriated for public transportation the significant elements were $4.7 billion in Urbanized formula grants, and $2.9 billion in State of Good Repair Grants from the formula grants section, and $2.6 billion in Capital Investment Grants from the* *competitive program. On the Intercity side of funding $1.9 billion of the $2.8 billion was allocated to Amtrak. $1.2 billion was enacted above the $14.8 billion authorized by the FAST Act.*

Excluding funding provided for the Public Transportation Emergency Relief Program, public transportation program funding was between $10 billion and $11 billion annually in the period FY2010 through FY2015, but has risen to $13.5 billion in each of FY2018 and FY2019(Figure 1). As we noted earlier appropriations in FY2017, FY2018, and FY2019 have been above the FAST Act authorized levels. Typically, about 80% of federal public transportation program funding comes from the mass transit account of the highway trust fund and 20% comes from the general fund of the U.S. Treasury. The FY2018 and FY2019 appropriations acts provided additional general fund money for several programs typically only trust funded, thereby raising the general fund share to about 28% in FY2018 and 26% in FY2019. Public Transportation Emergency Relief Program funding comes exclusively from the general fund. The fact that 20% of funding is from the general fund means that only 80% of the funding is more securely derived from the mass transit fund. Funding for most federal capital grants comers from the mass transit account. The Capital Investment Grants (CIG) is funded from the general fund and is dependent mostly on congress allocating those in every annual appropriations bill.

As the public transit industry has been deliberating their position on a potential bill to replace the FAST Act, several issues caused by the last bill are being debated and compromises are being sought. I serve on the APTA Board as the designated board member

365

representing the Legislative Committee and am a witness to the effort to get consensus. I hear the discussions.

The issue of funding allocations under a reauthorization bill has been a source of controversy among the transit systems, partially because of the competing needs of different entities looking to solve their capital problems. One source of contention has been that under the FAST Act bus and bus facility allocations have fallen below the 20% goal in the reauthorization process. The FAST Act authorization had a 14% of the distribution of funds for bus and bus facility allocations while Capital Investment Grants (CIG) were set at 39.7%, and State of Good Repair Grants (SOGR) at 46.3%. Meanwhile in the FY 2019 appropriations Bus and facilities were appropriated at 17.1% of the funding, while the appropriations for SOGR were at 44.1% and 38.8% for CIG Smaller and mid-sized transit systems that rely on bus grants felt that their needs were viewed as less greater than the larger systems which had more significant state of good repair issues. Smaller and mid-sized systems have been pushing for a restoration of a balance on funding. The general consensus in the industry is that the 40/40/20 ratio should be restored in the next reauthorization process over time. Specifically, setting Capital Investment Grants at 40%, SOGR at 40% and Bus and Bus facilities at 20%. Until the compromise is achieved, this will continue to be a major source of discussion at the American Public Transportation Association's Legislative Committee and Board meetings. Meanwhile if any area receives a funding increase the sense is that not any one of program result in an actual decrease in the other, like it did in the FAST Act.

Another issue being deliberated for the next reauthorization bill is funding for intercity and high-speed rail. The FAST Act was the first major surface transportation authorization bill that included a substantial rail title authorizing high-speed, intercity passenger and freight rail programs, The current discussion is for congress to create a Passenger Rail Trust Fund and identify new revenues other than revenues that are dedicated to the Highway Trust Funds, to support intercity passenger rail. Rail programs in the Fast Act are funded from the general fund and not from the mass transit account. The FAST act authorization level is 1.2 billion for funding in three separate programs – Consolidated Rail Infrastructure and Safety Improvements, Federal-State Partnership for State of Good Repair, and the High-performance Intercity Passenger Rail Grants. Current discussion in the APTA Legislative Committee and board is to increase each allocation over the next reauthorization and to use contract authority and ramp it up so that by the year 2026 $1.9 billion would be allocated. Under current political conditions this is not an easy task to accomplish. There could be tensions if this funding increase is not firewalled from the existing trust fund.

The elimination of earmarks in reauthorization acts or transportation bills is another problem that transit systems have been contending with. Previously many systems relied on earmarks to get funding for exceptional bus replacement or expansion needs. For example, when I was the CEO of the Rapid, we received a $17 million earmark in SAFETY-LU. This allowed us to secure an increase in our local funding from property taxes and to purchase buses for expanded service. We also got a New Starts earmark to perform an alternatives analysis study which ended up identifying a Bus Rapid Transit in the Division Ave, Corridor, subsequently this resulted getting a CIG Grant to start the Silverline, Michigan's first BRT and more recently were allocated a CIG grant of $54 million for 80% funding for the Laker Line, the region's second BRT. Apart from earmarks there was also an exceptional opportunity under The American Recovery and Reinvestment Act of 2009 (ARRA). The act more familiarly known as the Recovery Act, was a stimulus package enacted by congress and signed into law by President Barack Obama in February 2009. The purpose of ARRA was to assist with effects of the great recession. Jobs needed to be created and existing ones saved. Other objectives were to provide temporary relief programs for those most affected by the recession and invest in infrastructure, education, health, and renewable energy. The approximate cost of the economic stimulus package was about $831 billion. The effect at The Rapid was that we got another $10 million in funds apart from the formula funds to invest in transit. We passed another increase in our local property tax revenues and bought buses to expands service again. ARRA was however an unusual program passed under unique circumstance. Republicans voted against it. In fact, it stimulated the creation of the Tea Party. Once again it helped transit systems especially small and mid-sized systems to meet some of their capital replacement or expansion needs. Smaller and mid-sized transit systems relied on earmarks or ARRA stimulus dollars to meet exceptional needs especially since up to 50% of their federal formula capital funds can typically be allocated for operations rather than meeting bus or bus facility needs. Many large transit properties have also have used capital funds in the operating environment to support "preventive maintenance" or ADA related expenses under special provisions of the transit act that would allow such diversions.

Public transportation expenses are in two main areas, operating costs and capital needs. Operating expenses consist mostly of operating transit service, maintaining the vehicles and facilities and the administration of transit service. Also included are the purchase of transportation from private providers usually for paratransit services. Capital needs are usually the replacement of buses that have reached the end of their useful life, and maintaining the transit facilities is a state of good repair. Generally, federal public transportation programs allow an 80% maximum matching share for capital projects and a 50% maximum share for operating expenses. Typically, about one third of public transportation funding is for meeting the capital needs, and two thirds are expended for operating the various services. Fares and other operating revenues cover only one-quarter of the total cost, with the remainder provided by federal, state, and local governments. The federal government supports less than 10% of operating expenditures, but almost 40% of capital expenditures. (Source; Congressional Research Service May 2019). Capital needs for expansion purposes are usually funded through discretionary grants such as bus and bus facility program commonly referred to as Section 5339, the CIG program and state and local funds.

Operating expenses are not only diverted from the federal capital formula funds but are also affected by the ADA. The passage of the Americans with Disabilities Act of 1990(ADA), meant that many public transit facilities, bus shelters and stations as well as buses or trains had to be made accessible. This was probably the greatest impact. The ADA also mandated that individuals with disabilities should have access to public service in an equivalent manner. "Except as provided in paragraph (c) of this section, each public entity operating a fixed route system shall provide paratransit or other special service to individuals with disabilities that is comparable to the level of service provided to individuals without disabilities who use the fixed route system" (§ 37.121(a)).

This meant that complementary paratransit service must be provided wherever and whenever other routes or transit services are provided. Traditionally many transit systems use a dial a ride type service to provide this service. Usually this service means that a separate vehicle usually carrying about 2 persons is provided. The complementary service must be provided within a ¾ mile of a route and during the same hours as other service. The cost of operating this service is subsidized with local or state operating assistance but not federal assistance other than meeting the requirements as part of acquiring buses and constructing bus facilities as part of their capital expenditures. This equivalent service can be a significant part of a transit system's cost. Equivalency must be maintained in various aspects of the service. Fares cannot be more than double the regular fare, service areas and service times must be equivalent and there cannot be trip denials or capacity constraints. Also, in the regulations, there exist prohibitions regarding waiting lists and limiting the number of trips. Reservations for trips must not exceed a 24-hour period. Compliance with these federal requirements is strictly reviewed by the Federal Transit Administration and other federal agencies. Meanwhile systems can also offset the higher relative cost of ADA paratransit by using their federal formula funds. This diversion also affectes the availability of needed capital dollars.

The cost of providing a complementary paratransit service trip can be 3 to 4 times the cost of providing a transit trip. Transit systems therefore have explored cost effective ways of providing all service. Paratransit is almost always more expensive to provide than traditional fixed-route transit because it requires more labor per passenger and it generates minimal passenger revenue. On average, paratransit makes up about 1 percent of total ridership, but about 9 percent of operating costs. Source - Transit Cooperative Research Program. TCRP Synthesis 74: Policies and Practices for Effectively and Efficiently Meeting ADA Paratransit Demand." 2008. In part, because it is so much more expensive to provide paratransit service, it is very common for transit providers to contract out to private companies. Contracting out this service is often less costly than operating it directly. The 1990 Americans with Disabilities Act required cities to provide paratransit service for residents with disabilities but provided no operating funds. Nationally, paratransit now accounts about 12 percent of transit budgets, according to the report. It typically costs far more to operate than bus or train service — the national average is $29 per paratransit trip, compared to a little more than $8 per trip for fixed-route services. Source: NYU Rudin Center for Transportation Policy & Management.

*Five years after the passage of the Urban Mass Transportation Act the investment for public transportation has changed. From a $375 million allocated under the UMTA Act, $14.1 billion has been* *enacted in FY 2019. But as the earlier chart indicated federal support for public transit had not increased in comparison to other investment, especially for the highway program.* In the appropriations bill, The Federal Highway Administration gets $45.3 billion for Highway Trust Fund highway programs, which is $1 billion more than fiscal year 2018 and is consistent with the authorized levels of the FAST Act. And in addition, the bill provides $4.1 billion in formula highway funding above the FAST Act levels from the general fund, which is $2 billion higher than similar supplemental funding in fiscal year 2018.

*The following chart from the APTA 2019 Fact Book indicates that local funding for capital projects is as important to transit systems as federal funding for capital projects.*

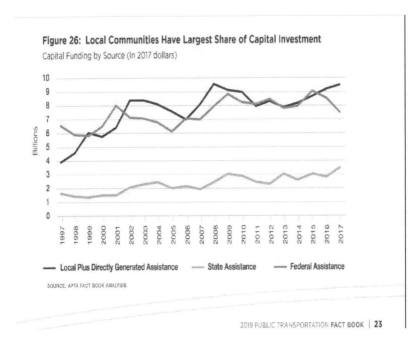

Figure 26: Local Communities Have Largest Share of Capital Investment

Capital Funding by Source (In 2017 dollars)

—— Local Plus Directly Generated Assistance    —— State Assistance    —— Federal Assistance

SOURCE: APTA FACT BOOK ANALYSIS

*As you observe over the years* the failure of federal funding to keep pace with program growth is shifting increasing responsibility on State and local governments. This is a form of devolution, and it has been occurring over an extended period.

*Meanwhile over the years there have been many grants for New Starts or Capital Investment Grant projects. These were discretionary projects that were approved annually by the Federal Transit Administration in their risk review processes. This year is no exception. The following discretionary projects are being proposed in 2020 - Bus Rapid Transit in Flagstaff, Indianapolis, Pittsburgh, Vancouver and Chapel Hill among others; light rail in Portland, Minneapolis and Phoenix; streetcars in Tempe, Sacramento and Tampa; Second Ave. Subway Phase 2 in New York City and the Hudson Tunnel between New Jersey and New York. In recent years we had seen many projects come out of this program – Bus Rapid transit in Eugene, Oregon and Grand Rapids, Michigan. Light Rail extensions in Seattle and Charlotte, Streetcar in Tucson and the Fort Worth Tex Rail Project. Over the years we also have seen investments occur from the formula programs.*

*A major example of growth of transit in the last twenty years is the development for example of the Dallas Texas light Rail network.* DART Light Rail, the Dallas Area Rapid Transit Light Rail, is a system in operated by Dallas Area Rapid Transit, better known as DART. The system comprises 93 miles (150 km) among its four lines. It is the longest light rail system in the United States. Another example is in the city of Eugene Oregon where the development of a network of Bus Rapid Transit routes were implemented. The Emerald

Express (EmX) is the BRT system in the region operated by the Lane Transit District (LTD). LTD chose bus rapid transit after a review process in which several transportation options, including light rail, were considered. BRT option was the best fit for Eugene-Springfield's size and current transportation needs. The first route, named the Green Line, was opened in early 2007, connecting downtown Springfield to downtown Eugene. Less than a year later, ridership had doubled in the corridor. Extensions to the system were added in 2011 and 2017.

American Public Transportation Association states, "Yet, as a nation, we have neglected to make necessary investments in this vital public service. Our public transit infrastructure is on the verge of failing; the U.S. Department of Transportation estimated in 2015 that more than $90 billion is needed just to bring bus and rail assets into a state of good repair. And communities are clamoring for even more public transportation as a way to reduce traffic congestion and ensure clean air. APTA calls for a federal investment of $145 billion over six years to fund critical projects that will repair, maintain, and improve our public transit systems today and in the future." Source: APTA Surface Transportation Authorization Recommendations October 2019.

Americans for Transportation Mobility state, that "Because the federal fuel tax has not been raised in a quarter of a century, the purchasing power of the Highway Trust Fund (HTF) continues to decline. Increasing the gas tax is deemed one of the most equitable and prudent policy options Congress can pursue to devise sustainable transportation funding." The Americans for Transportation Mobility Coalition is a collaborative effort of business, labor, and transportation stakeholders advocating for improved and increased federal investment in the nations aging and overburdened transportation systems. www.fastersaferbettter.org

The critical hurdle for FAST Act reauthorization is how to pay for it—in the language of Congress, what are the "pay-fors"? The "pay-fors" have been an issue in every surface transportation authorization bill since the gas tax was last increased in 1993. For more than 25 years, Congress has been unwilling to adjust the gas tax and create the dedicated, sustainable revenue needed to fund the level of investment it authorized. As a result, past bills have included a patchwork of pay-fors—from selling oil from the Strategic Petroleum Reserve to pension smoothing—to provide the necessary budget offsets to fund the bill.

Unlike these prior efforts, any patchwork of budget gimmicks will not solve the significant amount of revenue necessary to fund an infrastructure bill. The Highway Trust Fund already faces an enormous deficit—$176 billion over the next 10 years—to fund current highway and transit funding levels. To offset the Trust Fund shortfall and increase surface transportation investment, Congress will have to identify significant budget offsets. The American Public Transportation Association, together with the U.S. Chamber of Commerce and others, will continue to advocate for increasing the gas tax by five cents per year for five years to create the dedicated, sustainable funding necessary to provide this type of increased investment. Coalition partners are also open to other possible revenue options that can achieve bipartisan consensus.

As of this writing, for this surface transportation cycle, the Highway Trust Fund will be insolvent as of October 1, 2020 and payments out will only equal payments in. Without a dedicated and sustainable funding source or an infusion of General Fund monies, we will see a slowdown of the construction market in Spring 2020 and transit agencies having to dip into reserves or reduce service with uncertainty as to when Congress will come up with a fix. The challenge is that the hole keeps getting deeper, so short-term fixes get an increasingly expensive and harder to secure support for General Fund transfers. This will be a topic in congress as it deliberates the next authorization bill and among all transportation advocates until it is resolved. Meanwhile a long-term solution for fully funding transportation needs requires strong political leadership.

In the development of expanded or new services we can see that part of the vision "for the provision of good urban transportation" expressed by President Kennedy has been achieved. Many local transit projects were developed in the years since the Urban Mass Transportation was passed. Mass transit investment has grown in the United States, but because there was not a fundamental shift of funds to transit as opposed to highways and roads, we do not observe a resurgence that matches what transit looked like before World War II or as it compares with transit development in Europe or other parts of the world. A big example is the level to which high speed rail has been developed in places, like Spain, France or China and Japan. The United states currently does not have a high-speed rail corridor, the closest to it is the Acela, the Amtrak Corridor between Washington and Boston. China has the largest and fastest high-speed rail,

19,000 miles of rail at up to 200 miles per hour. But in the United States we went from an extensive rail system to a highway network – The National Interstate system. As we dream of the future of public transportation federal funding for urban and rural areas must increase in balance to local and state resources. There should be a greater shift of federal dollars to public transportation relative to other mobility options. The Highway Trust Fund shortfall must be addressed and the varied needs of the public transit providers, whether state of good repair, new starts or other capital needs must be made available without the demand to further devolve to local or state sources. The next reauthorization bills must meet the needs for these communities and the funding must keep pace with the growth of demand for good public transportation in the United States. Beyond Urban Mass Transportation Act, fifty-six years later, where will the leadership come from now to make the next big leap in federal public transportation funding in the United States.

*You can contact Peter Varga at*
*peterjsvarga@gmail.com*

# Chapter 40

# Smart City Mobility Includes Taxi

**Matthew Brownlie**

Managing Director
Trapeze Group Middle East

*Matthew Brownlie has an interesting life. He has spent nearly a decade working in the middle east on technology and transit. He now heads my company's Middle East operations.*

*Take a glimpse into this amazing world of smart (and uber rich) cities, transit and taxis.*

E ssentially, a smart city is the re-development of a city using information and communication technologies (ICT) to enhance the performance and quality of urban services such as energy, connectivity, transportation, utilities and others. A smart city is developed when 'smart' technologies are deployed to change the nature and economics of the surrounding infrastructure.

In essence, cloud-based IoT applications receive and manage data in real-time to help enterprises and residents make better decisions that improve the quality of life. But the owners of all this data are going to be the ones who get to make the decisions, regardless of what others may think.

How does public transport fit into this vision? How do we see public transport working together in these smart cities?

The smart city will only exist to its citizens if smart transportation is in the centre. Without a mobile city, all the information and cool features in the world won't matter if people can't move to where they want to go.

Public transport is the heartbeat of a city. We need to make sure that we don't make the same mistakes of our past and allow these tools, these modes, to be combative. Mobility is no longer just about a bus, a tram, a car, a bike, or someone walking.

In the past, these modes were mutually exclusive from one another. Now, things like Mobility as a Service (MaaS) fill our dreams of what could be. And seamless mobility is one of the main benefits of the smart city concept. All modes need to work together leveraging the data and connectivity of a smart city and IOT to mean that using Public Transport is more efficient, convenient and cost effective then driving a car.

Cities around the world are seeing clear benefits from smart public transport solutions:

**New York's** 14th Street Busway increased potential passenger movements from 1,000 people an hour to

25,000 people an hour. (http://inrix.com/blog/2019/10/nyc-busway/)

**London's** central city congestion charge reduced traffic by 15% and congestion by 30% (https://theconversation.com/london-congestion-charge-what-worked-what-didnt-what-next-92478)

**San Francisco's** Better Market Street project aims to improve travel times and safety on the city's busiest transit corridor. (https://www.citylab.com/transportation/2019/10/car-free-san-francisco-market-street-design-bikes-streetcar/599983/)

To deliver on this premise or dream of MaaS then Taxis and eHail, need to be a core part of the city's transport solutions. In particular, delivering on-demand as well as first and last mile, taxis have always been doing this, because they are there and available. But without being intelligently integrated into the rest of the public transport network, we continue to hear about proposed or upcoming first and last mile "solutions".

To be able to integrate, it is key that the data from all of the public transport systems, including taxi & eHail can be integrated together with an intent to drive improved services. However, it can only be done by whoever owns the real-time data from each system.

In typical mass-transit systems, it is accepted the data is either fully owned by a government agency or made fully available in real-time to a government agency by a trusted and contracted private party.

So why in taxis has this been so different? And has this contributed to an inability to work together? In cities where taxis already form an integral part of the public transport landscape, you can see this data availability problem is being addressed such as in Singapore and Dubai.

Difficulties in achieving this improved integration are already being felt in places like London, where some eHail providers, because they are not a part of the public transport network, are bringing too many taxi drivers into areas unsuitable for them and are directly impacting the performance of the city's road and transport networks.

This is unnecessary and only occurring because all modes are not working together, rather they are again competing against each other.

It is not the technology improvements that eHail has brought to the industry that has created this problem, but rather than the lack of being able to integrate them properly to become part of the regular landscape. Taxi is not the blocker to MaaS, it can be the solution with proper technology.

In Dubai, we have been working with RTA (local transit authority) for more than 20 years. Our efforts having been mostly focused on developing their platform to allow each of the taxi operating companies to continue to manage themselves independently. While simultaneously enabling the integration of all 12,000 vehicles real-time data to a multitude of government agencies and services.

The data and so the power is at the hands of the RTA making them well placed to integrate both modes into a strong Public Transport mix and enables them to achieve a true MaaS vision. What this leads to is the ability to find and innovate new ways of assisting the industry to grow and remain profitable while working towards this vision.

Here are some of the integrations being handled by the system live and in real-time: EC3, Dubai Police, real-time traffic data, Dubai Smart government, eHail (RTA's Careem venture is integrated through the common platform), S-Hail bookings, MLT advertising, CDM for driver cash collections, In-Vehicle Cameras, etc. Even tolling charges are handled independently within the RTA taxi system and not using any external hardware or interfaces.


So how does this technology work?

You can see here the fundamental design is about a platform with a multitude of interfaces and APIs that allow various parties involved in the industry, from the taxi operators themselves to others looking to work with or feed bookings into the environment. The aim here is to allow as much independence or control as desired or needed by all involved. Future integrations become a straightforward matter when the right platform with the right design in place.

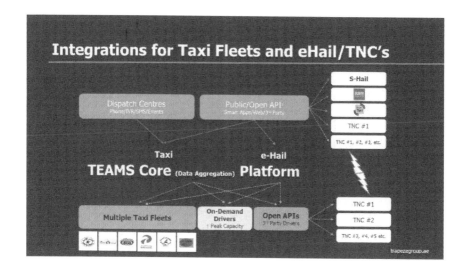

It is critical that to be able to integrate the sort of vision we all see in the highly integrated smart city future, the data is being owned and aggregated by a party with the city's best interests at heart and the ability to fairly balance the needs of all parties.

## What makes up a smart city?

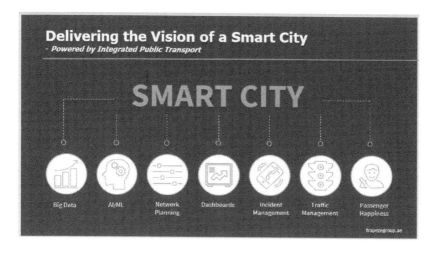

These Smart City capabilities enable taxis, eHail, and other on-demand services to be rationed out to where they are needed, increasing each party's return on investment and giving the people wanting to utilize public transport, the benefit of effective services being in all of the right places at all of the right times.

*You can contact Matthew by email at: matthew.brownlie@trapezegroup.com*

# Chapter 41
# Equity is the Future of Public Transportation

## Bacarra Sanderson Mauldin

Director of Policy and Innovation
New Orleans Regional Transit Authority

*I first met Bacarra Mauldin several years ago through APTA. She and I served on a panel discussing Employment Needs in the Transit Industry and she also has appeared as a guest on our podcast, Transit Unplugged.*

*Bacarra is a passionate advocate for mobility for those in need both in the Birmingham, Alabama area and nationally. She is a recognized leader in our industry serving on the APTA Board and Executive Committee. Her input on what's next for public transit here is integral to ensuring we maintain a focus on some of our most important customers.*

P ublic transportation as we know it historically, is evolving. It is far, far more than the simple bus routes and rail lines of years past. Public transportation today is a series of complex networks that may include on demand-like micro-transit zones that feed into optimized bus routes, that feed into a rail-line, light rail line or bus rapid transit line. It includes car fueled rideshare options, scooters, bicycles and autonomous vehicles; however, not necessarily the ones we saw as kids on the *Jetson's* cartoon. From rural areas to midsized cities to large metropolises, cities have experienced shifts in population and demographics that dictate a major change in how we think about public transportation. In some cases, evolution leads to extinction. However, this is not the case as long as industry leaders meet the changing needs of today and the demands of tomorrow by shifting its focus from public transportation to "public mobility." As a part of the industry's evolution, public transportation of the future must address the following areas in order to maintain it position in the center of the transportation ecosystem: Equity, Paratransit, Workforce Development, and Innovation.

Public Transportation must be the great equalizer. Equity does not mean equal. Although this might be a no brainer to some, there are many that have failed to fully embrace what it means to have an equitable transportation network. Fare equity is and will continue to be a driver in the future of public transportation as well. How can public transportation serve both the "Haves" (i.e. tourists, working execs) and the "Have nots" (i.e. working poor, the homeless) safely and harmoniously? Many systems have gone to a fare-less system. There are pros and cons on each side of that debate. The riders of each system make up a subcommunity of sorts. The "community" aspect is often overlooked when leaders make decisions like rate hikes and service cuts. This why there is such an outcry around these issues. The future of public transportation depends on how the industry responds to this growing debate. In addition, agencies are pushed to provide a higher level of service to the communities they serve in an equitable way. In the past, transportation service areas were viewed in simple terms: urban or rural. Today transit systems serve more complex areas that may include urban or inner city, rural and sparsely populated to suburban which is a step in between the two concentrations and the main driver of the need for "first and last mile." Each of those areas need public transportation; however, there is no longer a one size fits all way of serving those communities effectively and efficiently. The equity question drives us towards offering in the not so far future an array of services that may not be available in every community served, but the offerings selected for that particular community make it reasonable and feasible that its customers have access to the places that they live work and play.

Paratransit is often referred to as the biggest "unfunded mandate" in public transportation. However, the future of this industry is in its ability to take care of our aging and disabled customers. This customer base is growing in alarming numbers. A generation of baby boomers reaching senior citizen status combined with a corresponding uptick in chronic illnesses, has challenged how the medical and social services communities address the critical need of providing care for our nation's low-income elderly population.[27] In a similar way, persons with disability are desiring and demanding, in great numbers, the ability to lead full and productive lives. Without adequate access and transportation, this is simply not possible. This crisis of sorts has greatly impacted by our industry's ability to design transportation networks that are accessible by both seniors and persons with disabilities. "Currently, 3.6 million individuals do not access medical care because they experience transportation barriers."[28] Nationwide this is the third leading cause of missed appointments. Transit agencies have a great opportunity to serve this population in non-traditional ways, including brokering non-emergency medical transportation to access additional funding from sources outside of traditional FTA programs. During my tenure as Executive Director at the Birmingham Regional Paratransit Consortium, we began to explore direct partnerships with medical providers to close the missed appointment gap. During that six-month pilot period, missed appointments were reduced by 30% and our overall ridership went up by 15%. Technology also plays a large role in providing access for seniors and persons with disabilities. Advances in demand response dispatching software will make traditional paratransit operations flow more like its micro-transit counterparts with shorter lead time and greater efficiency due to the advances in mapping. Technology makes it easier for family, social workers, personal care attendants etc. to assist with securing the transportation needed to get their loved one or patient where they need to go. The landscape is full of

---

[27] Car, Ellis Stanford Social Innovation. *"Caring for an Aging Population, Ideas to help address the challenges of providing better care to low-income elders." 10/21/2016*
[28] https://revcycleintelliigence.com

challenges, but also many emerging potential solutions and promising examples that lead us to believe that there is a bright future ahead for our seniors and customers with disabilities.

If public transportation is going to sustain and stand the test of time, it must as an industry, replace its aging workforce. The aging of the U.S. workforce has been called the "silver tsunami." Ten thousand Baby Boomers turn 65 *every day*[29] *The public transportation industry has been hit particularly hard. Unfortunately, in the last decades, there have been fewer and fewer kids growing up saying that they want to be a bus driver, bus mechanic or any of the other careers that are a part of the industry. One example of this is in New Orleans, Louisiana, the home of the St. Charles Streetcar line, the oldest continuously operating street railway the world. The streetcars themselves are created and serviced by skilled craftsmen, artisans in their trade. The unfortunate thing is that 80% of that department is eligible for retirement TODAY. If they all left today, decades of experience in a lost art that is admired and appreciated by the thousands, would be gone in an instance. This why CEOs like Alex Wiggins are working to create career pipelines and apprenticeship programs to ensure that the needs of his agency are filled for years to come.*

Public Transportation must use technology to move from a service of necessity to a service of convenience. Each of the foregoing sections referenced some aspect technology. It goes without saying that technology is at

---

[29] Hirsch, Arlene, www.shrm.org, "4 Ways to Overcome Aging Workforce Issues" 10/11/2017

389

the center of what will drive the public transportation of the future. It was amazing to be in the hills of Reinhardt, Switzerland and see all of the information about their autonomous bus. I am inspired by the accounts from CEOs like Tina Quigley, who just retired from Las Vegas, Nevada's transit system and Nat Ford of the Jacksonville, Transportation Authority who are both pioneers in the U.S. Autonomous Vehicle movement. We have witnessed a major technology shift within the transportation industry that has caused everyone -- from users to providers -- to reimagine what public transportation really is. As a result, we have seen the rise of ridesharing, micro-transit and *Mobility as a Service* as the industry buzz. That trend will continue lead the industry's evolution into the future as riders are using the power choice, fueled by technology, to drive public transportation into a service that is tailor-made for their specific schedules and needs. But what about those who do not have the "power" to choose? There is a great opportunity to design and deploy technology that can level the playing field and make the inaccessible, assessable, obtainable and affordable in the future. The brightness of that future depends on the swiftness of our response and the limits of our creativity.

*You can contact Bacarra at her email: bacarra.mauldin@gmail.com and through her LinkedIn Profile https://www.linkedin.com/in/bacarra-sanderson-mauldin-5b983553/*

# Chapter 42

# How Autonomy Will Become the Norm in the Busing Industry

## J.D. Redmond

VP Marketing
TTN Fleet Solutions

*J.D. Redmond is an experienced Fortune 500 executive and a fleet maintenance expert. I met him through a chance encounter and was so impressed I asked him to join us in the venture to explain more about artificial intelligence's role in fleet maintenance in the coming decade.*

*I found it fascinating and I think you will too.*

The busing industry, just like any industry, is subject to the shifting tides of technological disruption. Even though we may not like it or may think that change is happening too quickly, advances in technology will change the way that business is done in our industry. Business models will change, and some hard-working employees may have to find new work. While technological disruption has occurred throughout history, it does not make it any easier to swallow.

One of the most fascinating technological advancements that will affect the busing industry centers on automation. It is easy to read the business and technology headlines and see the hype for things like cognitive automation and artificial intelligence. At times, it can be difficult to not only estimate whether the hype is real, but how it will affect the busing industry.

While it is impossible to predict the future with complete accuracy or certainty, we believe that automation has a good chance of causing several distinct shifts in the industry. Understanding these shifts now and how they will *affect all actors in the industry can help you and your team better prepare for the automation revolution.

### How Automation Will Become the Norm in the Busing Industry

In releasing our projections here, we believe that it is helpful to separate them into short-term and long-term projections. Specific time frames are extremely difficult to provide, yet this basic distinction between the short and long-term can still be helpful.

## Short-Term Trends

So, in the short-term, we are likely going to see the rise of scheduled maintenance. This isn't just a phenomenon that is going to occur in the busing and logistics industries. It is going to be extremely important in all industries. Scheduled maintenance that is overseen by artificial intelligence will make companies more efficient and productive. Instead of humans spending time determining when to best service their equipment and vehicles, machines can do it automatically.

While fleet maintenance is still a human job, we have already started to see the promise of automated scheduled fleet maintenance. Several different software companies have transformed the manual and time-consuming processes of fleet maintenance with automated systems, which save companies both time and money. By leveraging GPS tracking data, current driver behavior, and historical data in its algorithms, this fleet maintenance software can know the precise moment when a bus should come in for maintenance. It intuitively knows when certain vehicles should be inspected or repaired for certain maintenance events, whether it is a basic oil change, air filter replacement, or even a full Department of Transportation safety inspection. As far as payments for these maintenance events, cryptocurrencies like Bitcoin will become increasingly relevant. Busing and logistics companies will be able to easily track their costs and payments through blockchain technology, which will add another layer of transparency to their maintenance ecosystem.

While the automation of scheduled maintenance is certainly helpful for all busing companies, it is especially relevant for larger bus companies whose massive fleet canvasses the entire country. Controlling the deviations in maintenance, even if they are quite small, can go a long way in increasing uptime. Less time can be spent diagnosing and repairing a mechanical problem that "unexpectedly" occurs. Instead, by leveraging this software, busing companies can implement scheduled maintenance at the most optimal times possible.

From the rise of scheduled maintenance, new technologies are focusing on automating the last mile. Startups have already jumped onto this idea, with several creating Android-like robots to act as delivery professionals in last mile logistics. The general idea here is to remove all variables surrounding the extra mile so that cargo can be delivered as quickly and efficiently as possible. This is similar to reducing the lag with last-mile in the busing industry that it is facing a decline in passenger usage due.

Last mile automation has already made significant progress, yet a key inflection point centers on the advancement of self-driving vehicles. Tech juggernauts like Uber and Amazon have invested a significant amount of capital into automating the entire freight journey (including the last mile). As with scheduled maintenance, the increasing automation of the last mile will inevitably help busing companies trim their operating expenses, which they can reinvest into other parts of their businesses.

## Long-Term Trends

From short-term trends, let's talk about long-term trends. As we referenced at the start of this post, autonomy is going to be second-nature in the long-term. Many behaviors that require human oversight or control today will be taken over by machines. Yes, there will be developers, data scientists, and other humans programming these artificial intelligence algorithms and gathering insights from the gathered data. But putting aside those roles, software algorithms powered by artificial intelligence are becoming so sophisticated that what was once thought to be a quintessentially human job (like driving) will increasingly be replaced by machines.

In the busing and logistics industries, it is hard to see a future where automation does not replace many components in maintenance. This is not an original thesis, as technology experts have been sounding the alarm for years. Nevertheless, as artificial intelligence technology gets better and busing companies increasingly see the potential to eliminate a significant portion of their operating expenses, it makes intuitive sense as to why busing companies would seriously consider replacing their drivers with automated fleets.

This replacement thesis doesn't just end with the drivers themselves. You will likely see scheduled and unscheduled maintenance events that are transmitted out through a dispatching artificial intelligence platform. As a simple example, you will likely see autonomous tow trucks that are sent by these platforms (backed by blockchain technology) to maintenance events for the asset. Upon arriving, the asset will be towed (once again, autonomously) to a breakdown center.

Human interaction may still exist—depending on the service required. If parts are needed to fix the asset, they will be delivered accordingly (whether they are dispatched at the time of the scheduled event or once faults are run). While intelligent robots may do much of the grunt work in repairing the affected assets, humans may be in the background, ensuring that the job has been successfully completed. Nonetheless, robots and artificial intelligence will be doing much of the grunt work in terms of maintenance.

To be clear, all of this is in the far future. We haven't yet reached a point where many of these automation applications are ready to roll out on a massive scale. It is going to take continued investment and hard work from developers in order for these applications to become widespread. When it does occur, however, it will utterly transform the way that business is done in the busing and logistics industries.

## Forecasting the Future

While the future is inherently difficult to forecast, we strongly believe that automation is going to have a significant effect on the busing, trucking and logistics industries. Regardless of your specific role in your company, it is critical to monitor this trend. Along with this, think about the potential applications that automation will unlock in your business. Anticipating the future and thinking about the possible opportunities will substantially increase the odds that you will be able to leverage them when they do occur.

# Chapter 43

# A Better Future

## Jeff Maltz

### Co-Founder and CEO
### SilverRide

*Jeff Maltz is a compassionate futurist, focused on creating a world where there is true accessibility to all life has to offer for the elderly and people with disabilities. He believed in that vision so strongly that he created a company to help make it possible.*

*SilverRide provides door-through-door TNC service for passengers who need that extra "helping hand". The drivers are not only back-ground checked but also drug tested and fingerprinted (unlike many other TNC's). Using its platform, the company provides direct retail transportation services to clients by matching them with appropriate drivers, and also operates as a sub-contractor to transit agencies and companies around the country to provide this higher level but lower cost style of service.*

*Jeff is a popular speaker at mobility conferences on creating the kind of future we want for our parents, children and ourselves.*

'm Jeff Maltz, the Co-Founder and CEO of SilverRide, a company offering door-through-door and specialized assistance for seniors and those with disabilities, including offering accessible vehicles for those riders who need one. Having led SilverRide for over a decade, I've observed the challenges facing this population as we provided rides to thousands of customers both through our direct to consumer business and through our work with organization like transit agencies. Through these experiences, I have gained useful insights into potential solutions to problems facing the public transit system, mostly from the perspective of the needs of our older population and those with disabilities.

I'm going to focus on two problem areas that are important for transit agencies to address going forward. First, riders who need door-to-door service, or even door-through-door service, do not benefit much when curb-to-curb options are added, even if those options utilize accessible vehicles. Many of the innovations currently being implemented in the transit system are often only curb-to-curb, and even the soon to come driverless car solutions by definition are only curb-to-curb. Second, there is little innovation in how to handle transit for senior centers and dialysis clinics where rides can often take an hour or more to go for what should be a twenty-minute trip.

In looking at the "first twenty feet / last twenty feet" problem or "twenty feet" problem, as we call it at SilverRide, many good options are available in the market but do not seem to be a focus. The problem for many riders is that they cannot get to the vehicle because they use a walker, cane, crutches, are unstable or are simply fearful of navigating the stairs, uneven pavement and other obstacles between them and the ride. Often, an accessible vehicle can be even more difficult for someone in this situation to tolerate as the ride is bouncy and even getting on the bus can be more difficult than getting into a non-accessible vehicle. To help with this twenty-foot problem, door-to-door service is often offered by transit agencies to help people get to the vehicle. It is typically defined as helping a rider from the car to the door and back. This does not include physical transfer assistance in and out of the vehicle or home, or much physical assistance at all. However, the door-to-door service is a critical solution for many riders and helps solve much of the twenty-foot challenge.

Traditionally, for riders who need more help than door-to-door service, or need help getting from the front of the hospital to the doctor's office inside, a caregiver would be needed to travel with them, skyrocketing costs to serve this person. Door-through-door service helps alleviate this problem for very little added cost because a caregiver is not needed much of the time, and often no extra cost is incurred for the ride itself, if done right, as we have experienced at SilverRide. Door-through-door service involves helping a rider travel from inside their home or location (such as a doctor's office), to the vehicle and back, and usually implies a greater level of physical assistance. This physical assistance is provided to help riders who may use canes, walkers or wheelchairs to get to and from the vehicle by potentially escorting them from the

400

doctor's office to the front of the hospital, up or down stairs, along uneven surfaces and in and out of the vehicle. To be clear, what we are talking about is physically assisting a person from their wheelchair, for example, into or out of the vehicle using proper body mechanics and a light or mod physical transfer. Of course, if a rider cannot transfer out of their wheelchair, an accessible vehicle will be needed for that rider. Note that this door-through-door process is also helpful for those who have cognitive challenges because it reduces the risk of something going wrong since the rider is with a person from leaving their home and going inside the destination and same for trip back. For agencies looking to add door-through-door service, please be aware it is critical that eligibility services get boosted to be able to know who can best use the service and that it is set up properly.

Another problem area for transit agencies is the difficulty serving senior centers and dialysis clinics. What we have learned at SilverRide by providing a higher level of care with door-through-door service, is that the extra care it takes to offer that service translates to doing a better job with the dialysis and senior centers with pooled rides. To do a door-through-door ride properly, more information is needed for each rider and each pickup and drop-off destination because the driver is providing more assistance. More importantly, the driver and, consequently, the organization has a more direct connection to the pickup and drop-off points because the driver is typically going inside and can report pickup details and/or feedback to dispatch. All of this extra information helps to better schedule rides for return trips, but also helps for scheduling future trips as well. For example, while inside, a driver can get a precise update from the clinic on when a dialysis patient will be ready and can then update the system so a ride can come at the right time at pickup, versus coming and missing the trip and causing a will-call situation. For the future rides, if the changed time is a regular change, the system can be updated properly.

Note that to do the trips correctly, the technology has to be able to comprehend all the extra details of these trips and factor that information into ride scheduling and optimizing, often in real time. This is where driver app technology and more innovation in dispatch and scheduling systems such as we use at SilverRide is critical. For pooled trips, more information is available to group riders together more efficiently. Sample useful information would include knowing which riders typically take longer at pick-up, which riders have physical issues that prevent other riders from riding comfortably, which riders cannot be left alone for any period of time, etc. Thus, having door-through-door service, and utilizing all the extra information obtained in the process, leads to a greater ability to do pooled trips for physically and/or cognitively challenged riders better. At SilverRide, we have seen pooled trips improve with typically double the utilization rate, or more, for senior centers by adding the door-through-door option while at the same time decreasing ride times considerably.

As transit agencies and other organizations struggle to properly accommodate this difficult to serve population, and hope to take advantage of self-driving vehicles and other technology going forward, my hope is that they do not lose focus on the "twenty foot" problem, or the challenges facing group or pooled trips for riders who need this extra assistance. Although, in my experience, door-through-door service actually leads to lower costs for each ride serving this population, even slightly higher costs to fix problems with the most difficult riders (a small subset of the overall rider population) should lead to not only greater overall system performance and happier riders, but to significantly lower overall system costs as well.

*You can contact Jeff by email at: jeff@silverride.com or visit his company website: www.silverride.com*

# Chapter 44

## A Generation Z Perspective

## On the Future of Transportation

**Bronwyne Sawyer**

Introduction: **Steve Sawyer**
General Manager
Trapeze

*Steve Sawyer is the GM of Trapeze Group and ultimately my boss. He brings a wide and varied background to his position having served at senior roles for Microsoft and a number of tech and service companies. Prior to his current position, Steve was COO at Trapeze for five years and it was in that capacity that I really got to know him.*

*Steve is passionate about a customer-centric approach to all we do. In that vein, when we discussed the book and what he might write for it, he decided that he wanted a customer viewpoint from Gen Z on what the future of public transportation should look like to attract and retain them as a rider. So, he turned to his daughter, Bronwyn who is a member of Gen Z and works for a tech company. Her take on what young people need from transit and mobility is a nice way to wrap up the look into the future from our industry experts. Read and enjoy.*

My name is Steve. It is highly likely that my name alone gives away the generation that I am from; a tail end baby boomer. I grew up in farming country. Growing up, my modes of transportation were cycling, hitchhiking, walking, and the bus. I always felt a sense of joy from riding the bus. The drivers were friendly and helpful. I could relax and take in the sights or just think while moving easily and effortlessly from one place to another – like being on a magic carpet. I still have that same sense of joy taking public transit today. That said, at that time, I am sure that the lifestyles of others living within a 20-mile radius of me varied significantly based on their values, dwelling, work, transportation needs etc. My country boy experience was and is becoming more uncommon.

According to the UN, the global population will exceed 8 billion in the next 20 years and about 60% of people worldwide will live in cities, a 10% increase compared to the beginning of this century. Some reports claim that North American cities already hold 65% of the population and the percentage is growing. The lifestyles of most people, the future of cities, the future of transit and mobility are inextricably linked. The younger generations, continually driving for change, desire a different life experience; one of work-life balance, equality, inclusiveness, responsible consumption, preservation of the environment, control, safety etc..

This chapter is about the future of transit from the perspective of the most recent Generation Z, born 1996 and later. I would like to introduce you to Bronwyne, Gen Z, a city dweller, who's lifestyle relies on mobility options. From here on in, it's all Bronwyne.

"OK Boomer" - A dismissive, Generation Z slang response to the perceived obsolete perception of the baby boomer generation. The disrespectful nature of this sarcastic term is open to debate; however, the basic concept is undeniable- we are a unique generation with differing perceptions. This translates into novelty mobility demands and guarantees a progressive future for the transportation industry. Older generations have extensively examined the transformational mobility patterns of the Y generation in an attempt to manage evolving transportation trends. However, less effort is directed at the succeeding Generation Z, whose older members are approaching their mid-twenties and influencing these trends with increasing strength. The most accurate prediction for the future of transportation and mobility is therefore achieved through an open dialogue with the young "leaders of the future".

Born in 1998 and in my twenty-first year, I am included in the earlier Generation Z population. I relocated from a small town to downtown Toronto, three years ago, 65 km (40 miles) and have expanded my experience using a diversity of transportation services. To address progressive trends and their influence on the future of transportation, I began a discussion between thirty of my fellow Generations Zs, located in Toronto and the surrounding area.

As the first generation to be raised in a period of advanced technology and global connectivity, we not only value, but also expect, constant and immediate control. Through the use of mobile applications, we have developed a dependence for the control of most aspects of our lives; from our acoustic environments with the iPod to our personal brands on social media. According to our collaborative discussion and supporting research, this demand will likely assume the foundation for future transportation and mobility trends, as Generation Z anticipates: an obvious increase in environmental sustainability, a decrease in structure, and a blending of private and public alternatives.

Past generations have left the earth in environmental crisis and we are prepared and willing to respond. This argument is receiving global-recognition and is becoming the focus of research, as it concerns the existence of humanity and continues to threaten business operations. Though it is already an extensively-discussed concern, it is briefly included in this essay to acknowledge its undeniable influencing power on the future of transportation and mobility. This aspect is the most challenging for Generation Z, as we desire complete control and struggle to individually assume this control over the health of our environment. Yet, research reveals that we are prepared to face the challenge and continue to collectively strive for improved environmental conditions.[30] We are forceful in choosing products and services that will align with our environmental values and threaten the longevity of businesses that fail to accommodate. Our discussion revealed that environmental awareness encourages the top predicted trend for the transportation and mobility of Generation Z, as respondents identified environmentally sustainable transportation options as the future of the industry. Public transit services may have provided a temporary solution for the harmful effects of individual vehicle use. However, majority of these services are still harmful to our environment. We

---

[30] Frost and Sullivan, "Generation Z as Future Customers, Forecast to 2027," (2019)

are encouraging city streets to develop mechanisms for a safer commute, designed to promote pedestrian use, as we prefer these completely environmentally-sustainable options. Several respondents intend to use a bicycle, skateboard, or their own feet as their main transportation mode, but do not feel that the streets currently have adequate mechanisms in place to do so safely. Many predict the continued relocation of transportation modes either above or below ground-level to solve the issue of pedestrian space limitations. Several cities have introduced this concept with underground pedestrian or vehicle routes. However, Generation Z will remain unsatisfied until a collective, global effort is achieved.

Generation Z's recently reported demand for flexibility in the workplace[31] appears to be equally influential to the current structure of transportation, as we prioritize flexibility in where and when we travel. According to our discussion, multimodality in cities is a preference of the past, as Generation Z urges trends for decreasing locational-structure. Research suggests the presence of a greater multimodality in current post-secondary students in the suburbs of Toronto.[32] As the gap between the student's residential location and Toronto's immediate downtown decreases, single-modal transportation increases. Likely, these are evidential of single-modal location boundaries and limitations, as affordable transportation alternatives fail

---

[31] Holly Schroth, "Are You Ready for Gen Z in the Workplace?" *California Management Review* 61, no. 3 (2019): 7. doi:

[32] Khandker Nurul Habib, Adam Weiss, and Hasnine Sami, "On the heterogeneity and substitution patterns in mobility tool ownership choices of post-secondary students: The case of Toronto," *Transportation Research Part A*, 116 (2018): 664. doi:

to provide service between downtown and suburb areas without requiring a transfer between modes. The stationary pick-up/drop-off locations and routes of current transit services guarantees a multimodal trip for passengers who are required to travel to and from transit stops and stations. This limits the ability of Generation Z to control their choice in transportation method and dissatisfies the traveler, as we experience stress in the transferring process.

We are equally dissatisfied with the predetermined operation schedules of certain modes of transportation. Operational schedules are subject to alteration as busy cities always seems to result in service delays and cancelations. For Generation Z, this means additional factors influencing time management, which are beyond the user's control. Additionally, transit service schedules are determined on a demand-basis and increase frequency during periods of high user-density. This results in less reliability or control during off- periods and dissuades our use of schedule-based transportation modes.

Ridesharing applications like Uber and Lyft have creatively developed an alternative, which provides travelers with complete control over point A and B locations, as well as when services will be used. These solutions are marketed as premium services; not a realistic alternative for the 81% of Generation Z currently experiencing significant financial-related stress.[33] Our discussion revealed, majority of us are willing to exert greater amounts of energy for self-controlled transportation, including walking and biking,

---

[33] American Psychology Association, "Stress in America: Generation Z." Stress in America Survey (2018): 5.

as these modes avoid the added loss of control. The ideal dynamic mode of transportation offers users the ability to travel directly from any point A to any point B, at any time, without additional expenses.

The economic disadvantage, concern for safety, and social anxiety of Generation Z continues to influence the blurring of private and public transportation services. Financial and environmental costs, associated with private transportation, are unreasonable for Generation Z. A larger percentage of Generation Z experiences financial and work-related stress,[34] decreasing their likelihood of owning a personal vehicle. Obtaining a driver's permit is no longer a necessity, as research shows Generation Zs are the least likely of all generations to earn or use one.[35] Though we may be financially unable to afford private transportation alternatives, majority of my thirty interactions reported that if we were financially able, we would choose private over public. Not surprisingly, concern for safety and the generation's social anxieties are threatening the sustainability of public transportation alternatives. We were raised in a post 9/11 society and are familiar with the circulation of negative media.[36] From stories of terrorism and a divided political environment to several foreign wars, we learned to fear our safety in public spaces and have developed a higher desire for risk aversion.[37] For the transportation and mobility of Generation Z, this translates into a greater desire for private, as we

---

[34] American Psychology Association, 5.
[35] Sarwant Singh, "Car Companies Get Thinking Out Of The Box for Gen Z," *Forbes*, Apr 9, 2019.

[36] Geoffrey A. Talmon, "Generation Z: What's Next?" *Medical Science Educator,* (2019): 1. doi:
[37] Talmon, 1.

experience higher levels of anxiety using public alternatives.

Generation Z is additionally coping with the highest levels of depression and anxiety-related disorders; [38] a result of our overprotective parents obstructing our social development and our dependence on technology for communication.[39]Our population, especially women and minority groups, are more likely to feel discomfort using public transportation. These results are supportive to my discussion, which unanimously presented safety and social comfort as desired characteristics for transportation. Ridesharing and demand-responsive alternatives provide solutions for Generation Z and may increase in popularity, assuming the continued reduction in their environmental impact and the improvement of Generation Z's financial ability. Until ridesharing or demand-response services are performed with minimal environmental impact, Generation Z predicts a trend towards private-feeling, public alternatives to service their security and social concerns. We are looking for in-transit accommodations to encourage our sense of security. Majority of discussion responses determined GO Transit train services (a regional public transit system) as the most desirable and comfortable form of public transit in the Greater Toronto Area. The organizational arrangement of seating within each cart is beneficial to the socially- anxious generation. Seats are creatively arranged in groups of four, limiting the feeling of human density in the immediate environment and reducing the stressors associated with public space. Recently, a petition to receive cellular service throughout Toronto's

---

[38] American Psychology Association, 4.
[39] Schroth, 13.

underground subway lines has circulated through the city, as a survey revealed over half of TTC riders would feel more secure underground with access to communication.[40] Generation Z is demanding control for their own security and comfort, and transportation services will continue to respond with added accommodations.

While every generation presents unique challenges for the transportation industry, Generation Z, being the first generation raised in the new world of technology, guarantees revolutionary and difficult challenges. We are demanding control of external and internal conditions simultaneously and are choosing transportation and mobility modes accordingly. Generation Z anticipates an environmentally-sustainable and dynamic blend of private and public alternatives as modes evolve to accommodate the global environmental demands as well as the flexibility, affordability, security, and social-comfort demands of this generation. According to our collaborative discussion and supporting research, our ideal transportation could consist of: (1) underground and above ground public transit options that offer the perception of private transportation, are geographically and temporally controlled by the user, environmentally-friendly, and affordable; and (2) space for the ground-level use of personal mobility modes, such as walking or biking, that are unobstructed by vehicle and road safety concern. Whether the transportation and mobility ideas, presented in our discussion will become a reality or not remains unknown, however, they provide important insight into the preferences of Generation Z. The novelty perceptions of this generation, coupled with continued technological

---

[40] Iwantaccess.ca

development, are creating an exceptionally demanding industry. Involving Generation Z in the design and decision-making processes is significantly important for companies. These individuals are responsible for leading the future of the transportation and mobility industry – consider reaching out to and listening to their differing perceptions.

Bibliography

American Psychology Association, "Stress in America: Generation Z." Stress in America Survey

(2018): 1-9.

Geoffrey A. Talmon, "Generation Z: What's Next?" *Medical Science Educator,* (2019): 1-3. doi:

Holly Schroth, "Are You Ready for Gen Z in the Workplace?" *California Management Review*

61, no. 3 (2019): 5-18.

Khandker Nurul Habib, Adam Weiss, and Hasnine Sami, "On the heterogeneity and substitution

patterns in mobility tool ownership choices of post-secondary students: The case of Toronto," *Transportation Research Part A,* 116 (2018): 650-665.

Singh, Sarwant, "Car Companies Get Thinking Out Of The Box for Gen Z," *Forbes,* Apr 9,

2019.

Iwantaccess.ca

Frost and Sullivan, "Generation Z as Future Customers, Forecast to 2027," (2019)

*You can contact Steve Sawyer at his company website www.trapezegroup.com*

# Chapter 45
## One More Thing

**Paul Comfort**

Author and Host of Transit Unplugged

*I hope you have enjoyed the book, learned something new and been inspired to help create the Future of Public Transportation in your own region.*

*As I was reading over all the chapters during my final edit, the thought kept popping up in my mind, "oh, there's one more thing.." about various topics that I felt weren't sufficiently addressed in the current chapters. So, I decided to add this chapter called "One More Thing" about several additional matters that are an important part of the Future of Public Transportation. Here goes:*

### Public Private Partnerships (P3)

While I was Administrator and CEO of the Maryland Transit Administration (MTA), we started what was at the time, the largest Public Private Partnership (P3) project in America, the Purple Line. This was a $5+ billion, 16.2 mile light rail line connected to the Washington Metropolitan Area Transit Authority's (WMATA) Metro line with stations on the Maryland side. I selected a great Executive Director of the project who is still there today and hired much of our tremendous MTA staff to help kick it off. The project is moving forward toward completion.

I like the concept behind these big P3s because they take advantage of the innovation from the private sector while ensuring quality service delivery for the public. These P3s often don't dictate all the "hows" but mainly the "whats" of the project. What does that mean?

Well, in a traditional government procurement an agency would typically define in explicit detail, for instance, the type of metal and equipment to be used by a private sector contractor in designing and constructing an elevator for a transit station. It would detail the height and width and weight of the elevator, the type of electronics, and all the fine details of it. But in many P3s now the agency details more what they want the end results to be, and less exactly how they are to do it, such as wanting "X" number of passengers to be able to ride the elevator per hour, safely and the agency will pay "availability payments" to the contractor for achieving that goal.

This P3 approach allows for more current technology to be used and updated over the life cycle of the project as advancements becomes available. These contracts normally cover a multi-year construction timeline and then also perhaps a 20-30 year operating contract. So, this approach doesn't limit what technology can be used 25-30 years from now.

Steve Butcher, CEO of the John Holland company in Australia told me during his Transit Unplugged podcast interview, "In recent years, it's moved from just the separation of design and build and operations and maintenance into having a fully integrated model that's a full end-to-end service.

In the rail division of John Holland currently, we design and build the railway. We overlay with the track and the signals, and the signal integration, the testing and commissioning. But also, then we would put skin in the game. We are then going to be responsible for operating and maintaining it for however long the concession is. Sometimes that may be five years. Sometimes the longest might be even 30 years. What it does is it gives our clients and the transit agencies security that they've got a continuum - all the way from designing a railway through building it in the best possible way because, to be honest, you're then going to have the responsibility of operating and maintaining it."

So, my takeaway is, look for multi-faceted consortiums of companies to continue to be utilized for construction and operation of large, capital projects into this decade of the 2020s to design, build, operate, finance and maintain them. Much of the benefit can also be achieved for government when they pass off the financing of these projects to the consortiums and maybe allow them to collect tolls or fares as their primary repayment methodology. This keeps the government from having to issue large bonds and reduces direct taxpayer subsidies for these mega-projects like new rail projects, bridges and facilities.

## Air Travel

Recently, I was in Las Vegas moderating a panel on the Future of Public Transportation for a day long symposium called GONV 2020 Summit that looked at what's next for the state of Nevada when it comes to public transportation. On my panel were representatives from Uber Air, Virgin Hyperloop One and the Nevada Institute for Autonomous Systems (which works with drone technology). Wow, there is so much that could be said about all these upcoming modes of travel.

Suffice it to say that these three new technologies are happening and will potentially come to full fruition in this decade. Drones are already being used to deliver packages to homes in select cities and human organs to hospitals for surgeries. Uber Air announced and displayed (the day after our GONV Summit) their new shared VTOL (vertical takeoff and landing) aircraft at the 2020 Consumer Electronics Show. By 2023 they plan to allow you to take rides between Skyports in a city for an "affordable shared flight" – kind of like you do now with Uber, Lyft or taxis on the ground. And the folks overseeing drone technologies say they can see the same type of thing happening for their vehicles. Maybe even calling for a drone to pick you up on your front lawn and take you to your appointment in the city. Are you ready?

### Rail

Well, there are so many new developments in rail transportation that it's hard to know where this technology is headed, except to say it's here to stay.

When I visited Australia last year, I was impressed by their commitment to rail mass transit. The Sydney Trains system there under the leadership of my pal, CEO Howard Collins is drilling tunnels and expanding rail at an amazing rate. Expect this to continue both in Australia and in major cities around the world. Nothing beats rail for mass transit in cities - be it light rail, heavy rail or underground subways.

Here in the US  the Virgin Trains/Brightline brand, the only privately owned and operated intercity passenger railroad in the nation, is expanding their vision of rail in places like Florida where they are now offering luxury, high-speed passenger train service that runs at speeds up to 79 miles per hour, between Miami and West Palm Beach. They plan to extend service to Orlando by 2021, 235 miles from Miami, linking Florida's two major tourist destinations.

In Las Vegas, my friend Tina Quigley (former CEO of the RTC of Southern Nevada) recently joined Virgin Trains to help them do similarly between the Los Angeles area and Las Vegas. Wow will that make a difference for the tens of thousands of people who travel that way often.

While I was CEO of the Maryland Transit Administration (MTA) we were studying the possibility of bringing a high speed, mag lev, rail system between Washington DC and Baltimore. As of this writing, they are still studying it. Meanwhile, Elon Musk's Hyperloop company has already met with the state government here to get permission to build on the Baltimore/Washington Parkway right of way. We'll see who gets it done first.

In California there has been a much-publicized effort to bring high speed, mag lev rail to the state. Due to funding concerns the initial length of the route has been scaled back but they are still moving forward with the project. There also is the Texas Central, a 240-mile high-speed rail that connects the Dallas and Houston regions, two of the largest economies of the country, in less than 90 minutes. This rail system will operate with the same technology as the Central Japan Railway, the world's first high-speed line. Plans are for this line to be operational in 2026.

I also wanted to comment on Commuter Rail in North America and beyond. This heavy rail service transports passengers mostly to work and city centers from the suburbs and is one of the only modes regularly increasing ridership, year after year; and growing in the US, from only a handful of services in 80's – 90s to nearly 40 systems now. I found it amazing that folks would ride 90 minutes or more one way on a train from Western Maryland on my MARC Commuter Train service into Union Station in downtown Washington DC every day to work – but they did and do. Right now, there are billions of dollars of investment going into further expanding commuter trains in systems like Caltrain and Metrolinx around Toronto. An interesting fact is that approximately 80% of all Commuter Railroads in USA have private sector Operations and Maintenance companies like Bombardier and even Amtrak running some piece or part of their railroad. I look for Commuter Trains to continue to grow and prosper in the 2020s as commuters want to stay in the suburbs but work in the city.

There are many other innovative and non-traditional rail type projects on the books or in planning stages around the country and the world from pods to gondolas to other types of raised/lowered/in ground high speed, electric trains and the like. New technologies are being developed on a regular basis encompassing all modes and what we have at the end of this decade may be very different from what we are looking at now. That's why the cover of this book offers multiple options showing the past, present and future of Public Transportation modes. They are shown moving upward on the primary color bands against the backdrop of cities which rely on mass transit for their mobility on the face of a clock indicating the movement of time toward an event horizon of the 2020s.


## Payment Methodology

In earlier chapters we have touched on this topic but there is a little more to say. Traditional transit systems used to use tokens for payment. Then tokens went the way of gas lanterns and we moved to cash. After cash many systems introduced their own branded fare payment cards – first paper then plastic. Now systems are leveraging technology more and moving to credit card readers to allow for "contactless" or "tap and go" payments, while maintaining the option of cash to comply with US federal requirements to allow those who are "unbanked" to keep paying their fares. The latest fashion is "wearables" mobile and BIBO. Wearables are similar to branded fare cards but allow bracelets or necklaces and the like to be used for fare payment. With mobile payment we are moving away from using plastic credit cards to e-payments through smart phones and smart watches with similar "tap and go" technology. Finally, the proximity-based technology or BIBO (be in-be out) is another form of contactless payment that identifies the presence of a person through detectable devices and calculates fare based on the duration of their presence; a person simply hops on and off the vehicle without interacting with any payment system.

Fare boxes are changing too. They have become so complex to handle the myriad of these fare payment options along with day and monthly passes and more. Now in a countervailing move, some agencies are opting for the opposite. They want to go back to a simple cash only fare box with separate card readers or validators in the front and back of the bus for those using all of the other card, smart phone, wearable payment options. I had one top industry official tell me that the next order of fare boxes most transit systems make will be their last. Meaning, fare boxes are becoming an anachronism of the past and soon all these other payment options will mean it's no longer really necessary.

The free fare movement is also taking root. For these transit systems they certainly won't need fareboxes. Transit advocates like Robbie Makinen, CEO of Kansas City Area Transit Authority (KCATA), who wrote the Forward to this book, are moving ahead with finding other funding sources to pay for the unsubsidized portion of transit services, meaning riders can ride for no fare. One of the practical reasons to pursue this free fare is the cost of collecting fares; which can top 30% of the actual fares collected with fare enforcement, collection and counting personnel along with the capital cost of replacing fareboxes, armored car services and more.

Will transit eventually be considered as a basic city service like parks, streets or public schools with no additional subsidy requested from the user? In the past, the small percentage of citizens who take transit as compared to those who use these other public services has kept government leaders treating transit more like a public golf course or airport (enterprise funded service) that requires an extra payment from the user, while remaining publicly subsidized. There seems to be some traction to this free fare movement, and you can look to see more cities adopting the approach that transit will now be a basic city service not requiring a fare payment.

## Human Capital

As I write this book there is much being made of driver shortages in places like Denver, Colorado where bus and light rail routes are potentially being cut back to compensate. But that is a problem all over the world, largely because Generation X (my generation ~1961-1981) workers are now retiring from jobs like bus operator, bus and train mechanic, radio/catenary/signal technicians etc... and there doesn't appear to be a huge surge of replacements.

So, what to do? Some agencies like Los Angeles Metro with visionary leaders like my pal, CEO Phil Washington, are building transportation schools to train up a new generation with the interest and skills to meet the growing job demand in the transportation skilled trades. Other agencies are thinking that autonomous shared vehicles may soon be needed not just on tourist routes in downtown areas or on college/business campuses but also to backfill regular routes that don't have drivers. Many rail systems already have the technology to be driverless. Will public housing or housing vouchers for transit bus drivers and mechanics be introduced in some cities soon?

## Summary

The collective body of wisdom from this book will hopefully both inform and inspire you. I am a believer that transit=mobility and mobility=life. So, I see transit having a bright future in all its forms. Since more people are moving to the cities and more cities are expanding to become mega-city regions, public mobility will continue to be integrated into these smart cities not as an afterthought, but as a key component of the city infrastructure.

Private companies have figured this out and are making public mobility one of their core focuses (see recent moves from Ford/GM and other major auto manufacturers into the new mobility sphere). I don't see private companies taking away the need for public transit services, but the role of city transit agencies may adapt to become provider of mass transit and enabler of micro transit – run by private, for profit companies. The companies that are currently dominating new mobility may make way for new conglomerates combining service provision under contract to public transit agencies along with their own private micro-transit services (shared car/bike/scooter etc...).

In the end, bold leaders will take us to new horizons as they always have, but they will do so using modern technology to move us in ways we never thought possible, and in the process,  eliminate barriers that have too long stood in the way of true mobility for all. **And THAT is the Future of Public Transportation.**

**Visit our website at:**
www.futureofpublictransportation.com

Find blog posts, updated information, opportunities to meet the authors, info on seminars, order an autographed copy of this book and shop for themed merchandise.

Find Paul's first book on Amazon:

***Full Throttle -
Living Life to the Max with No Regrets***

Stories from Paul with 10 CEOs on career management and tools to reach the top

Check out Paul's #1 Transit CEO Podcast at
www.transitunplugged.com
and on most podcast platforms.

Follow Paul on LinkedIn, Twitter (@comfortpaul) or Instagram (paulcomfort2020) to stay connected.

Printed in Great Britain
by Amazon

55570772R00253